Praise for *Leadership Resu*

A great read. In *Leadership Results*, Sebastian addresses the challenges of leadership and provides valuable insights and tools to help leaders at all levels of an organisation. Leadership is a critical factor in so many roles in today's organisations as the complexity of operations, the removal of geographic borders and the ability to create value challenges many companies. Sebastian's data driven analysis, supported by real and diverse experiences, makes this book a great reference point for anyone looking to take on the leadership challenge.

— **Joff Allen**, Chief Executive Officer, EduCo International Group

Leadership Results pulls together leadership wisdom from a remarkably inclusive set of thinkers and doers, and the result is an engaging and useful book to enhance the effectiveness of leaders in any sector. Illuminating the most powerful tool of the leader, Salicru distinguishes between the language of action and the language of possibility. In short, leadership is ultimately relational, and language is the material upon which relationships are built. The book offers simple exercises to practice and deepens the reader's leadership effectiveness.

— **Amy C. Edmondson**, Novartis Professor of Leadership and Management, Harvard Business School and author of *Building the Future: Big Teaming for Audacious Innovation*

Leadership Results will challenge every leader's thinking about what effective leadership really is. Sebastian Salicru makes clear that we are experiencing a leadership crisis like we have never known before and he urges us to become part of a movement to overcome that crisis. In detail, he eloquently outlines how leaders can become strong performers who are adaptive to new circumstances in their global operating contexts. A must read for anyone with even a remote interest in leading into the future.

— **Professor Gary Martin** FAIM FACE, Chief Executive Office, Australian Institute of Management WA

A compelling view of leadership as social performance. Timely, relevant and full of insights.

—**Vip Vyas**, CEO of Distinctive Performance and contributor to INSEAD Knowledge

With essential elements of leadership at his fingertips, Sebastian Salicru in *Leadership Results* has created a wonderful tapestry to help organizations find their way. Myths, dreams and lessons in growing up are woven together with comprehensive research findings to provide the reader with practical examples of how organizational leadership can really make a difference. Sebastian makes it very clear that we are lost without good leadership and shows us all how to develop this important capability."

—**Warren Parry**, CEO LifeMap Research and author of *Big Change Best Path – Successfully Managing Organizational Change with Wisdom, Analytics and Insight*.

Sebastian's deep understanding of leadership behaviour is unique and impactful. This is a very inspirational book that addresses the leadership crisis and its failure in developing trust, motivation, and effectiveness to bring out the best in self and others. In a world of relentless change and uncertainty, Sebastian has clearly hit the mark. All leaders must understand and do what he is emphasizing to be truly effective. His ideas are thought-provoking, timely, and daring—a must-read for every leader.

—**George Kohlrieser, Ph.D**, Professor of Leadership and Organizational Behavior, IMD, Lausanne, Switzerland, and bestselling Author of *Hostage at the Table* and *Care to Dare*

It is almost cliché to say that the world is changing faster than ever, and the sad truth is, in most organisations, leadership practices haven't caught up. In *Leadership Results*, Sebastian Salicru unpacks a research-based model that offers a relational approach that yields innovation, extraordinary performance, and business results for twenty-first century leaders. He presents a broad range of anecdotes that will not only make you smile, but help you understand why he has created this road map to navigate modern leadership. If you want to be a successful leader in our constantly changing world, *Leadership Results* is critical reading.

—**Peter Cook**, CEO, Thought Leaders Global

The book reveals several important insights about the nature and evolution of human beings and why leadership is relational, contextual and as ever evolving as we who practice it. It's inspirational with a clear message. This evidence-based book uses a systematic research-based approach in building the arguments and in describing the thinking behind the leadership results framework. Readers who appreciate scientific and evidence based-books will like this – it's a complete guide to leadership as a discipline and how leaders can elevate their own capacity and quality in practicing it.

—**Niklas Nordling**, PsychDr, Head of Culture and Organization Development, Nokia

This book provides a wide perspective in a growing field of leadership literature. Sebastian is humorous in that he rarely makes the mistake of taking himself too seriously. He does however take the subject matter seriously and attempts to bring together research and global experience in a coherent manner. Of particular interest is his exploration of relational models of leadership; his own research into the field and the implications for how to develop leadership. I also enjoyed his frequent use of stories together with his anecdotes about his personal journey: a rare combination in a leadership text. This book will appeal to beginners in the field because of its comprehensive coverage as well as to advanced practitioners because of its practical insights.

—**Michael Johnstone PhD**, co-founder and Executive Director, Vantage Point Consulting, Australia

Sebastian Salicru starts by throwing down the gauntlet, challenging readers to be part of the solution to the leadership crisis across the world. Through his 'Leadership Results' model, he succinctly captures the complex interrelationships between self and collective leadership without oversimplification, reminding us that leader development is not the same as *leadership* development, while providing examples and context to help illustrate the differences. Interspersed with instructive and entertaining stories throughout, this well-written book provides a valuable perspective on leadership, leadership development and the possibilities for our future if we can collectively exercise better leadership to tackle our toughest challenges.

—**Joe 'Hark' Herold**, CEO & Founder, Hark Leadership

Leadership Results is an essential book for all leaders dealing with the challenges and opportunities presented by the cyber-physical age. Salicru crystalizes decades of the most relevant thinking and leadership theory, effortlessly bringing together reasoned insights and science-backed tools to help leaders adapt to complexity. Replete with engaging stories, as well as experienced wisdom, suggested practices, authoritative studies, and practical measures, a central treatise of the narrative is that that there's no such thing as a perfect leader, or indeed one 'best' way to lead in all contexts. This impressive work supports that all leadership requires connection, however, whether to people or purpose. Highly recommended reading.

—**Dr Natalie Ferres**, Director of strategic leadership advisory Bendelta Pty Ltd, and author of the book *People Development: An inside view to developing individuals, leaders and organisations*

Leadership Results is a thoughtful, thoroughly researched, well written and timely blend of Salicru's lengthy experience and deep psychological insights. It is evidenced based, pragmatic and a must-read for any leader's library.

—**Jim Grant**, Partner, Dattner Grant

In *Leadership Results*, Salicru is tackling the greatest leadership challenge of our time, the role of the leader in the future. His thesis that leadership has always been and will increasingly be about the relational dynamics in a business is critical for knowing what to do next.

—**Matt Church**, Founder, Thought Leaders Global

Of all the leadership books I've read, *Leadership Results* is the most accessible. Salicru has advanced the art and science of leadership with this well researched practice based guide. A must read for aspiring leaders.

—**Dan Buchner**, founder, praktikel Innovation Leadership Learning

In an era that is characterised by a crisis of leadership, Sebastian Salicru has done all of us and our leaders a great service in compiling the thinking and practice of prominent researchers, authors and practitioners of leadership. The result, *Leadership Results*, is practical and down to earth and full of insightful questions as well as informative examples and anecdotes that allow us to see great (and not so great) leadership in action. Sebastian has utilised his comprehensive research to create a new model of leadership based on the understanding that all leadership is based on relationships and that an organisation's journey towards greater engagement of their people begins with the integrity and individual personal development of its leaders.

—**Mandy Geddes**, General Manager, Education, Institute of Executive Coaching and Leadership (IECL)

Sebastian has written an insightful and useful book which will appear at precisely the right time. Now. Right now, as we as a species (all 8+ billion of us) are immersed in a transformative moment. It is quite unclear what the new forms and forces of the emerging world will look like. It is very clear that most of what we have taken to be normal and expected will pass on by. Getting from Here/Now to There/Then is the issue, and finding the way is what leadership is all about. Leadership is not the private preserve of The Leaders. It is the opportunity and obligation of every human being—in families, workplaces, and the community at large. Some do it well, others poorly. We can all do it better—and Sebastian can help. Read this book.

—**Harrison Owen**, President of H.H. Owen and Company, author, consultant and creator of Open Space Technology

I really enjoyed Sebastian's book and admire his passion. We proceed from different perspectives: I believe the world is very well led and we have reached an incredible level of human prosperity. However, leaders today face a new challenge, 24-hour a day broadcast of criticism with an emphasis on bad news. Our well-being and the planet's health requires new modes of thinking and leadership and this is where Sebastian nails the need for change. Sebastian's book and his insights will help many people understand and improve their leadership capacity and leadership!

—**Victor Perton,** leadership adviser and advocate, editor and publisher, *The Australian Leadership Project*

As Sebastian Salicru demonstrates in his thoughtful new book, *Leadership Results*, it is relationships that are of paramount importance. No matter what the company, success depends on the psychological wellbeing of those who work there. Salicru makes a convincing case that the successful leader knows how to foster the successful relationships that drive organizations.

—**Ellen Langer**, Professor of Psychology, Harvard University, author of *Mindfulness*

Salicru has performed an enormous service and a prodigious feat of intellectual dexterity by mining the exhaustive canon of writing and research on leadership to create a holistic, synthesised yet original theory, assessment tool and practice which will be an invaluable resource for anyone who seeks to make progress on daunting challenges in the world, the workplace, or even personally. His core insight that leadership is at its essence a relational activity is an important and timely note of reality, especially for the times in which we live, when the seemingly intractable challenges communities face can lead to a yearning for authoritarian saviours who promise more than they can deliver.

—**Marty Linsky**, faculty, Harvard Kennedy School

If you want a comprehensive view of the leadership literature and how to create adaptive leaders for this ever-changing workplace, *Leadership*

Results is that book. It is highly readable, practical and thorough and a must if you want to understand what leadership is all about.

— **Professor Sir Cary Cooper**, ALLIANCE Manchester Business School, University of Manchester, UK

Amidst a dearth of innovative leadership literature, this book is a gem. Referencing grounded theory, the reader is guided towards new models of collective leadership with a focus on performance and results. In an age where leadership seems to be regressing towards the charismatic, Sebastian presents a compelling and progressive model for the 21st century.

— **Dr Graham Ward**, Adjunct Professor of Organisational Behaviour. INSEAD Business

In this book Sebastian Salicru skillfully weaves together a rich tapestry of theory, research, examples and personal experience to provide a thoughtful yet practical guide for leadership practitioners, students, scholars and developers. It is a timely and compelling call to action that encourages the reader to reflect on their prior learning and experience, embrace new ideas, discard out-dated practices, and to work collaboratively to build a better future.

— **Richard Bolden**, Professor of Leadership and Management, Bristol Business School, University of the West of England

Finally, an evidence-based book on leadership written for managers as opposed to scholars. This highly readable book makes clear what leaders must do in their respective organisations to bring about a high-performing workforce.

— **Gary Latham**, Secretary of State Professor of Organizational Effectiveness, Rotman School of Management, University of Toronto

We are in an era when many of the conventional myths about leadership—to develop leadership we need to develop leaders; leadership and authority are one and the same—no longer apply to contemporary organisations. Sebastian Salicru is bold enough in *Leadership Results* to introduce us to new models of both leadership and leadership development. In particular, having pushed for years to re-imagine leadership as a collaborative property, I am—and readers of this book will be likewise—grateful that this author has come up with such a firsthand and practical way to illustrate collective leadership and collective leadership development.

—**Joe Raelin**, Knowles Chair of Practice-Oriented Education, Northeastern University, Boston, USA

Leadership is arguably the most written about topic in the field of organisational management and operations. Yes, much of what is written is based on popular myths and misconceptions about what leadership is and why it exists. In this book, author Sebastian Salicru cuts though all the hype to make it clear that good leadership is first and foremost about forming and maintaining relationships with other human beings for the benefit of the whole society. By talking a relationship perspective, Salicru delivers a straightforward and easily digestible account of what leaders need to do in order to obtain real results in today's fast-moving and complex world. A particular strength of the book is the way the author combines a deep knowledge of the evidence-based literature with his own real-world experience. The result is a 'road map' of effective leadership that tells how organisational leaders can engage with their followers to produce exceptional results that matter.

—**Neal M. Ashkanasy OAM, PhD**, Professor of Management, UQ Business School, The University of Queensland

Our understanding of leadership—what it is, how it works, and even how people know it when they see it—is changing. In *Leadership Results*,

Sebastian combines the latest research with his power of storytelling to speak in simple relatable terms about what makes a twenty-first-century leader—relational dynamics! This book requires nothing less than a revolution of mind and a shift in order of thought to see relationships as both a context for action and as an outcome of leadership. The world is changing—*Leadership Results* will help you keep up.

—**Jennifer Gippel PhD (Finance)**, Emeritus Faculty, Australian National University

Sebastian Salicru's extensive experience as an international business psychologist and scholar provides a strong foundation for his powerful insights into driving innovation in organisations through his Leadership Results model. He provides key resources and extensive personal experience outlining a model to build leadership capacity based on a social process that emerges from the dynamics of relationships in the organisation. *Leadership Results* is compelling in its call for growing exceptional leaders who think deeply and act boldly to lead global innovation with authenticity and integrity.

—**Dr Susan Keller-Mathers**, Associate Professor, International Center for Studies in Creativity, Buffalo State

FRESH, ENGAGING and DEEP, this is how I would describe *Leadership Results*. Academically sound but it captures you like a novel. Sebastian brings a harmonious combination between theory and practice with many stories and quotes that make the text more interesting and appealing to the average reader. At the same time, *Leadership Results* is a very comprehensive book that covers and uncovers many aspects of leadership, questioning some of the established wisdom about leadership and its development in a way that will make you reflect and expand your previously adopted ideas. Are you already initiated into leadership?

—**Enric Bernal**, Global Solutions Faculty and Latin America Manager, Center for Creative Leadership, San Diego, California

In his wonderful new book *Leadership Results*, Sebastian Salicru illuminates the new paradigm of relational leadership with wisdom and clarity. This book reframes effective leadership in the world today as a creative and above all *relational* activity shared among many people working together across all kinds of boundaries. The old maps don't work anymore and the world is in crisis. It is time for us all to wake up and get on with the agenda Sebastian masterfully describes in this book.

— **Charles J. Palus PhD**, Senior Fellow,
The Center for Creative Leadership

In this relational look at leadership development, Salicru weaves together compelling stories, historical perspectives, and relevant case studies into a work which thoroughly covers the terrain of leadership theory. Each chapter is chock full of frameworks, tools, and insights for achieving more powerful leadership. With examples from many different fields and industries, he demonstrates how leaders can use their understanding of relational principles to make shifts towards 'extraordinary performance', build 'collective leadership capacity' and achieve results.

— **Karen Jo Shapiro, Psy. D.**, Adjunct Faculty, Center for Creative Leadership

Reading the manuscript, the word 'beautiful' appeared in my notes more often than it does when I read most books. This is an immense and impressive work. Sebastian does not shy away from the crises that we face on our finite planet and, without apology or ego, firmly places the notion of adaptive leadership at the heart of a successful future world. The book combines attention to the big picture, alongside practical wisdoms that are implementable right here right now. Drawing deeply on existing wisdom, Sebastian weaves that together with his own evidence-based insights, stories and experience creating new awareness and ways of being. This book will be a companion for you for as far as you are happy to take it on your leadership journey.

— **Dr Alison Whybrow**, chartered and coaching psychologist

Early in his book, Salicru points out that leadership is more than art and science; it also contains a healthy dose of mystery. Through stories, case studies, research insights, ancient wisdom and personal experiences, he takes the reader on a journey that accesses both the head and the heart, while encouraging imagination and courage, to navigate the new landscape of leadership. The magic of this book is that Salicru masterfully makes the insights stick and provokes leaders to move out of their comfort zones and self-created echo-chambers, and engage others of myriad political, ethnic, and cultural stripes, in their quest for meaningful achievement. The timing of his manuscript and the introduction of his novel ideas are of paramount importance to the modern leader. *Leadership Results* is designed to launch leaders into a new way of thinking and being, and is a must-read for leaders seeking to challenge old paradigms, and open their minds to an adaptive and relational approach for building collective leadership.

— **Jacque Merritt**, Senior Workplace Consultant and Executive Coach, GALLUP

Sebastian Salicru's *Leadership Results* is a reliable and urgently needed book about the state of leadership in the world in an age of inconceivables: instability, change, uncertainty, group think and political turmoil and dis-ease. His timely focus is on urgent questions concerning the very existence of viable leadership in a world, personal and workplace, in which old paradigms about leadership are seriously in question, and new paradigms about leadership arise from new questions. What is shared here is an invaluable model of what leadership can, and needs, to be. And not a moment too soon.

— **Jeff Olma**, Professor of Creativity, Florida State College, Jacksonville

At a time when leadership definitions are becoming broader and more complex by the day, Sebastian provides an invaluable text which seeks to re-evaluate what leadership means, not just in business, but also through practical daily life. In refreshing style, this consistent interpersonal narrative includes key insights by chapter, a rich variety of additional reading material, and references to many prevalent real-world historical and current examples, all with the aim to provide answers to the golden question about what is expected from leaders versus the behaviour of those at the top. I thoroughly recommend this book for both a thought-provoking read and as a guide to best practice leadership!

— **Richard Want**, Registered Psychologist, Partner,
Kendall Want Associates

Leadership
RESULTS®

Leadership
RESULTS®

How to Create Adaptive Leaders and

High-Performing Organisations

for an Uncertain World

SEBASTIAN SALICRU

WILEY

First published in 2017 by John Wiley & Sons Australia, Ltd
42 McDougall St, Milton Qld 4064

Office also in Melbourne

Typeset in 12/14 pt Adobe Garamond Pro

© PTS (Professional Training Services) Ptd. Ltd. 2017

The moral rights of the author have been asserted

National Library of Australia Cataloguing-in-Publication data:

Creator:	Salicru, Sebastian. author.
Title:	Leadership Results : how to create adaptive leaders and high-performing organisations for an uncertain world / Sebastian Salicru.
ISBN:	9780730345374 (pbk.) 9780730345473 (ebook)
Notes:	Includes bibliographical references and index.
Subjects:	Leadership Executive coaching. Industrial management. Corporate governance.

Cover design by Wiley

Cover image © aarrows /iStockphoto

Printed in Singapore by C.O.S. Printers Pte Ltd

10 9 8 7 6 5 4 3 2 1

Disclaimer

The material in this publication is of the nature of general comment only, and does not represent professional advice. It is not intended to provide specific guidance for particular circumstances and it should not be relied on as the basis for any decision to take action or not take action on any matter which it covers. Readers should obtain professional advice where appropriate, before making any such decision. To the maximum extent permitted by law, the author and publisher disclaim all responsibility and liability to any person, arising directly or indirectly from any person taking or not taking action based on the information in this publication.

To Lisa

CONTENTS

FOREWORD

Sebastian Salicru has mastered the use of my Stakeholder Centered Coaching process and in *Leadership Results* he continues to strive forward on the subject, offering a very fresh and thought-provoking perspective on leadership. This book comes at a time when we all need to enact personal, meaningful and lasting change, and organisations need to build real leadership capacity to achieve real results.

In *Leadership Results*, Sebastian's vision and core message are clear and simple. He invites us to make the world a better place by exercising leadership that forges meaningful and trusting relationships, and he tackles the subject of leadership development with great boldness, determination and pragmatism. He also addresses some of the most pressing leadership challenges we are experiencing in the world today. This includes the main reasons why leadership efforts have failed despite the huge investment made by organisations. Sebastian hits this nail firmly on the head.

Throughout his book, Sebastian uses a balanced mix of personal and professional experience, research and vivid narratives — cases, stories, fables, allegories and metaphors — to illustrate sophisticated concepts, evoke strong emotions and provoke original thinking, while offering wisdom and insight. *Leadership Results* inspires and infuses hope and enthusiasm towards taking action and delivering results.

Sebastian walks the talk by candidly sharing his personal challenges and feats. He exemplifies what I refer to in my book *Triggers* as 'creating behavior change that lasts — becoming the person you want to be' and leaving a positive impact on people's lives. Many of us recognise the benefits of behavioural change, but few of us have been able to make those changes happen. Sebastian's story is testimony that such personal behavioural changes are possible. He shows us how not to lose hope when facing adversity, how to have courage and creativity, build reliance, and come through situations with flying colours. He also explains nicely the importance of one of my personal favourites, 'feedforward' — providing future-oriented suggestions for improvement, which is critical for successful people to become even more successful.

None of this can be done alone. As I explain in *Triggers*, to become the person you want to be you need others. Sebastian demonstrates this using a relational approach to leadership and leadership development.

Leadership Results offers content rich in experience, research, and stories that present new perspectives of leadership and leadership development for our times. Sebastian is a wonderful thought leader and deserves kudos for tackling a difficult topic in times when we are facing unique challenges and unprecedented change. *Leadership Results* is a must-read for anyone wanting to take their self-leadership, and the leadership capacity of their organisation, to the next level.

Dr Marshall Goldsmith

Dr Marshall Goldsmith has been recognised by the American Management Association as one of 50 great thinkers and business leaders who have impacted the field of management over the past 80 years — and by Business Week *as one of the most influential practitioners in the history of leadership development. Marshall was recognised as the #1 Leadership Thinker in the World and one of the Top 5 Most Influential Business Thinkers in the World, as well as the #1 Executive Coach at the 2015 biennial Thinkers50 ceremony in London.*

PREFACE

Leadership across the world is in crisis and, while fixing it won't be easy, I think there are ways stop the rot and achieve much better leadership results. And while I can't possibly change the world single-handedly, I choose to connect to this cause intellectually and emotionally because it allows me to contribute and be part of the human race.

Harrison Owen created open space technology (OST), which is a deceptively simple and productive purpose-driven leadership approach in which groups of up to a thousand people organise themselves to deal with complex issues in a very short time. In the preface to his 1999 book *The Spirit of Leadership: Liberating the leaders in each of us*, he writes that '…leadership, along with everything else in our lives, has become or must become something quite different from what it has been'. This statement embodies the constantly evolving nature, understanding and practice of leadership.

It is no surprise, then, that leadership remains a much-debated topic and a universally undefined phenomenon. It's not only an art and a science; it also has a touch of mystery—just like life itself. And it is critical to businesses, organisations and communities, and to the evolution and survival of our species. Leadership is a determinant of our future and I cannot imagine anything more exciting, meaningful and rewarding than helping shape the destiny of humankind. This book is my humble contribution.

Sebastian Salicru
Sydney, Australia
March 2017

ABOUT THE AUTHOR

Sebastian Salicru is a business psychologist who specialises in leadership and organisational development. He is the director of PTS Consultants, an associate of Melbourne Business School—Executive Education, and Fellow of the Institute of Coaching (McLean/Harvard Medical School).

Sebastian has more than 20 years' experience working across sectors and industries with some of the top Fortune Global 500 companies in Australia, the United States, Europe, the UAE, China and Singapore. He helps organisations build leadership capacity to successfully navigate change and thrive in an increasingly demanding global economy where hyper-complexity and adaptive challenges are the new normal. Sebastian assists global leaders to minimise the business risks of working with people from diverse cultural backgrounds, acquire a global mindset, drive innovation, and achieve unprecedented levels of performance and business results. He also assists emerging leaders to unleash their leadership potential.

Sebastian's passion is moving from opinion-based discussions to evidence-based solutions by developing best practices. His uniqueness lies in his ability to apply them creatively to take his clients to the next level.

As a thought leader and author, Sebastian regularly presents at national and international conferences and industry events on the latest developments in leadership. His latest publications include two articles in the *Journal of Business Strategy* and *OD Practitioner*, and two book chapters on global leadership.

In addition to being a registered psychologist, Sebastian holds a Master of Creativity & Change Leadership from the State University of New York, and a Master of Management Research from UWA Business School at the University of Western Australia; he is also a graduate of the Art and Practice of Leadership Development program at Harvard Kennedy School. Sebastian is a PhD candidate at the University of Technology Sydney.

ACKNOWLEDGEMENTS

This book draws on and integrates a towering body of research on leadership, and on extensive practice of leadership development. You have probably heard from other authors that writing a book requires collaboration and teamwork. Today, I confirm to you this is absolutely the case.

The writing of this book has been possible through the assistance of four distinct groups of people. To begin with, those who taught, challenged, and inspired me experientially through my work by serving them. Next, those who by fed my appetite for learning and curiosity, taught me about doing research, simulated my thinking, provoked me with new ideas and perspectives, and uncovered many of my blind spots. Further, those who took my writing to the next level by assisting me to put my thoughts and ideas into narrative and stories. And finally, are those who supported me from behind the scenes throughout the whole process.

Firstly, I wish to thank the many client organisations and thousands of people at all organisational levels, from around the world and from all walks of life, I worked with and served during the last twenty five years. I have learnt from all of them, and they have contributed to my own personal and professional development. They have become a boundless collective repository of wealth and wisdom, a catalyst for writing this book, and they have inspired the many stories and cases presented in this book.

I am also grateful to the many world-class practitioners and researchers, with whom I had the privilege to undertake advanced professional training and development through my career. Namely:

Professor Ronald Heifetz, Marty Linsky, and Dr Michael Johnstone, who serve on the faculty of the John F. Kennedy School of Government at Harvard University; Dr Susan David, faculty of Harvard Medical School and CEO of Evidence Based Psychology; Professor Gerard Puccio, Dr Susan Keller-Mathers, and Dr Mary Murdock *RIP*, faculty of the International Center for Studies in Creativity at Buffalo State, State University of New York; Dr Stephen Covey *RIP*; and the legendary Harold Bridger *RIP*, founding member of the Tavistock Institute of Human Relations, London.

Thank you to the following leading researchers and authors I had the pleasure to meet personally, and whose work has enriched my thinking and professional practice: David Guest, Professor in Organizational Psychology at King's College in London; Professor Sir Cary Cooper, ALLIANCE Manchester Business School, University of Manchester; Professor Gary Latham, Secretary of State of Organizational Effectiveness, Rotman School of Management, University of Toronto; Allan Bird Professor in Global Business, D'Amore-McKim School of Business, Northeastern University; and Dr Marshall Goldsmith, Professor of International Business at the Tuck School of Business at Dartmouth College.

A special thank you to the many great thinkers, scholars, authors and practitioners whose work has further informed and galvanised my thinking, and focussed and sharpened my work, many of whom without knowing me, generously agreed to review my book and contributed with their invaluable feedback and accolades. They are: Dr Barry Posner, Professor of Leadership, Santa Clara University, and author of *The Leadership Challenge*; Professor Amy Edmondson at Harvard Business School; Professor Ellen Langer at Harvard University; Joseph Raelin, Professor of Management and Organizational Development at Northeastern University; Professor Richard Bolden, Bristol Business School, University of the West of England; Dr Jennifer Martineau, Senior Vice President, Research, Evaluation, and Societal Advancement, Centre for Creative Leadership; Dr Charles Palus, Senior Fellow at the Center for Creative Leadership; David Day, Professor of Psychology and Academic Director of the Kravis Leadership Institute; George Kohlrieser, Professor of Leadership and Organizational Behavior at IMD Business School. Harrison Owen President of H.H. Owen and

Company, and creator of Open Space Technology; Kevin Cashman, CEO of Korn Ferry and best-selling author; and Dr Niklas Nordling, Head of Culture and Organization Development at Nokia.

I also wish to thank a handful of committed practitioners and colleagues who have also contributed to this book with their feedback and endorsements. This includes: Dr Alison Whybrow, Chartered and Coaching Psychologist; Joe "Hark" Herold, CEO & Founder, Hark Leadership; Jeff Olma, Professor of Creativity, Florida State College at Jacksonville; Richard Want, Partner at Kendall Want Associates.

Long before I even thought about writing this book, and worked on many projects, often with colleagues and friends with whom I shared memorable fun times. One that stands out and which I cherish is that of Ron Kemp from iikon, one of the greatest facilitators I have ever met. Ron, your collegiality, sense of humour, and feedback was very special to me, and are things I still remember fondly today. Thank you.

During the early stage of conceptualising the book, I wrote whitepapers that served as early experiments. I wish to thank my two colleagues and friends Ingo Susing – Managing Director of Leadership & Succession Capability, and Kenton Smith, Director of Leaders Aligned, for their reviews and feedback on this preliminary work.

Above all, writing a book requires putting thoughts and original and ideas into serious writing. This requires developing a distinct voice by going through a learning curve. Thank you to Marian Edmunds who assisted me by reviewing and challenging my writing with the first draft proposal for Wiley. I'm also thankful to Donna McTavish for her assistance with the many blogs and other pieces I wrote as part of my early work. Grant Butler and Peter Arnold, who form the Editor Group, assisted me to shape my manuscript with the first round of serious editing. Thank you both.

Thanks to Scott Eathorne from Quikmark Media, who told me that my initial book proposal was an 'excellent document' and introduced me to Wiley.

Experiencing the professionalism of the Wiley team was my next stage. Thank you to Lucy Raymond, Senior Commissioning Editor, my initial contact at Wiley; Theo Vassili, Marketing Coordinator; my copy editor Jane Thompson; and to Chris Shorten, my Project Editor, who really impressed me with his mastery and finesse.

The last group of people who have been indispensable for writing this text are those individuals who had supported me before, during and after the writing of the book. I wish to thank my coach Jacque Merritt at Gallup, who assisted me to explore and appreciate my talents themes, and hone into my strengths. Jacque your unique empathic listening allowed me to access and to rejoice the very depths of my being. Thank you to my good friends Patrick Gallagher and Tony Pagliaroli for their words of encouragement. Gracias to our friend Rowena Prasad for sharing my excitement in writing this book. And finally, but not least, I wish to thank my wife Lisa Sundheim who has always supported me unconditionally. Lisa, I thank you for your ongoing patience and dedication. You have always helped me to see and appreciate a different perspective, and you are the great organiser in my life. I love you!

INTRODUCTION

I have had the privilege of working all over the world with people at all organisational levels, and from many socioeconomic and cultural backgrounds throughout my career as a business psychologist specialising in leadership and organisational development. The most valuable thing my 25 years' experience has taught me is that relationships and integrity used in coordinated collective action have a unique power to achieve the extraordinary.

My first full-time job as a psychologist was with a large international management consulting firm. One of the questions I was asked during the interview process was whether I had a current passport. As soon as I accepted the job offer, I was sent on my first assignment overseas. It was a seven-hour flight from Perth, where I lived at the time, to Auckland in New Zealand. Needless to say, it felt exciting and glamorous. But things changed dramatically after just nine months and disappointment set in. This wasn't a function of having to travel week after week across time zones. It was the actual work.

I realised I was being asked to do the opposite of what I believed in. The promises to clients of increased productivity, cost savings and enhanced profitability came mostly from slashing a significant percentage of their workforce, although it was debatable whether this was good for the company in the long run. The worst part of the job was that we said to the client before the project started that we didn't know where the savings would come from, as this would be determined through our audits and calculations. But in fact, we knew very well that we would recommend massive cuts to the workforce.

I wish I could say that once I realised the job wasn't for me, I quit and moved on—perhaps the best decision with the benefit of hindsight, who knows. Instead, I decided to stay in the hope that things would change. But they didn't, and eventually I was fired. It became obvious to my employer that I wasn't cut out for the job. For me this became a lesson in the importance of being true to yourself, and in sometimes having to do things you don't like but which need to be done. By this time, however, learning from failure, loss and disappointment was already well entrenched in me.

* * *

I was shaken to the core when I was 13 years old. My father died. The first thing my mother said to me, rightly or wrongly, was, 'You're now the head of the family and you must take care of me and your two younger brothers.' It was the highest expectation I had ever had put on me. And I failed miserably.

What I didn't know then was that I was not the first nor the only 'leader' to fail. It took me decades to understand, fully accept, reconcile and live with the idea that it was okay to fail. In fact, it wasn't until I began to study and research leadership seriously, and came across quote after quote from great leaders in history, that I realised that failure was not only inevitable, but also desirable and indispensable to our personal growth and development. Abraham Lincoln said, 'My great concern is not whether you have failed, but whether you are content with your failure.' This really made me think. Then I read Winston Churchill, who said, 'Success is going from failure to failure without losing your enthusiasm.' Nelson Mandela said, 'The greatest glory in living lies not in never falling, but in rising every time we fall.' Even Bill Gates stated, 'It's fine to celebrate success but it is more important to heed the lessons of failure.' The list goes on!

I realise that leadership can be learned, but—paradoxically—cannot be taught. It is a unique journey and entails initiations or rites of passage that enable us to make life transitions. These are often associated with a confronting and painful experience or crisis. For me, losing my father was my rite of passage into adulthood. It laid the groundwork for me to be able to exercise leadership one day. It clearly signified to me the transformation I needed to make in developing a strong sense of my own identity and forging my role in life. Then, by realising that failure is a vital part of growth and success, I was able to question my 'script' in life and reshape my identity.

My greatest breakthrough came in my early twenties when, as a confused young man in search of identity, meaning and purpose, I came to understand myself through the unique value and power of relationships. Possibly my greatest epiphany was the realisation that I had considered myself a victim and believed this was a licence to be self-indulgent. I had been too scared to face up to life and put my best foot forward with confidence and drive. I had uncovered a huge blind spot, and no longer had an excuse for not growing up, taking life by the horns and getting on with living. I had to face the music! As nineteenth-century humourist Henry Wheeler Shaw said, 'It is not only the most difficult thing to know oneself, but the most inconvenient one, too.' How right he was.

I did not imagine at that time that I would become a practitioner of leadership development and an active member of its community. And, like many others, I did not foresee that we would be facing the greatest crisis of leadership the world has ever known, at a cost beyond estimation, causing incalculable human suffering and posing environmental, geopolitical and socioeconomic threats to the future of the world.

The leadership crisis

In our most immediate history, we have witnessed what I call the three Ds of leadership—distrust, doubt and dissent. These are the outcomes when leaders fail to respond effectively to both the changing context in which they must lead, and to the expectations of their stakeholders. In fact, distrust and lack of engagement flag the need for political and business leaders to rethink how to they exercise leadership and engage their followers. Traditional approaches are no longer working, and the game is changing—because people have had enough!

Not surprisingly, only 13 per cent of employees worldwide feel engaged in their organisation[1] and 86 per cent of the world's 1500 foremost global experts agree that we are experiencing a leadership crisis.[2] The obsession with leadership comes from the collective realisation that it has a profound impact on business results. The *Global Leadership Forecast* published by Development Dimensions International (DDI) in 2011 studied 1897 HR professionals and 12 423 leaders from 74 countries, and demonstrated the impact of good leadership on an organisation's bottom line. It estimated that a top-performing leader made an astounding 50 per cent higher impact on a business than an average leader, as well as being 13 times more likely to outperform competitors on key metrics such as financial performance. Plus, higher-quality leaders create levels of employee retention and engagement that are up to three times higher than their average counterparts.[3]

The obsession with leadership and with becoming a leader, however, also stems from the view that leadership is the path to making money, attaining power and social status, achieving prestige and being able to create change. Becoming a leader has become the new mantra in the corporate world. It's no wonder, then, that leadership is such a popular topic. Just about everyone wants to understand it better. Many want to practise it. Others practise it without realising it. Sadly, many more don't understand it, but believe they practise it. This explains the explosive growth of the leadership development industry in the past two decades. It also explains the escalating trends in the abuse of power, corruption and other unethical business practices—which show few signs of declining. The examples are many—Bernie Madoff, Kenneth Lay, Jeffrey Skilling, Robert Mugabe and Richard Nixon, to name a few. The result has been a growing lack of faith in leadership. This has been referred to as the dark side of leadership, or 'bad leadership'.[4]

The crisis is being fuelled by ineffective, unethical and untrustworthy leaders. Individuals and stakeholders caught up in this crisis are frustrated and angry. Many potentially high-performing leaders are ill-prepared to deliver what is required of them, often through no fault of their own, and they are increasingly disillusioned and at risk of burnout. In short, many current leaders lack the skills, qualities and attributes to deal with the challenges. This can be seen in both business and politics and it is affecting economies and societies globally.

Even in politically stable and very prosperous nations such as Australia there are leadership-related business issues of great concern, and challenging social problems. For example, Grant Thornton Australia—one of the world's leading independent assurance, tax and advisory firms, notes 'Losses from fraud and corruption are a significant impediment to achieving growth and strategic objectives of organisations in the Australian Banking and Financial Services sector.'[5] This has prompted the government to demand real leadership from bank heads over cultural issues and it warned that their reputations were at risk.

At work, 75 per cent of employees surveyed in 2016 reported that Australian workplaces needed better managers and leaders.[6] A federal parliamentary inquiry conducted in 2012 estimated that abrasive leaders (commonly referred to as 'bullying bosses') were costing the economy between $6 billion and $36 billion a year.[7] That is unlikely to have improved. Not surprisingly, Australia's leadership capability has slipped significantly compared with other nations, as Australian managers overestimate themselves.[8] The cost of the resulting lack of engagement was put at $54.8 billion a year in 2013.[9]

Does this mean Australia lacks good leadership? Yes, Australia does have a chronic problem as a nation that struggles to distinguish between leadership, authority and power. A saving grace may be that Australia also has many well-documented cases of leaders with exemplary character,[10] who inspire high levels of engagement and extraordinary results.[11] Still, it is not without reason that in 2013 Geoff Aigner and Liz Skelton, senior managers at Social Leadership Australia, published the book *The Australian Leadership Paradox: What it takes to lead in the lucky country*, which emerged as a wake-up call. Paradoxes—situations that appear to be impossible or are difficult to understand because they contain contradictory facts—are a perfect example of what the rest of the world is encountering. In today's world, paradoxes abound.

If a picture is worth a thousand words, the briefest glance at the newspapers or television news or newspapers paints a vivid picture of the global leadership crisis, with escalating trends and all-pervasive images to dismay even the most casual viewer.

I would contend that data, facts and figures say far more than even a thousand words. Let's look at the story that the most credible research at the forefront of contemporary thinking is telling us. Lack of trust and lack of ethical leadership have been identified as the greatest problems organisations face.[12] The ethical expectations and trustworthiness of those leading have declined sharply.[13] This leaves a void that is being filled by unethical business practices, and escalating bribery and corruption, which in 2013 cost more than 5 per cent of global GDP (US$2.6 trillion) annually, with more than US$1 trillion paid annually in bribes.[14] People around the world lack confidence in public and private sector leaders, and organisations are worried that they do not have enough good leaders.[15] According to Deloitte's 2016 *Global Human Capital Trends Report*, which surveyed 7000 business and HR leaders in 130 countries, only 6 per cent of executives said they felt 'very ready' to meet their leadership challenges.[16]

This precarious state of affairs exists despite the fact that organisations invest heavily in preparing their leaders (an estimated US$15.5 billion in the United States in 2013),[17] which in turn has generated explosive growth in the leadership industry. You don't have to be a rocket scientist to figure out that despite the vast expenditure, something is not working. This growing multibillion-dollar leadership development industry is clearly failing to deliver results[18] and corporations have become victims of 'the great training robbery'.[19]

How about that as a paradox?

How this book can help you

Leadership is fundamentally a relationship. The best leaders are authentic, respectful, empathetic, inclusive, consultative and collaborative. They lead with integrity and an uncompromising commitment to ethical excellence. This is how I aspire to work. But it wasn't always that way.

Reflecting on my own life, it's only through objective and fearless self-evaluation that I have learned and made significant progress. From my early, failed attempts at being the 'head' of my family, through my twenties as a restless and disconnected young man, I struggled with many leadership crises of my own. Once I finally decided to do something proactive, I threw myself into fearless self-examination and faced my doubts, fears, insecurities and defects of character, as well as my future. But I discovered that willingness and my own drive was not enough. I could not be a successful leader by myself. I had to reach out for help. I needed to be in relationships with other people. Only then did I begin to fully understand that leadership is fundamentally relational—and there is more on this subject in the next section.

Leadership is a hotly discussed topic. It is the subject of countless research projects across multiple sectors and disciplines. An internet search for 'leadership' yields some 284 million results. Refining the search doesn't help, as 'corporate leadership' returns a staggering 302 million possibilities. Add to that the thousands, possibly hundreds of thousands of books on the topic, and it's easy to feel overwhelmed and confused about how to become a more effective and ethical leader.

I think global leadership is in crisis and after 20-plus years of working in management education and leadership development, I see it only deepening. I know we can do better.

That's what this book is all about and it's why I decided to write it.

When I look at the world today I see despair, violence, depravation, injustice, coercion and the abuse of power. I also see division and disconnectedness, social fragmentation and a lack of fairness in communities and organisations. In the business world, I see wasted talent, lack of critical and creative thinking, risk aversion, ignorance and missed opportunities. But what concerns me most is that the majority of organisations lack the empowerment and leadership capacity that would enable them to counter these issues. This concerns me deeply. It makes my heart sink. But I know there is a way out that promises a better future for us all. The timing is critical—and it's right now!

The question of what constitutes effective leadership and how it can be achieved is now a high priority for all organisations and nations. And despite the fact that the term 'leadership' means many things to many people, it's important to realise that there is an intuitive and unspoken shared understanding of leadership as a 'big social concept'—one of great size and importance. Leadership determines access to health care, education and justice, as well as fair trade, successful business practices, and economic and social prosperity. And this matters. The quality of today's leadership is the key to our future.

From this perspective, I treat leadership and leadership development as a critical social phenomenon, a research discipline, and an essential organisational practice and business imperative. This means separating real outcomes and results from wishful thinking, slogans and vague aspirations. Understanding what leadership is and exercising effective leadership are different things. We need clear vision, fresh thinking, focus, resilience and bold, relentless collective action to effect change. We also need the wisdom to choose what to keep from what we have learned about leadership, and what to get rid of because it no longer serves our needs. This is at the heart of the adaptation (and adaptive leadership)[20] we need to secure our future.

These measures are far from easy. We need the courage and strength to abandon what's no longer working despite our natural tendency to remain in our comfort zone. This means outgrowing our former selves and it means identifying our blind spots—those things we don't know about ourselves—which is the only path to individual and collective self-awareness. Finally, it means developing a greater capacity to relate—and relational leadership is at the heart of this book. In essence, relational leadership is understanding and responding to the unspoken expectations and commitments that bind us. Only then can we build sustainable collective leadership capacity.

Such journeys, even collective ones, always begin with individual personal development. This means finding and owning our unique personal stories to clarify and strengthen our identities. It's important not to confuse this search for self-knowledge with the pursuit of education or the acquisition of new knowledge (knowing), or even the acquisition of new skills or behaviour (doing). What we are looking for ultimately are the ways we must be (being). The latter relates to our identity, character and world view and it's about making a choice, taking a position and a stand in the world. Without this, most so-called leadership training fails to produce effective leaders and build leadership capacity. It just teaches theories, concepts, principles and competency frameworks but ignores the 'being' dimension of leadership.

In 2016, I conducted an extensive review and synthesis of all major works written about the current state of affairs in leadership development. The results clearly pointed to a significant problem—a global leadership crisis. Using the same method, I identified the major causes of the problem. Organisations make ten fundamental and interrelated errors when designing, procuring and delivering leadership development programs. These are discussed in detail in chapter 4.

I also conducted an extensive review of the most prominent contemporary models of leadership, identifying 16 approaches from which I extracted and integrated the very best. The final result is the model presented in this book.

You will take your self-leadership to new heights on this journey and create, as Mahatma Gandhi said, the change you want to see in others and in the world. This will allow you to share your vision with the passion and purpose shown by Nelson Mandela. Then you will boost your credibility and reputation and elevate your leadership capacity to enable your team, organisation, constituency or community to achieve the extraordinary dream, just as Martin Luther King Jr did.

Are these extravagant promises?

Definitely not!

In the words of Nelson Mandela, 'It always seems impossible until it's done.'

A new road map

This book presents a model of leadership for our times. People the world over lack confidence in public and private sector leaders, and organisations are worried they do not have enough good leaders.

This book addresses a big problem in a simple way. We need to go back to basics — relationships — to tackle the leadership crisis effectively. Leadership is fundamentally relational. This means it is not about an individual's attributes — traits, personality, charisma, knowledge, skills, attitudes, competencies or stage of development. Instead it's a social process that emerges from the relational dynamics in organisations. This explains the emergence of social networks. It also explains the spectacular leadership failures of recent times, which I document in the following pages.

Organisations need a paradigm shift in the way leadership is considered, how leaders are developed, how leadership capacity is created, and how their people are engaged. Current leadership development practices remain rooted in old paradigms: the world is changing faster than our capacity to adjust our mental software to deal with it effectively. Despite the rhetoric, the ability to shift paradigms is proving extremely difficult for many organisations. Most keep making the same mistakes. Change is required as a matter of urgency.

To make this change successful and sustainable requires an open and inquisitive mind. This means moving from opinion-based discussions to evidence-based solutions by abandoning naive models of leadership. We need to question our assumptions by challenging our implicit models of leadership, and be prepared to change our leadership narrative and practices accordingly.

This book is based on the latest advancements in leadership, including my ongoing PhD research and professional experience in the field. It is a practical guide and will be of great interest to CEOs, senior executives, middle managers, HR and organisational development (OD) professionals, and enthusiasts and students of leadership.

Above all, this book is designed to deliver leadership results.

Leadership Results®

What if your organisation could build real leadership capacity by developing individual leaders, boosting employee engagement and building collective leadership across the organisation at the same time?

Leadership Results® (LR) is a holistic and integrated model of leadership development. It is a pre-eminent research-based model that offers a relational approach that yields innovation, extraordinary performance and business results.

This book introduces you to the model. It is divided into three parts.

Part I (Leading in context) outlines the new big picture that shapes contemporary leadership practices.

> **Chapter 1** explores the hidden power of relationships, and explains the genesis of this book and the research behind it.

Chapter 2 outlines the new context. It explains why organisations can't see the forest for the trees, and describes the current challenges organisations face.

Chapter 3 discusses what it means to lead without maps and it explains the language, narratives and speakership required to exercise leadership in this new world.

Chapter 4 explains why organisations keep making the same pervasive errors in designing and delivering leadership development programs.

Chapter 5 introduces the LR model, which addresses each of the errors discussed in chapter 4. The LR model has three main components: self-leadership, collective leadership and extraordinary results (which is covered in chapter 13).

Part II (Self-leadership and leader development) explains self-leadership and explores the various approaches to leader development.

Chapter 6 challenges the perennial and misleading closed-ended question as to whether leaders are born or made, explains initiation, and why and how leaders should to be initiated.

Chapter 7 discusses self-leadership and leader development.

Chapter 8 examines emotions, virtues, signature strengths, values, principles, morality and ethics.

Chapter 9 covers motivation, visioning, goal setting, feedback and feedforward, employee engagement, commitment, innovative behaviour and self-engagement.

Part III (Collective leadership and leadership development) explores leadership and leadership development, leadership development methods, spectacular performance and business results, and action planning for results.

Chapter 10 outlines the various forms of pluralistic leadership and explains collective leadership.

Chapter 11 examines leadership development.

Chapter 12 reviews a range of leadership development methods.

Chapter 13 discusses spectacular performance and business results.

Chapter 14 offers a summary and a call for action and results.

This book is designed to be a road map to extraordinary leadership. Consider the following. What if leaders could positively influence others more effectively than they do now? What if they exceed even their own expectations? How can they do this? And what does leadership really mean in the twenty-first century? If any of those thoughts have crossed your mind, this book is for you, because that's what it's all about.

If you work in the leadership development industry and want or are expected to provide innovative solutions for your clients, this book is for you. If you have any desire to become more effective, or to exceed your own expectations and deliver results beyond the predictable, this book is for you. *Leadership Results* details the latest developments: mental software, wisdom and capabilities.

Leadership Results is also for those who, whether they are recognised or not, exercise leadership through their efforts to make a difference in the lives of others, their organisations or their communities. Leaders are not necessarily those in positions of power or authority, but rather those who show leadership.

This is not a publication for bookworms who are happy to accumulate knowledge without putting much, if any, of their newfound learning into action. The leadership journey is not an easy one and it is certainly not for the faint-hearted. But like anything worth doing, the rewards are significant for those willing to venture into the world of personal transformation.

If you would like to unmask the most pervasive leadership myths, learn the latest advancements in leadership development, and take your leadership to the next level by forging strong and sustainable relationships, then read on!

Leadership Results is a book of action that will enable you to achieve results, and lead you to a brighter and better future.

PART I

LEADING IN CONTEXT

This section explains the genesis—and the *why*—of this book. In a world of turbulence, disruption, high velocity, fierce competition, social unrest and uncertainty, current leadership thinking and practices no longer hold water, and the struggling multibillion-dollar leadership development industry is failing to deliver results. I discuss the new context for leadership and its challenges, and examine the new ways of thinking, doing and being required in order to thrive and make a real difference.

There are five chapters in part I:

- Chapter 1 explains the origins of this book and discusses the hidden power of relationships.

- Chapter 2 explores the new context for leadership and its challenges.

- Chapter 3 discusses how to lead without maps: sense-making, storytelling, speakership and the power of language.

- Chapter 4 covers blind spots, naive models of leadership, and why organisations fail to develop effective leaders.

- Chapter 5 presents an integrity model of leadership for our times.

CHAPTER 1

The hidden power of relationships

The genesis of this book

A psychology student asked her mentor, the head of a research laboratory, to reveal the secret to truly meaningful collaboration and high performance in a team environment.

The mentor liked the question and respected the student's keen and inquiring mind, so he took her to a room where an experiment was in progress. The subjects of the experiment sat around a large round table, on which was a huge bowl containing a selection of healthy and appetising food. Exquisite aromas filled the room and the food looked so tempting the student's mouth watered.

However, the people appeared miserable and uncomfortable. Each of them held a spoon with an extremely long handle, and while they could reach into the bowl and take a portion of food, the handle was much longer than their arms, preventing them from getting the spoons into their mouths. The student watched in amazement for a while before the mentor suggested they move on.

(continued)

3

The mentor took the student to another room. The setting was the same as that in the first room — people were seated around a large round table containing a bowl of delicious, abundant foodstuffs, with the same long-handled spoons. The difference was that the people in this room were laughing and talking, enjoying each other's company and relishing the food before them in an atmosphere of conviviality.

It took the student just a moment to comprehend the difference. Every so often a person at the table would reach forward and scoop up a morsel of food before offering it to someone else. Occasionally someone asked another to feed them with something they found particularly tasty.

'I don't understand', said the student. 'Why has the other group not adopted the same practice?'

The mentor smiled. 'It's very simple', he replied. 'The people in this room learned very quickly how to cooperate with one another. In contrast, the people in the other room are trying to look after themselves — their mindset is still one of personal gratification and self-preservation.'

When individuals in groups, teams or within organisations seek to nourish only themselves, everyone goes hungry. But when they look after their fellow team members and colleagues, they discover a myriad clever ways in which to nourish one another, and the outcome is a healthier and happier whole.

This reinforces what I have learned over many years of working with high-performing teams in complex and high-value collaborative projects. My experiences in these exciting environments became the genesis of my research — and the foundation for this book.

The power of relationships is like an iceberg in relation to their impact on an organisation's or team's endeavours. There is extraordinary capacity and untapped potential beyond what is immediately visible and obvious. Here are some examples.

The National Museum of Australia is a record of the land, nation and people of Australia. Built on the Acton Peninsula in the centre of Canberra in 2000, it is also a unique achievement in terms of its architecture and construction. The museum was the world's first project alliance in building construction, and as such is the embodiment of what can be achieved through working relationships based on mutual respect, trust and integrity. The Wandoo Offshore Oil Platform—Australia's first project alliance, in 1999—is another outstanding example.

Leadership and effective team relationships are the keys to a successful project alliance, which is a procurement method based on selecting participants based on fit rather than tender price. It has been one of the most innovative and successful methods for delivering large and complex high-value capital projects, such as motorways, bridges, tunnels, dams, pipelines, railways, submarines, airports, public buildings and shopping malls. In essence, a project alliance is a superlative example of a high-performing team committed to achieving results that are often referred to as 'ground-breaking', 'extraordinary outcomes' or 'breakthroughs'.

The total value of project alliances in the Australian road, rail and water sectors between 2004 and 2009 was $32 billion. This represented 29 per cent of the nation's total infrastructure spend of $110 billion.[1] At that time, Australia was recognised as the world leader in such projects,[2] which were described as the embodiment of collective responsibility, innovation, high performance and authentic leadership for the twenty-first century.[3]

But project alliances have their own challenges. The project team—the project owner and its partners—must be a high-performing collective. A key requirement is to develop and sustain an 'open book' and collaborative approach with a 'no blame' culture. This is easier said than done and does not come naturally. The team must develop its own identity, sense of purpose, common goals and culture. This can be challenging because team members come from different organisational cultures in the government and private sectors, and must unite and work quickly to avoid project delays. This is when the magic of collaborative relationships becomes critical to success.

Highly effective and successful teams arise when each member thrives in relationships with others, enabling them to reach unusual levels of collaboration and achieve unprecedented results. The catalyst is leadership. I see the connection to my own experience; I know the amazing power leadership and relationships have to change peoples' lives—as they have changed mine.

All for one, and one for all

The famous mantra of the Three Musketeers hits the nail on the head, and perhaps that's why their story has held people in its thrall through the ages. It strikes at the heart of something we all know instinctively to be true and is a powerful model when put to use. It also encapsulates perfectly what it takes to form and sustain a project alliance—and for that matter any high-performance team.

Highly effective and successful teams arise when each member thrives in relationships with others

When all members of an alliance support its individual members, and each one pledges to support the alliance, that alliance can move mountains. Highly successful teams are formed by individuals who enjoy autonomy, possess unique knowledge and skills, are responsible and interdependent, and who can work confidently together to pursue the same goals and objectives. They are accountable to each other and their stakeholders, while each having unique responsibilities. Problems become everyone's problems. There is no blaming, and team members support each other. Their sense of identity is always aligned to the collective, with their position and point of view representing the alliance, not an individual's stand. As a result, the team's efforts are greater than the sum of its single members. This is known as 'synergy'; it characterises truly high-performing teams and is what makes an alliance uniquely powerful and potent.

One of the most high-profile project alliances I worked on was the Air Warfare Destroyer Alliance project in 2008, valued at $8 billion, the most significant shipbuilding project in Australia's history. The aim was to deliver three Hobart-class air warfare destroyers to the Royal Australian Navy between 2015 and 2017. I helped the senior leadership team with its alignment and development during the formation of the alliance. I also helped other teams across the alliance build leadership capabilities and culture, which included supporting and coaching the various teams while addressing the inevitable problems, issues and setbacks.

Two of my experiences working with project alliances stand out. In the first, everyone consistently spoke in awe and with a sense almost of reverence about the power of collaboration and relationships. They attributed the success of the alliance to the quality of relationships among team members. Intuitively, this made a lot of sense to them. However, no-one could explain what it was, specifically, that made their high levels of collaboration possible, or what characteristics were critical to success. Everyone spoke of trust, for example, but no-one could explain how this trust came about or was enhanced and sustained. They had no idea how it could be measured, described or used to predict the impact on team performance and project outcomes.

The second experience, which impressed me even more than the first, was several alliances in which most of the individuals became convinced that there was no way they could return to work with their own organisations. Usually, alliance members go back to their original employers at the end of the project. However, these individuals were downcast at the prospect of going back to the 'old' or 'traditional' ways of working. They felt transformed by the alliance experience and, like passengers upgraded to first class on an outbound flight, they did not relish making the inbound journey in economy.

In the context of the opening story of this chapter, who would want to belong to the group that wanted to feed only themselves, having seen the dynamics of the other, thriving and collaborative group?

In search of gold

As a psychologist and researcher, I found the challenge of identifying the exact nature of the relationships formed in alliances, as well as their transformative impact, irresistible. These questions led me to begin my PhD in 2009. My research was on how to identify the factors or variables that made some alliances more successful than others, and the effects of these factors. I had to put together a model that could measure the health of relationships to compare alliances. The model also had to be able to predict each alliance's performance through the quality of these relationships. So, I adopted a predictive model proposed by David Guest, professor of Organisational Psychology and Human Resource Management at King's College, University of London, based on psychological contract theory.

The term 'psychological contract' was coined by Chris Argyris (1923–2013), Professor Emeritus at Harvard Business School, who was known for his seminal work on learning organisations. Psychological contracts, unlike formal written employment contracts, are the unspoken and unwritten (tacit or implicit) 'promises' or 'expectations' between parties in employment relationships. These parties include employers, managers, individual employees and their peers. Psychological contracts are the lifeblood of relationships—critical aspects of workplace relationships and wider human behaviour. While most of the contract remains invisible, it doesn't mean it can't be measured. In fact, this was what I set out to do.

I conducted in-depth interviews with 24 of Australia's most experienced alliance practitioners, who had more than 600 years of combined industry experience. This enabled me to validate the premise of my proposed research model, that the quality of relationships in alliances could lead to extraordinary performance outcomes. This is a typical response:

> I often ask people to think back to the most successful contracts they ran and why they were successful. Almost without fail, they come back to the relationships. Successful contracts come from relationships.

Overwhelmingly, participants agreed that in an alliance, good relationships are critical at all levels and influence problem-solving and project outcomes in both positive and negative ways.

All participants identified trust as the key ingredient for alliance success and the health of alliance relationships at all levels. The most common sources of conflict in alliances are the breakdown of trust, communication and respect. This is how one interviewee sees it:

> Trust isn't something that just happens naturally. It is actually something that has to be earned. People have to understand when

other alliance participants are exposed or might be apprehensive about a situation. This becomes an opportunity to generate trust. Developing and generating trust is a key issue and something that is not easy at all levels, and it takes a while.

Trustworthy behaviour means being true to one's word, collaboratively and respectfully addressing differences and challenges, and listening to others to understand precisely what they are saying. This can generate insights, for example, into any issues that may require the support of others.

The most effective way to elicit trust is by modelling trustworthy behaviour. This may result in alliance team members making themselves vulnerable, and it requires risk-taking and courage from everyone. The benefits of trust are multiple, however. They include allowing team members to understand each other, providing alignment, reducing risk and uncertainty, maximising flexibility, enabling successful execution of work, and saving time and money.

Discretionary effort (willingness to voluntarily put in extra effort) is variable and an outcome of healthy alliance relationships that most participants considered to be very important. One interviewee commented: 'Discretionary effort returns incredible value to the project. If you can create a culture and atmosphere that breeds discretionary effort, you will be successful.'

Effort is not restricted to the physical, but includes any behaviour related to doing the job better. Examples include finding ways to better perform jobs; taking on additional duties; assisting others with their work; sharing information with other alliance members or stakeholders; and voluntarily allocating thinking time for work-related problems or challenges, outside working hours. Discretionary effort also can be thought of as the difference between a person's performance and their capability. It depends on an individual's level of motivation, inspiration and/or commitment.

Innovation is another outcome variable of healthy working relationships. Innovative behaviour refers to an individual's attitude towards change—the generation, acceptance and adoption of new ideas or practices. It also relates to a perseverance in implementing new and promising ideas. One interviewee put it this way:

> In the good alliances that I have been involved in, no-one says to you, 'You have only got so many hours to do this job.' What you are told is that if you can come up with a better way of doing this, then do it! It is amazing what this does. It throws off the shackles; it liberates people. When people are put in a position where the shackles are removed, it is just bloody amazing.

Innovation is encouraged and promoted by giving people the time, freedom and permission to think creatively and approach tasks and challenges their own way, as opposed to telling them what to do. This is how one interviewee approaches innovation:

> We should never stop thinking about innovation. Never stop thinking about making improvements, whatever they might be; we try and encourage that all the way through.

Innovation is linked to a leadership commitment that is demonstrated by continuing support and encouragement. This includes allowing people to take risks and make mistakes, as well as developing and supporting creative thinking.

* * *

Once I validated my research model, I collected data by surveying 17 project alliances across various industry sectors. In 2010 I presented my results at the twenty-seventh International Congress of Applied Psychology Melbourne, and at the Alliance Contracting Excellence Summit in Sydney. My most interesting discovery was that the award-winning alliance at the summit was the alliance with the highest scores in all relational dimensions in my dataset, such as fulfilment of expectations, trust and fairness. Furthermore, when I looked again at my data, I noticed that one of the key differences between the award winner and the other contenders was the high credibility scores of the alliance manager or leader.

At that point, I knew I was on to something. I had found gold!

This led me to formulate a new relational model which I named, at the time, the Leadership Psychological Contract (LPC). This refers to the unspoken and unwritten expectations of leaders and their teams. I presented my new model from 2011 at various industry events and international conferences, culminating with the presentation of the fourth version of the model at the twenty-eighth International Congress of Applied Psychology at the Palais des Congrès in Paris. This was followed by publication in the *Journal of Business Strategy* in 2014, a book chapter in *Leadership 2050: Critical challenges, key contexts, and emerging trends* in 2015, and another book chapter in *Business Psychology in Action: Creating flourishing organisations through evidence-based, and emerging practices* in 2016.

Conclusion

Relationships are critical to any endeavour. Every relationship is governed by a psychological contract or set of unwritten and spoken expectations, perceived promises or implied obligations. Despite being highly subjective, the psychological contract is the glue that holds relationships together. Healthy and trusting relationships are critical to achieving extraordinary performance.

Your leadership psychological contract with your team members and stakeholders is like the wind. It's invisible, but its impact is real and makes a real difference to your journey. It can slow you down, cause havoc, or make for very smooth sailing. You'd be wise to learn how the wind is likely to blow.

Insight questions

- Could your team legitimately claim the mantra 'All for one, and one for all'?

- Do they know how to feed each other?

- Do your team members understand the power of the psychological contracts they have with you and with each other?

- Are you fully leveraging the relationship with your team members and stakeholders?

- How could your team take the quality of their relationships to the next level?

CHAPTER 2

The new context for leadership

Do you still believe in leadership gurus?

For the first time in its history, a large organisation experienced what the CEO and his executive team described as an intractable challenge. The executive failed, time and time again, to resolve this unprecedented crisis. In desperation, they invited a world renowned leadership consultant to help them.

In the town hall meeting, everyone in the organisation gathered to hear what the consultant had to say, but to their surprise, he asked them just one simple question.

'Can you guess what I am going to say?'

'No,' they replied, puzzled.

'Then I can't teach you something that you don't already know,' the consultant replied enigmatically. And with that, he left without further comment. Everyone was disappointed, to say the least, and their problem remained unsolved.

Many weeks passed, but the problem remained unsolved. The executive deliberated and sent a second invitation to the consultant and in preparation for his arrival, the executive coached all managers and employees to this time say 'YES' in response to the consultant's question.

Once again, the consultant arrived and once again everyone from the organisation gathered to hear his counsel. As before, he asked,

'Can you guess what I'm going to say?'

The executive looked at the crowd and all at once they shouted 'YES!'

Unflinchingly, the consultant responded 'Then what use is there for me to tell you anything?' And again, he left without giving any further advice.

This time the executive, managers, and employees were perplexed and angry. They had prepared for the consultant's advice and been willing to listen to his words of wisdom.

They continued to struggle to solve their problem for months as they tried to understand why the consultant was offering them nothing. After many more months, and with some desperation, the executive issued a third invitation to the consultant, and this time they hoped to be ready for him. The organisation gathered around and for a third time, the consultant asked, 'Can you guess what I'm going to say?'

In response, half of the organisation shouted 'YES!' while the other half shouted 'NO!'

But the consultant was unruffled. He stared at the crowd and replied, 'Then those that know should sit down and talk with those that don't know, and then together you will all have the answers.' And with that the consultant left, never to return.

The next morning, and after much deliberation and reflection, the CEO elatedly gathered the entire organisation together once more. He had finally understood the consultant's message. 'The answer to all our problems can be found within our organisation, in our experience and in our accumulated wisdom, not from outside consultants like him. It is not our knowledge and wisdom that fails us, but our self-belief and self-assurance.'

This story reminds us that in times of unprecedented change, uncertainty, complexity and high velocity, traditional models of leadership no longer hold water. We need to grasp the new context for leadership using capabilities that have been largely ignored by organisational and leadership development practitioners. In this chapter, I explore some of the most fundamental knowledge, skills, insights and mental software we need in order to acquire 'the confidence to believe in ourselves'—as revealed by the CEO—to adapt to the new context for leadership.

Why can't organisations see the forest for the trees?

Leadership never occurs in a vacuum—it is a highly contextualised phenomenon. As the context changes, so, too, does leadership. The context for leadership, as we know it, has been turned upside down. The new context is one shaped by a complex, turbulent and high-velocity environment. Turbulence refers to the degree of change and complexity created by constantly changing economic conditions. High-velocity environments are characterised by rapid and continuous change in response to competition, new technologies and/or regulations in which information quickly becomes inaccurate, unavailable or obsolete. Business today is VUCA (volatile, unpredictable, complex and ambiguous).[1]

Like the people in the story, we need to shift our attention and hopes away from hero- and individual-based models of leadership to more contextual, relational and collective models. This is because leadership is—above all—a collective endeavour.[2]

As we face rapid change and complexity, contextual intelligence (CI)—the practical application of knowledge and information—has become as important as any other type of intelligence. CI relates to fully understanding the context in which we operate so we can successfully navigate complexity and respond appropriately to change.[3] This requires us to use hindsight, insight and foresight. Hindsight is about taking full advantage of what we have learned. Foresight is about clearly articulating what we wish to become and clarifying what we can do to reach this goal. Informed by hindsight and inspired by foresight, we can gain the clarity and understanding needed to make decisions.

By tapping into our experience and accumulated wisdom, as noted from the CEO's revelation in the opening story, we do more than use our CI. We also develop learning agility[4] — the flexibility and dexterity to adapt our behaviour to changing situations. This enables us to rapidly analyse and understand new situations and business problems, as well as learn from experience.

Equally relevant is the application of four high-level core leadership capabilities identified by Deborah Ancona, Professor of Management and Organization Studies, and the Director of the MIT Leadership Center at the MIT Sloan School of Management.[5]

First, sense-making — to understand and map the context in which a company and your people operate. Second, visioning — to create a vivid and irresistible picture of the future. Third, inventing — to develop new ways to reach this vision. Finally, relating — to build trusting relationships with all stakeholders.

The new context is a global village. Many organisations are richly diverse cultural, political and institutional systems built to achieve ambitions on a global scale. At the core of their business they manage multiplicities, tackle huge challenges, grapple with instability and ambiguity, and must be able to navigate these challenges to survive. They also need to face new kinds of problems, take on new and challenging tasks, perform across cultures, and work with virtual teams, often on a temporary basis.

A few years ago, I had the privilege to travel across four continents over four years delivering a leadership development program for a global industry champion at the frontier of engineering innovation. The company, with a workforce of 18 800 employees of 120 nationalities in

70 countries, wanted to generate and maintain a healthy pipeline of leaders with the strategic thinking, business acumen and intercultural competence to take the company into a successful global future. Many of its managers had to learn how to identify and tackle new types of challenges, adapt to local cultures and market needs, and shift to decentralised and collaborative decision making while preserving the company's unique DNA—its culture, values and behaviour.

This is what I learned: Culture is pervasive and has multiple layers that can often be invisible to the untrained eye. It acts like a pair of glasses that colours our vision. Culture works like a powerful filter through which we perceive and experience reality. It is like the mental software that we use to decode, interpret, encode and send messages. Culture determines how people 'do things around here'; it is the 'unwritten rules of the social game', and what we consider 'normal'. It is the glue that holds societies together. Leadership beliefs, expectations and practices are not readily portable from one culture to another. Hence, applying them uniformly across geographies is a fool's errand, much as we'd like to think otherwise. All this makes culture a critical business risk.

But old habits die hard.

The difficulty lies not so much in developing new ideas as in escaping from old ones.
—John Maynard Keynes

To achieve our objective of adapting to our new context, I draw on my own personal and professional experiences, as well as those of others—clients and colleagues—by using case examples and short stories. Above all, however, I resort to the latest research in the field—including my own. This means that, as a reader, you may feel challenged by findings that seem counterintuitive and contradict your current beliefs (especially if you consider your beliefs to be fundamental truths). This book introduces a new vocabulary that will become indispensable, not only for corporate and community leaders, but ultimately also, within the next decade, for mainstream society. Perhaps you will embrace the new language that may bring new meaning to your own experiences; or you may be inclined to dismiss it as jargon or buzzwords. Let me illustrate this by using the following historical reflection.

The word 'stress', for example, did not have the physiological meaning it has today before the 1920s. 'Stress' is now used very commonly in modern daily life to describe bodily responses to such things as fear or pain. Once upon a time, terms such as 'soft skills', 'emotional intelligence', 'sustainability', 'corporate social responsibility', 'learning agility', 'paradigm shift' and 'social capital' were considered specialist language or jargon. Progressively, over the years, these terms have been embraced more broadly. Many of these terms, in fact, are now in general use — at least in the corporate world and among leadership readers.

Here are more specific examples. The now commonly used term 'brainstorming' was popularised by Alex Osborn in his book *Applied Imagination*, published 1953. It was not used before then. Mihaly Csikszentmihalyi introduced the concept of 'flow' in his 1990 book *Flow: The psychology of optimal experience*. Clayton Christensen popularised the concept of 'disruptive innovation' in his 1997 book *The Innovator's Dilemma: When new technologies cause great firms to fail*. Today, the word 'disruption' is used everywhere. 'Positive psychology' was popularised in 2000 by Martin Seligman and Mihaly Csikszentmihalyi in their paper 'Positive psychology: An introduction' published in *American Psychologist*. 'Cultural intelligence' entered the popular language in 2003 through Christopher Earley and Soon Ang's book *Cultural Intelligence: Individual interactions across cultures*. Daniel Pink, in his 2005 bestseller *A Whole New Mind*, reminded us that we are moving from the information age to the 'conceptual age', and that the 'keys of the kingdom are changing hands'. In 2006, Carol Dweck popularised the term 'mindset' in her book *Mindset: The new psychology of success*.

These terms were already known to experts in the field but at some point, someone, not necessarily the originator of the concept, has taken the idea to the mainstream. Initially they were considered buzzwords. A good example was Daniel Goleman's popularisation of the term 'emotional intelligence' in his book of the same name. In 1999 Goleman, at that time a science reporter at *The New York Times*, borrowed the term (with permission) from two academics: John Mayer, currently at University of New Hampshire, and Peter Salovey, currently at Yale University, who had formulated the concept of 'emotional intelligence'. Another example is the concept of the Leadership Psychological Contract (LPC; the unspoken and unwritten expectations between leaders and their followers, teams or stakeholders) I introduced in the article 'Messing with corporate heads? Psychological contracts and leadership integrity' published in 2014 in the *Journal of Business Strategy*.

These new terms can sound technical or jargonistic—for good reason—at first glance. However, I have seen the benefits people derive from such terms once they are properly explained and demystified. Never dismiss new terms as jargon and never be afraid to learn new words. Imagine where you would be today if you had stopped learning new concepts after you left school. I hope this book makes such terms—their meaning and benefits—accessible, easy to comprehend and as easy as possible to apply. In this way, you—and everyone with whom you share your learnings—will benefit.

Adaptive challenges

The main challenges today are not technical, but rather 'adaptive'.[6] Technical problems are easy to identify, are well-defined, and can be solved by applying well-known solutions or the knowledge of experts. In contrast, adaptive challenges are difficult to define, have no known or clear-cut solutions, and call for new ideas to bring about change in numerous places.

> The main challenges we face are not technological, but adaptive.

Examples of adaptive challenges include climate change and other environmental challenges, social unrest, terrorism, poverty, homelessness, suicide, violence against women, and corruption. In organisations, examples of adaptive challenges include designing a new system or procedure, successfully implementing it, securing agreement for a policy change, and dealing with multiple complex people-management issues or stakeholder relationships.

Consider the following scenario. You are the sales director of a global company that wants to launch a new sales management system. Its successful implementation requires everyone across multiple geographic regions to use the system by certain date. One morning, while driving to work, you suddenly have a flat tyre. What do you do? Easy! You, or someone else, replace the flat tyre with the spare—problem solved!

When you arrive at the office, you find a stack of emails and telephone messages from multiple regional sales managers and other sales representatives questioning the implementation of the new system. Many people want to talk to you about it, saying you are missing key pieces of the puzzle. You already know, via the grapevine and conversations with others, that about 40 per cent of the sales force believes the old system did not need to be replaced, and that everyone is sick and tired of changes—this being the third major one this year. This is despite the communications department having sent multiple messages explaining the business case for this major and important change. You also know that if this change doesn't happen successfully on time, it will cost your company millions of dollars, and will risk losing many very valuable customers. How can you ensure that the entire sales force of 120 people will help implement the required changes on time? Can you treat this challenge in the same way you dealt with the flat tyre? I'll let you answer this question—although we both know the answer.

Adaptive challenges require very uncomfortable work, including, for example, changing attitudes, behaviour and values. It also entails increasing tolerance for conflict, uncertainty and risk. It is no wonder that adaptive change engenders resistance, because it challenges our habits, strongly held beliefs and values. Yet this adaptation is critical to our survival. This relates directly to Darwin's concept of adaptation, whereby we are better placed to survive or reproduce by becoming better suited to our environment through change.

Above all, we need different perspectives on leadership to make progress on adaptive challenges. In particular, inappropriate expectations of authority need to be eradicated. It no longer works to hold the individuals in formal positions of power or authority responsible for causing or solving organisational or community problems. Like the guru in the story, the C-suite and other senior managers are no longer the experts with prescriptive formulas or solutions. Adaptive challenges must be addressed by the people directly connected to the problems. They are the ones with access to their own collective intelligence and a reservoir of resources that is more likely to bring the needed solution.

Leadership traditionally has been—and sadly for many, still is—mistaken for authority and power in all of its many forms, such as legitimate, coercive, expert, informational, reward, connection and referent. Authority relates to exercising conferred and legitimate power to perform a service, and to the people who follow those exercising such power. This is because their positions demand such authority, irrespective of who holds the position.

Leadership, on the other hand, relates to exercising influence, with or without authority, that creates willing followers. That is, those who are not forced to accept anything thrown their way. Leadership relies on trust and fairness and, to a large degree, meeting mutual expectations. For example, Gandhi, for the most part, did not hold any official position to enable him to lead the freedom struggle in India. He did not gain followers because he held a position of authority; he became a trusted leader because of his strong vision, judgement, respected expertise and integrity.

Let's go back to the sales example. As a sales director, you are in a position of authority and, for example, could fire anyone who does not comply with the changes, but that's not enough to ensure the smooth introduction of the new system. What would be your strategy to ensure everyone embraces the changes?

Globally, the challenge is to prepare for a combination of macro socioeconomic trends that may herald a 'perfect storm'[7] of new forces. In this scenario, business leaders will have to grapple with new dilemmas and challenges. This will require considerable foresight and collaboration between internal and external stakeholders. As yet, though, current business, political and community leaders are still struggling to find their way and are still failing to respond effectively.

From this perspective, it is also important to realise that leadership occurs in a social context. This not only links to the relating capability of leadership, but also to the fact that relationships are governed by psychological contracts,[8] as highlighted in the previous chapter.

Global mindsets and cultural intelligence

A major global insurer with more than 15 000 employees in 50 countries decided to establish a new call centre in the Philippines, outsourcing hundreds of jobs to generate sustainable savings. However, underestimating the cultural impact put the forecast savings in jeopardy.

Filipinos use a 'high context' communication style that tends to be indirect and formal, combining verbal and non-verbal messages to convey meaning. The listener must 'read between the lines' and understand non-verbal nuances to fully comprehend the message. Individuals from high-context cultures find it extremely difficult to say no, as it can be construed as confrontational, unfriendly and disrespectful, causing loss of face and embarrassment. For Filipinos, maintaining harmony—a Confucian value shared across Asia—is far more important than being informative. As an example, remaining silent and not questioning customers' understanding of policies would be preferred over clarifying to confirm comprehension.

In contrast, 'low context' cultures (such as the United States, Canada, the UK and Australia)—where most of the insurer's customers live, and with whom the Filipinos in the call centre have to deal—use a direct communication style. This relies on literal and precise meaning with a preference for explicit conversations in which words convey the entire message, or at least most of it. Not surprisingly, the marked contrast in communication styles caused havoc during the early days at the new call centre. The lesson for the insurer was that it is very risky to ignore cultural differences and assume that English fluency equates to effective communication.

But the confusion in customer communication was only part of the story. Internal communications were also compromised. Requests commonly used by people from the insurer's head office (such as 'Would you mind sending the latest figures?') were indecipherable to the Filipinos. A more direct request, such as 'Please, send me the latest figures as soon as possible', would have been far more effective.

Further, it is important to be aware that Filipino culture uses holistic thinking (understanding the system by sensing its large-scale patterns and reacting to them), as opposed to an analytic style (understanding the system by thinking about its parts and how they work together to produce larger-scale effects).

Eventually, the insurer invested heavily in comprehensive intercultural training, both for key head-office employees and call centre employees in the Philippines. The training resulted in better understanding and appreciation of cultural differences and improved communication between the call centre and head office. This illustrates the importance of acquiring a global mindset[9] by identifying and understanding the implications of our thinking style when communicating with individuals from different cultures.

We now live in a global village. This means most organisations have diverse cultural, political and institutional systems to help them achieve their global ambitions while managing multiplicities, tackling huge challenges, grappling with instability and navigating ambiguity.[10] Consequently, they now rely on creative thinking, innovation and developing global mindsets—the ability to absorb information, understand traditions and cultural norms with openness and awareness of diversity, and to be able to exercise global leadership—to effect change. They can do this by building communities through trust in conditions of cultural, geographical, and temporal complexity involving multiple authority sources, multiple stakeholders, and multiple cultures.

Adding to the complexity are the challenges associated with transferring tacit knowledge into explicit knowledge. Explicit knowledge can be expressed easily and communicated verbally or in writing, formulae or codes. Tacit (or implicit) knowledge is difficult to write down, codify, visualise, share and transfer. And yet, as the insurer discovered, all these things must be shared across cultural and organisational boundaries if they are to become the explicit knowledge that enables organisations to build and sustain a competitive advantage.

Within this global context, it is also important to acquire cultural intelligence[11] — the capability to relate and work effectively across cultures. This is sometimes also referred to as intercultural competence.[12] The following example illustrates this capability in action.

In 2014, much to my surprise, I learned that I was perceived as arrogant and disrespectful after talking about my plans to work with a group of senior leaders from the Abu Dhabi police headquarters. I was quietly taken aside and told, very diplomatically, 'In the Arab world — we, Muslims, when we talk about the future, use the expression "Insha Allah" at the end of our sentences.' This translates as 'God willing', an expression that is part of every Muslim's daily vocabulary. Islam teaches believers not to make definitive statements about the future — only God knows what will happen. The phrase is also commonly used as a sign of respect. This was a humbling experience that allowed me to become more culturally aware and, therefore, more effective. During the rest of our week of working together, I used the expression and received smiles of acknowledgement and gratitude from my clients.

Showing respect is a universal expectation that I had unwittingly failed to meet until the gap in my cultural knowledge was bridged. Cultural intelligence creates the capability to relate and work effectively across cultures, which is also relevant to domestic managers and leaders working in their own countries because modern economies are multicultural environments. Australia, for example, is one of the most multicultural societies in the world. This explains the increasing number of workplace initiatives aimed at managing and leveraging cultural diversity to promote innovation.

But all this is just the tip of the iceberg. There is so much more!

The next chapter explores how having identified and understood the complexities of the new context, you can then quickly explain them to others and map them in your organisation. This is the essence of sense-making.

Conclusion

Context and leadership are inseparable. The context for leadership as we know it has been turned upside down. The world is now characterised by high turbulence and velocity, volatility, unpredictability, complexity and ambiguity. This calls for a shift from heroic or individual models of leadership to more contextual, relational and collective approaches. In acquiring the confidence to make this shift, we need to develop our contextual intelligence, learning agility and the application of four high-level core leadership capabilities (sense-making, visioning, inventing and relating). Further, we need to distinguish between technical problems and adaptive challenges to exercise effective leadership in the new context. Finally, as the new context is a global village, we also need a global mindset as well as cultural intelligence or intercultural competence. Only then will we be able to see the forest for the trees!

Insight questions

- Does your team believe in leadership gurus?

- Do they understand the new context?

- Do they have the confidence to face the new context?

- What specific factors are impacting you and your team in the new context for leadership?

- How have you adjusted your leadership practices to adapt to the new context?

- Does your team understand the difference between technical problems and adaptive challenges?

- Does your team understand the difference between authority and leadership?

(continued)

- Are your team members aware of their psychological contracts with customers and other key stakeholders?
- Is your team aware of the risks of working across cultures and with people from different cultural backgrounds?
- Do they have a global mindset?
- Do your team members display intercultural competence?
- Is your team open to learning new concepts?

CHAPTER 3

Leading without maps: Sense-making

Can any map work?

A small group of highly successful senior managers decided to challenge themselves by climbing Mount Everest to validate their legacy. They were all elated at first, savouring the adventure of their lives. But this was short-lived. Suddenly, things turned sour.

Extreme weather descended on them on the second day, sparking an avalanche; and to make things worse, their porter fell off a sheer cliff and disappeared carrying valuable supplies. Everyone was shocked and tried to come to terms with their predicament in their own ways. The group was paralysed—physically, mentally and emotionally.

On the third day, still dazed by their traumatic experience, the group resumed their journey. But after two days of feeling like they were going around in circles, they considered themselves lost. It was still snowing

(continued)

and their cold, hunger and isolation was amplified. Doubt, combined with the knowledge that about 280 people had died climbing the mountain in the past few decades and that fatalities occurred every year, crept into everyone's mind. Another avalanche was no longer a remote possibility. Morale and energy were low, the silence grew, and what had been a natural and unspoken fear turned into panic.

Unexpectedly, one of the group announced he had found a map in his backpack. Everyone surrounded him to study the map and gauge the situation for themselves. Once the group had inspected the map, located where they were and planned their way back to the base, everyone settled down. Hope had emerged and energy was restored. The group tracked the landmarks they had identified on the map and recalibrated their direction at various times. Their sense of progress and confidence was gradually restored.

At various points in the journey, different group members contributed their unique observations, suggestions and ideas. One, for example, shared that she had read it was important that they regularly correlate what was on the map with what they saw around them. This helped sharpen the group's senses and allowed them to use their imaginations to conceptualise a path to the base.

Another told the group a highly experienced Norwegian mountain climber had told him that keeping a steady pace and never rushing were critical to navigation in such conditions. He made the point that estimating their walking speed would be vital in calculating the approximate distance they had covered from their last known location. This encouraged the group to be fully present to their experience and to take the time to collect their thoughts while consuming their meagre supplies, and study the map and their surroundings.

After two days of navigation—much of which had seemed like trial and error—the group reached the base exhausted but safe. The big surprise was that the adventurers learned that the map they had been following was of the Yumthang Valley, which is surrounded by the Himalayan mountains in North Sikkim, India—about 175 km from Mount Everest.

So, what's the moral of the story and how does it relate to leadership?

Sense-making, as the term indicates, is about making sense of the world by creating a picture that enables us to act. It is one of the four core leadership capabilities (along with relating, visioning and inventing) for contemporary complex, uncertain and dynamic environments.[1] Sense-making is not concerned with accuracy, or finding the 'correct' answer, but about plausibility; that is, what seems reasonable, probable, believable or valid at the time. As is shown in the story, when you are lost, cold, hungry and in a panic, any map will do. This is because, when dealing with ambiguity, individuals 'search for meaning, settle for plausibility, and move on'.[2]

In the story, despite the fact the map did not accurately represent the surroundings, it gave the group the hope and confidence to make good decisions and not give up. This triggered their internal resources, as the climbers kept searching for answers by retrieving valuable knowledge from their reservoir of memories that related to the crisis at hand. The group was also able to slow down and develop mindfulness and presence.[3] They focused their full attention in the present and became aware of their thoughts and actions, thus becoming highly sensitive to their surroundings. Sharpening their senses, they were then able to respond to the crisis more instinctively while limiting distractions, and look after themselves without losing the plot. This is an example of how sense-making can allow people to reinterpret reality in a way that enables them to bring their very best to the fore.

> Sense-making is about making sense of the world by creating a picture that enables us to act.

Rapid and disruptive change propelled by technological developments in organisations are now the norm. This can cause confusion and uncertainty. Such upheavals often create unfamiliar and incomprehensible situations. When dealing with confusion and ambiguity, individuals search for meaning. Therefore, more than ever before, leaders need to demonstrate sense-making to enable individuals to understand experiences, events or issues that are confusing, unexpected and often unwanted.

A further lesson from the story is that where we choose to look, the place where we choose to put our focus and the parts of the area we choose to show, ultimately drive what we 'map' in life. Our choices (not the realities) are what govern the kind of life we live. Therefore, there can be no perfect path. The group's choice was to move, search and recalibrate. This demonstrates that making sense is an act of creativity, not just one of analysis.

The genesis of sense-making is chaos, crisis and confusion as people attempt to answer the question, 'What's the story?' by mapping the context and their ongoing unpredictable experiences. Ultimately, sense-making is to make something understood explicitly and in a way that will work as a path to action. The task for leaders is to help others respond to the crisis by linking perceptions and interpretations of external change, which in turn enables organisational adaptation to achieve outcomes and results. Just as the group did!

Leaders need to constantly try to understand the changing contexts in which their organisations operate so that they can make decisions and drive strategy. This requires asking questions such as:

- What role will customers expect the organisation to play in society?

- How will the new context affect talent management strategies, expansion plans and growth?

- What disruptions will technology bring to the industry?

Leaders create understanding in others by becoming 'sense-givers' and influencing their 'sense-making for self' skills. The key question is *how* contemporary leaders can become effective sense-givers.

Given that sense-making is a conversational and narrative process, the answer is through storytelling.

Storytelling

Speech is power: speech is to persuade, to convert, to compel.
— Ralph Waldo Emerson

The Walt Disney Company is a storytelling organisation par excellence. Have you ever wondered why the founder, Walt Disney, became so successful? What was the context in which Disney flourished?

Interestingly, it was during the Great Depression (between 1929 and 1939), which was triggered by the Black Tuesday stock market crash and crushed the economies of North America, Europe and other industrialised areas. It was the longest and most severe economic depression ever experienced by the industrialised Western world.

Banks closed, and many businesses cut wages and hours as consumers refrained, initially, from buying luxury goods. The lack of consumer spending deepened the downward spiral, and businesses cut wages further and laid more people off. Even so, these measures failed to save many businesses, leaving nearly 15 million Americans unemployed and bankrupting almost half of the country's banks by 1933.

The Great Depression, however, was an opportunity for Disney. His Mickey Mouse kept people entertained through the Depression, and Disney's business was buoyant. In 1937 the company released a blockbuster, *Snow White and the Seven Dwarfs*, financed by the Bank of America and produced at a cost of US$1.5 million. Was this timing a coincidence? No, it wasn't!

Mickey Mouse served a crucial role in that context and at that time. The character lifted people's spirits, and gave them a legitimate reason to smile. Mickey reminded people of the good in life. The cartoon mouse symbolised hope and unique power of the human spirit to overcome great obstacles, which people badly needed.

If Mickey epitomised hope and the power of the human spirit, *Snow White and the Seven Dwarfs* embodied the message that good could prevail against evil. This fantasy tale showcased qualities such as friendship, innocence and loyalty — just what was needed in the lead up to World War II. Both Mickey and Snow White are examples of how storytelling can create meaning, and build optimism and confidence in times of crisis.

Notice the similarities between Disney's stories, which brought faith and hope during the Great Depression, and the experience of reading the wrong map on Mount Everest. They provided the sense-making needed in each context, with comparable positive results.

Storytelling and narratives (I use the two terms interchangeably here) are used in different contexts and for other purposes—not just in times of acute crisis, but certainly critically in times of change. A perfect example is the way politicians use narratives to influence their constituencies.

US President Donald Trump, in his controversial inaugural address in Washington, DC, on 20 January 2017, declared a 'new vision' for America. This included a pronouncement that every decision on trade, taxes, immigration and foreign affairs would be made to benefit American workers and their families. Americans' confidence reached new heights (from 11 to 13) in Gallup's US Economic Confidence Index by the end of that week. In fact, Americans viewed the economy more positively after Trump's election than in the nine years prior.[4] Clearly, his narrative provided sense-giving to many Americans.

Former president Barack Obama littered his acceptance speech with a heavy sprinkling of personal anecdotes, stories of gratitude, an overflowing of humility and inspiration, and a great sense of intimacy, evoking solidarity and empathy for diversity.

In business, whether you want to inform, sell, educate, inspire, convince, persuade, provoke, instigate, promote your brand, or enlist and move others to action to drive cultural change, storytelling is essential in communicating your message clearly and credibly. Great businesses have great stories behind them.

Individual leaders and entrepreneurs use personal and corporate brand stories to convey who they are, their convictions and values, and to champion their products and services.[5] Some prominent examples of individuals who have done this well include Steve Jobs of Apple, Herb Kelleher of Southwest Airlines, Anita Roddick of The Body Shop and William Bratton of the New York City Police Department.

Bell's Whisky, Guinness, John Deere, Nike, Lego and Weight Watchers are organisations that have used storytelling successfully to promote their brands and engage their customers. Xerox and Amcor have used stories to challenge conventional wisdom and drive change.

As noted by David M Boje in 'The Storytelling Organization: A Study Of Story Performance In An Office-Supply Firm', 'storytelling is the preferred sensemaking currencies of human relationships.' Boje further explains that a 'collective storytelling system in which the performance of stories is a key part of members' sensemaking and a means to allow them to supplement individual memories with institutional memory.'[6] This is because storytelling is a powerful way to explicitly or implicitly transfer both information and emotion. It also serves multiple organisational purposes, such as socialising new employees; communicating complex ideas and persuading others to change; problem solving; conducting action research; and generating organisational renewal.

During times of strategic change, for example, contemporary leaders use storytelling to drive the transformation and mobilise others to act and thrive in what can be turbulent and high-velocity environments. In this way, they attempt to support people's adaptation (survival) to the new context. This is what adaptive leadership is — 'the practice of mobilising people to tackle tough challenges and thrive'.[7]

Stories can be delivered using multiple communication channels, written or spoken, formal or informal, or in combinations of these. Stories can include rumours, gossip, retelling of information or tales, and negotiations. For example, managers may tell mixed and ambiguous narratives during times of change to influence employees' attitudes. In response, employees may exaggerate, overstate or elaborate these narratives to make sense of, champion, accept, or resist the change. This is why 'speakership' is so important.

Speakership

Speakership is a core leadership competency. Matt Church, the founder and chairman of Thought Leaders, who is consistently voted as one of Australia's top conference speakers and is former Australian Speaker of the Year, says speakership—'the art of oration and the science of influence—is the new leadership imperative'.[8]

From ancient times, great speeches have motivated the masses to fight for worthy causes such as justice, freedom from tyranny, the restoration of dignity and the preservation of democracy. Speeches have enabled great leaders to empower people to never give up, to win wars, advance human and civil rights, liberate nations, send men to the moon, win presidential elections, and heal and transform lives. They have helped entrepreneurs apply their ideas and pass on their benefits and legacy.

Powerful oratory is much more than speaking. It evokes the noblest values and principles, brings forth our sentiments, moves souls, stirs passions and emotions, and inspires and commits others to take courageous and virtuous action to shape the future and change the world. A good speech can turn crises into opportunities and even initiate massive cultural changes in large organisations.

On 17 September 2015 General Motors agreed to pay a US$900 million fine to settle federal charges and another US$575 million to settle civil lawsuits related to a mishandled recall that was blamed for more than a hundred deaths. The car company recalled 2.59 million small cars due to a fault whereby the ignition switch could be stuck in the 'accessory' position. This fault then lead to the air bags, brakes, and power steering being disabled or shut off.

The crisis hit the company just days after Mary Barra was appointed CEO in January 2014. Significantly, she repudiated GM's traditional approach to handling blame—minimise importance, fight, and settle reluctantly. Instead, she saw the opportunity to change GM's problematic culture and took a completely opposite approach. 'I never want to put this behind us', she said during her speech to employees at a town hall meeting that shocked many. 'I want to put this painful experience permanently in our collective memories.' GM executives said her words were unlike anything they had ever heard from a GM CEO.

At a more personal level, whether you want to develop greater presence by delivering better presentations in the boardroom, present your ideas convincingly and persuasively to your clients, address your professional body or association, or present with authority at a breakfast meeting or conference, speaking effectively to an audience is a must.

Being a great storyteller who can deliver a message with competence, clarity and confidence that moves others to action and secures results requires a certain knowledge, specific skills and competencies, and imagination. A powerful transformation story, for example, needs to bridge the gap between top management and the rest of the organisation. This requires thoughtful and skillful work.

Typically, this is done by choosing a suitable type of narrative or a combination (for example, metaphors, analogies, fables, allegories, symbolic anecdotes, images and archetypes) that clearly and simply communicates what is at stake while addressing four key issues:

1. the case for change

2. the challenges and opportunities ahead

3. the expected impact on employees

4. the coping/empowering strategies to support them.

This is why senior managers need specific storytelling and speakership skills.

This is Barack Obama's formula: address your audience's concerns; keep your message simple; anticipate what your audience is thinking; pause, and master your body language.

The way to develop speakership is through practice and feedback.

The power of language

Language is a fundamental human action. Humans are linguistic beings — language is our preferred method of communication. Through language we can communicate and also create new realities. We can describe the world around us, our experiences, thoughts and feelings, and invent new worlds. The language we use also has an impact. It can influence, persuade, deceive, explain, manipulate, comfort, inform, coerce or create, and yet it is still a much misunderstood dimension of leadership. In fact, I dare say that in many ways, for most people, language remains as invisible as water is to a fish. In her book *Storycatcher*, Christina Baldwin writes:

> We live in story like a fish lives in water. We swim through words and images siphoning stories through our minds the way a fish siphons water through its gills. We cannot think without language, we cannot process experience without story.[9]

Essentially, there are three main types of language: descriptive; the language of action; and the language of possibility or the language of leadership. Each is designed to achieve different outcomes.

Descriptive language

As the term indicates, this kind of language simply describes something that already exists and is before us. In fact, it is the language that describes either what's happening now (present), or something that has happened (past). Stories, for example, fall into this category by definition. They describe something that has happened. You may also argue, however, that we can tell stories about the future (more on this soon).

Descriptive language can also be either objective or subjective. Objective language constitutes statements of fact that are unbiased. For example, yesterday was Monday; today it is raining; the colour of my car is white. These statements can be verified by other parties as an objective reality, or 'truth' shared by most people.

Subjective language includes opinions, assessments or judgements, interpretations and complaints. Subjective language can often land us in trouble, especially when we treat it as 'the truth', because the views expressed may not necessarily be shared by most people. In fact, this kind of language has very little power to move others to action and, unfortunately, tends to be overused.

Consider for instance, how often you express your opinions, assessments or judgements and interpretations of situations. All the time, right? When I ask this question during my workshops and seminars, most people say they do so between 80 per cent and 90 per cent of the time. This means that, at most, they use another kind of language only 20 per cent of the time. This explains, of course, why so many people struggle to implement change and get things done. It certainly would be very different if they used the language of action 80 to 90 per cent of the time.

Language of action

The language of action, also referred to as 'performatives' or 'performative utterances', is very different to descriptive language in that it generates action. Test the following: Ask someone standing or sitting near you to pass an object such as a pen, glass of water or book. It's very likely that they will hand you that object. An action has taken place. Your language—a request—has generated action, the passing of the object. Requests are a type of language of action.

Here's another test. Take out a $50 note and ask someone, 'Would you like this?' It is likely there will be another action and the note will vanish from your hand. This is because you have made an offer—and in this case, one that's easy to accept!

An offer is an expression of your readiness to take action—to give, or do something. If you make an offer to someone who needs what you are offering, it is very likely they will accept it. Hence, the importance of researching your prospects' needs as part of the sales process before you make an offer: an offer only has value when fulfils a need. (Otherwise, it's not an offer, but a request).

The third kind of locutions, or expressions, that generate action are orders, or commands. The term 'order' implies a relationship in which someone in a position of power instructs, directs or mandates a subordinate to take a certain action. Here are some examples: 'Send this report to your HR manager'; 'Write a memo for distribution'; and 'Call an emergency meeting immediately'. These expressions employ a more direct language and are used by individuals in roles of authority, often in hierarchical relationships, such as boss and subordinate, and mostly in certain organisational cultures such as the military, police and emergency services. Orders are an expression of power. In certain roles, this kind of language dictates rapid action and response.

As strange as it may sound, it is important to remember that language (verbal, written or gesture) is the only tool we have for communication. Organisations can coordinate effective action only through requests, offers or commands—the language of action.

Promises

A promise is also a 'performative', and a very important one. A promise is a commitment of future action and therefore creates expectations in others. One of the secrets of high-performing teams and organisations is that individuals in those team consistently fulfil their promises or commitments to each other. This is why 'promise-based management'[10] is regarded as the essence of successful execution.

When people keep their promises, they 'become their word'. Consistently doing so builds trust, respect and credibility with others. It also builds a strong reputation for being reliable and trustworthy. This is possibly the best thing you can ever do to practise relational leadership effectively. It becomes a unique branding strategy and a source of authenticity and competitive advantage. As we see in part II of this book, when this happens, your team members will be prepared to move mountains for you.

> The language of possibility is the language of speculation, vision and creation.

Language of possibility

The language of possibility is future-based and creates what is possible. It is the true language of leadership. Language of possibility is the language of hope, inspiration, speculation and creation that anticipates possibilities and the action needed to reach goals, desires, outcomes or dreams. Visions and declarations are some examples of this type of language. John F. Kennedy's 'We choose to go to the Moon' speech, made in Houston at the Rice Stadium on 12 September 1962, is a classic example: 'We choose to go to the moon. We choose to go to the moon in this decade and do the other things, not because they are easy, but because they are hard.' Kennedy shaped the future in this speech, with a new possibility—which became a reality—by declaring something unimaginable for most people at that time. It is one of the most well-known examples of the language of possibility.

Martin Luther King Jr's 'I Have a Dream' speech during the March on Washington for Jobs and Freedom on 28 August 1963, is another example: 'I have a dream that my four little children will one day live in a nation where they will not be judged by the colour of their skin, but by the content of their character.' In this speech, King painted a reality that for most people was also unthinkable at that time. In doing so, he also shaped a new future—a future of freedom!

Winston Churchill's 'We Shall Never Surrender' speech also used the language of possibility: 'We shall fight on the beaches, we shall fight on the landing grounds, we shall fight in the fields and in the streets, we shall fight in the hills; we shall never surrender...' And they never did!

Those three speeches are great examples of how effective leaders enlist their constituencies or followers by painting a strong vision, dream or picture of the future. By using the language of possibility, they 'implant' a new future in their followers' minds. And as history tells us, the rest takes care of itself.

Note the difference between telling a story—a narrative about something that has happened—and a narrative about something yet to come. From this perspective, the language of possibility is sometimes referred to as telling stories about the future. Clearly, the use of such language inspires others to see new perspectives and often (not always) to act to achieve the suggested outcomes.

Declarations

Declarations are the most powerful form of language, as they have the power to change the world and the future. They literally create a new reality; they are decisive and immediate—right here, right now! Declarations create instant action.

Consider the Declaration of Independence adopted by the United States Continental Congress on 4 July 1776: by 'declaring' themselves an independent nation, the American colonists became free. The sentence 'I now pronounce you husband and wife' in a wedding ceremony creates a new state of affairs for everyone. Other examples of declarations include: 'I resign from this job', 'You are hired', 'You are fired', 'You are under arrest', 'I sentence you to death', 'I apologise', 'I accept your apology' and 'I love you.'

Here's an interesting question that I ask in some of my workshops: When does a team score during a football match? Most people say, 'When the ball goes through the goal posts.' Wrong! It actually occurs when the umpire declares it a goal!

Notice that often the person making the actual declaration has to hold a position of accepted authority, such as celebrant, police officer, judge or umpire.

Taking a stand

Taking a stand entails publicly declaring a decision to make something happen, such as changing yourself, your team, your organisation or the world, by behaving according to your cause and values. Taking a stand can involve opposing or supporting something, having an opinion about something and asserting your position. This evokes the military spirit to stand, or 'hold one's ground against the enemy', or to achieve an ideal or cause, as Churchill, King, JFK and other great leaders did.

To be powerful, a stand needs to be personalised, based on something you know well and care about deeply, and be for the common good. It will then resonate with the people you lead.

How does this all relate to leadership?

Imagine if everyone in your team or organisation were to use 'performatives', or the language of action (making offers and requests, and fulfilling their promises) instead of descriptive language (stating opinions, making assessments or judgements, complaining, or telling stories) most of the time, or at least more often.

Imagine what it would be like if everyone in your team or organisation made meaningful offers and requests that related to achieving their common goals, keeping their promises, taking stands to be accountable to each other, and made significant and positive contributions to others every day.

Conclusion

Descriptive language—opinions, assessments or judgements, interpretations, and complaints, in particular—is overused and overestimated to a point that it can get us into trouble. To command respect and establish credibility, you always need to keep your promises. If you want to inform, inspire, motivate or connect with people, tell stories. But if what you really want is for others to take bold action, stories alone are unlikely to work. You need to use the language of action: requests, offers, or commands when appropriate. Performative language is the language used by high-performing teams and organisations. To offer a vision and inspire others, tell stories about possible futures by using future-based language or the language of possibility. If you want to enlist others to change the status quo and create a better world, make bold declarations and take a stand for something you care deeply about, for the common good.

Regard your team and organisation as a network of conversations. Conversations are the only route to coordinating effective and collective action, and achieving results.

Insight questions

- How are you offering sense-making to your people?
- How do you use your language to generate action, outcomes and results?
- How do you create possibilities for yourself, your team and your organisation?
- Do your team members know how to make requests of, and offers to each other?
- Do they keep their promises?
- Do you keep your promises?

(continued)

- What requests and offers would be useful for you to make today, and to whom?
- What have you taken a stand on lately?
- What stand would be useful to take today?
- What powerful story are you preparing at the moment?

CHAPTER 4

Blind spots and naive models of leadership

When an organisation needs a new lens

Ruben was a senior manager in a global company and was based in the Netherlands for some years. He managed a large team of people by being egalitarian and collaborative. This style suited the team, which was made up of open and collegiate individuals.

Then Ruben was transferred to Italy. Very quickly, he began to sense that his collaborative style, which had been so effective in the Netherlands, was perceived by his new colleagues as a lack of leadership. They complained that he was weak, indecisive and ineffective.

Culture was the problem. Ruben's Italian colleagues had never experienced collaborative leadership and had no idea such a thing

(continued)

43

existed. Their 'implicit' model was more hierarchical in style, using command and control. Implicit in the Italian team was the expectation that a manager or leader would always have the answers to the problems and questions they raised. In Ruben's model, the team solved problems under his direction.

It didn't take long for the hostility towards Ruben for his perceived lack of management prowess to have a negative impact and cause a drop in performance. As a remedy, Ruben and his team were given leadership and intercultural coaching to make them aware of their unconscious cultural programming and assumptions.

Once both parties were aware of their implicit leadership models and once the impact of those was made explicit, everyone could see their own blind spots. To Ruben's undoubted relief, tensions diffused.

This chapter, like this story, is about blind spots, stereotypes and naive or implicit models of leadership. We may think we are aware of many of these things but they may unconsciously govern our behaviour and leadership practice to an alarming degree. I will look at the root causes of the current leadership crisis, and the ten pervasive and interrelated errors organisations repeatedly make when designing, delivering or procuring leadership development programs.

Blind spots and stereotypes

The final mystery is oneself.
— **Oscar Wilde**

I often ask workshop participants to identify some of their blind spots as a warm-up exercise. While some attempt to answer the question, others point out the contradiction implicit in the request. If it's a blind spot, by definition an individual is blind to it. The assumption is that if they could identify their blind spots they wouldn't be blind spots. A blind spot, therefore, refers to any aspect of yourself that you are unaware of. This includes a broad spectrum of things such as your actions, feelings, habits, idiosyncrasies, thoughts, traits, values so on. Uncovering blind spots requires courage and a willingness to scrutinise your own thoughts, words and deeds to highlight strengths as well as unhelpful behaviour that may be influencing your perception of and response to events.

Consider the following story.

The power of conditioning

On a dark night a father and son are travelling home after the boy's football practice. The mood is relaxed as the pair chat about the prospects for the weekend's match. The son is excited and animated as he describes a new training routine his team had tried for the first time that night. He laughs as he recounts the awkwardness of the group as they got used to the routine, falling over each other and dropping the ball as if they were newcomers to the sport. The son is in full flight describing the scene and the father is laughing along with him when, without warning, a vehicle slams into the side of their car at full speed and kills the father instantly.

People run to assist and an ambulance is called. An ambulance officer pulls the boy from the vehicle and within minutes he is being raced to the nearest hospital. He is alive but critically injured. On reaching the hospital, the boy is stretchered quickly into the emergency room and passed to the care of a waiting group of nurses and a doctor.

The doctor takes one look at the patient and turns to the nearest nurse, saying, 'I can't work on this boy. He's my son.'

When I share this story in my workshops or seminars, most people are immediately confused, scratching their heads and wondering how that's possible. After all, wasn't the father killed in the accident?

Some of the solutions people come up with depend on their perception and willingness to find another point of view. Invariably someone will suggest that the boy has two fathers—a natural father and a stepfather. Another common response is the 'soap opera' solution, which involves some convoluted and usually far-fetched possibility that the doctor is the boy's uncle but also, unknown to the boy, his father as a result of an unwise dalliance. Or that the boy was adopted and didn't know it.

Very few people even consider the correct answer — the doctor is his mother. Most people are still conditioned by the old stereotypes, even though there are many female doctors. This blind spot assumes all doctors are male. Incidentally, women are just as likely to assume the doctor is male.

The same assumptions are made about leaders and leadership. As soon as the word 'leader' is mentioned, the stereotype is the hero or lone ranger (who, naturally, is male) with the capacity to solve everyone's problems and make everyone happy. But this paternalistic style of leadership no longer holds up in the post-heroic twenty-first century. Nevertheless, it is pervasive. Have you ever wondered why gender inequality persists despite the efforts by governments, organisations and individuals to break the glass ceiling by encouraging more women to take leadership positions? It's because the blind spots that condition people to see doctors as males dressed in white coats, and leaders as males in their ivory towers, are pervasive.

Michael Porter, a Harvard Business School professor, refers to blind spots as truisms that while no longer valid, are still used to inform strategic decisions. Effective leaders today must admit they have blind spots, and seek to identify and manage them. The way we grew up, where we grew up, our family environment, culture, religion, education, our own expectations, past experiences, prejudices, motivations and emotional state all play a huge part in how we perceive reality.

The story about the car accident illustrates the power of conditioning and the prevalence of blind spots. Most people simply cannot see the most obvious solution because it doesn't tally with their inbuilt, almost subconscious belief that all doctors are male. It also highlights the fact that perception and reality are not always the same. We behave in keeping with our perception of reality, not reality itself. Therefore, a leader's task is to manage the current perception of reality.

Let's take a deeper dive into what creates and perpetuates these blind spots, which psychologists refer to as 'implicit mental models'. As with Ruben and his Italian team who are unable to see beyond their own conditioning and perceptions, implicit mental models act like a pair of coloured glasses filtering everything we see and experience.

Naive models of leadership

Ruben and his Italian team's blind spots—their unconscious cultural programming and assumptions, and expectations about leadership—collectively is called a naive or implicit model of leadership. The Italian team had an implicit model of leadership that shaped the way they expected Ruben to act even before they met him. This, of course, informed how they went on to evaluate their new leader. Unfortunately, Ruben didn't fit the criteria.

Implicit mental models, our mental software, filter, shape and distort reality to fit what we believe. In fact, it would be more accurate to say that they are what we have been led to believe are 'unquestionable truths'; they are sometimes referred to as belief systems or core assumptions. They are difficult to detect because they work behind the scenes, just like a program in your computer—hence, the term 'mental software'.

So, how do we acquire these implicit mental models?

Monica's story

When Monica was little, like all children, she curiously observed her parents. She progressively noticed that her parent's reactions to different situations contrasted dramatically. When she didn't achieve good grades at school, Dad reprimanded and blamed her, and demanded higher grades from her next semester. Mum, on the other hand, encouraged her to study differently, and also helped her with homework. In addition, Mum also rewarded her for her efforts. As a result of being exposed to these contrasting parenting

(continued)

styles during her early life experiences, Monica learned two very different styles of leadership. Dad tended to blame and punish, while Mum helped and encouraged. While Monica learned both types of responses, she was far more inclined to respond positively to the encouragement and support her mum demonstrated throughout her school days, and later in her life. By internalising her belief about the best or most effective style from her primary care givers, Monica formed experientially her own 'implicit' (internal and unexpressed) model of leadership.

We first pick up our implicit models (or ways of thinking and behaving) via our early learning process by modelling the behaviour of those around us. Our parents, of course, are our first role models and their behaviour becomes the exemplar, standard or model to emulate, so we encode or internalise our parents' behaviour in our programming. At school, our teachers, peers and friends also become potential role models. Eventually, we develop a full repertoire of behaviours to respond to most life situations — how to react to approval or disapproval, agreement or disagreement, frustration and anger, and so on. Our culture 'indoctrinates', or teaches us how to think and respond to just about everything. This learning, or socialisation, process is largely unconscious in that we learn how to behave without realising that we are. By the time we reach adolescence, the social norms are so ingrained we don't even notice them.

This socialisation continues as life goes on, mostly within a cultural context. We acquire new ways of thinking, new attitudes and more complex behaviours that determine how we respond to situations and shape and reinforce our attitudes, prejudices or biases — hence the term 'unconscious biases'. These are the biases that are triggered by our mental programming and happen beyond our control.

The fact that these implicit models (assumptions, beliefs, attitudes and expectations) are formed early in our lives is critical. First, we tend to treat them as the 'truth' — that which is, or ought to be. Second, they are difficult to change. If someone challenges our attitudes or behaviour we feel surprised, confused, or even attacked and humiliated. It's as if our sacred cows—core beliefs or customs we support and consider exempt from criticism or questioning—have been challenged. So, how does this relate to leadership?

The root cause of the current leadership crisis is similar, in that the expectations organisations have of their leadership development programs (LDPs) are also unmet and out of sync with the ever-changing world. Many organisations and OD practitioners find it extremely difficult to shift paradigms. This is obvious, given that most LDPs are still using obsolete practices and most organisations and practitioners are still using implicit models of leadership. They are unaware of the assumptions that have informed and shaped their thinking about leadership. These unspoken assumptions, biases (whether conscious or unconscious) or blind spots are perfectly human, and guide people's behaviour. Yet, if not addressed, they distort reality and skew decision making. It's like wearing a pair of sunglasses on a dark, rainy day or walking down the street blindfolded. Researchers also refer to this as 'naive theories' of leadership.

This explains why organisations keep making the same mistakes and fail to develop leaders who can deal effectively with the current challenges at hand, let alone future ones. Change is required as a matter of urgency.

Ten fundamental and interrelated errors

The first step is for organisations to recognise the ten fundamental and interrelated errors or assumptions I have identified through my research:

1. using outdated models of leadership

2. mistaking 'leader' for 'leadership' development

3. confusing authority with leadership

4. maintaining a fixation with competency-based models

5. underestimating learning agility and adaptation

6. ignoring relational measures of leadership

7. neglecting global and intercultural dimensions of leadership

8. being inattentive to creative thinking and innovation

9. disregarding the measurement of collective outcomes and results

10. failing to conduct impact evaluations.

1. Using outdated models of leadership

The most popular leadership models organisations now use have an intra-personal focus and were developed from theories of personality, psychotherapy, psychoanalysis, developmental psychology, ego development, moral development, spirituality or even mysticism. Not to mention a barrage of competency-based and personality tests.

These models tend to assume that by reaching the highest possible level of development, psychological stability or enlightenment, an individual will become a better leader. In practice, such models focus on assisting individuals reach the peak of their personal development or transformation. They do this via one-to-one coaching — often crossing the boundary between coaching and therapy. This is not surprising given that these approaches explore deep individual psychological structures, or stages of ego development such as early life experiences, core assumptions, beliefs, behavioural patterns, ego states and stages of consciousness. There is nothing intrinsically wrong with personal development. I have experienced its benefits and firmly subscribe to the notion that all leadership development begins with self-awareness and self-development — the foundations of self-leadership. However, this is only the first step and the assumption that to exercise effective leadership requires one to be well-balanced and a good all-rounder is misleading. In fact, a degree of positive deviance, or eccentricity, can be a great source of creativity and inspiration to challenge the status quo and drive change — which is what true leadership is all about.

Take Steve Jobs, who built Apple, one of the world's most valuable companies. Following his death in 2011, many people said they had disliked his way of doing business. They claimed he was elitist, belittled the views of competitors, made hypocritical statements and acted as if normal rules didn't apply to him. He was also a perfectionist who was petulant and impatient. Yet he is acclaimed as the most successful CEO of the past 25 years, and his legacy has completely changed the world. 'The people who are crazy enough to think they can change the world are the ones who do', the quote from Apple's 1997 'Think Different' commercial, rings true for Jobs.

Nassir Ghaemi is a professor of Psychiatry at Tufts University School of Medicine. In his book, *A First Rate Madness: Uncovering the links between leadership and mental illness*, Ghaemi explains that mildly depressed people tend to see the world more clearly and objectively, or more 'as it is'. He states that 'creativity and resilience is higher in people with mania and realism and empathy is higher in people with depression compared to normal subjects'.[1] Ghaemi's research also reveals that leadership icons Mahatma Gandhi and Martin Luther King Jr tried to commit suicide as adolescents and had severe depressive episodes in adulthood. It is also well-documented that Abraham Lincoln suffered from depression and Winston Churchill from bipolar disorder. For these individuals, their weaknesses became sources of strength. It was not their levels of personal development or psychological stability that made them great leaders; it was their strong vision, clarity of purpose, commitment to making a difference and to drive change, and their ability to inspire and enlist others to action.

Of course, I'm not suggesting that to exercise effective leadership one has to experience mild depression or be eccentric. Nor do I imply that it is undesirable to promote and cultivate personal, psychological or spiritual development. I know from personal experience that promoting such practices is highly desirable as a precursor to developing self-awareness — the foundation of leadership development. However, effective leadership also can be exercised without necessarily attaining complete psychological stability, the highest possible levels of personal or spiritual development, enlightenment or self-transformation.

Shelley Carson is a Harvard University lecturer, researcher of the psychology of creativity, and author of the book *Your Creative Brain: Seven steps to maximize imagination, productivity, and innovation in your life*. Ellen Langer is a professor in the Psychology department at Harvard University, and author of the book *The Power of Mindful Learning*. In their paper 'Mindfulness and self-acceptance', they explain:

> Self-acceptance is crucial to mental health. The absence of ability to unconditionally accept oneself can lead to a variety of emotional difficulties, including uncontrolled anger and depression. Living mindfully entails living daily life without pretense and without concern that others are judging one negatively.[2]

Self-acceptance, clarity of goals and purpose, integrity, ethical behaviour, respect for others, and true collaboration and teamwork can go a long way. They can, in fact, move mountains!

You don't need to wait to be perfect to exercise leadership.

2. Mistaking 'leader' for 'leadership' development

David Day, professor of Psychology, S.L. Eggert Leadership Chair and academic director of the Kravis Leadership Institute, contends:

> The proposed distinction between leader development and leadership development is more than mere semantics. At the core of the difference is an orientation towards developing human capital (leader development) as compared with social capital (leadership development).[3]

Joseph Raelin, Knowles Chair of Practice-Oriented Education, and professor of Management at Northeastern University, in his 2010 book *The Leaderful Fieldbook: Strategies and activities for developing leadership in everyone*, explains:

> Leadership need not be centered on the traits of any one individual ... we can find it in the everyday practice of those who are engaged. It is less about what one person thinks and does and more about what people do together to accomplish important activities.[4]

Leadership development historically has focused on enhancing the knowledge, skills and abilities of certain individuals only—those holding senior managerial positions. Current leadership thinkers refer to this as the development of 'human capital'.[5] The focus needs to expand. It needs to be on improving the leadership capacity of the whole organisation through greater efforts to develop teams, business units, functions and departments. This must entail developing and improving the

> *While leader and leadership development are distinctly different, they are not mutually exclusive.*

relationships that knit these groups and networks together—which is referred to as 'social capital'.[6] 'Leadership' development then is a collective activity, as opposed to 'leader' development, which is an individual activity.

A key reason that current leadership models fail is that they mistake 'leader' development for 'leadership' development. Self-awareness and personal development are definitely the foundations of leadership development. It starts with self-leadership, but this alone does not guarantee effective leadership. It is like having a very creative or promising idea; unless it is put into practice, innovation never happens. Most current approaches to leadership development are still built on implicit models of leadership based on leader development. They use traditional 360-degree feedback supplemented by coaching, which is accessible only to selected individuals—those in formal positions of management or authority.

This approach assumes effective leadership happens by developing individuals, or so-called leaders. From this perspective, leader development concentrates on developing the intra-personal domain and skills competencies of individuals. On the other hand, leadership development assumes that leadership is a social or collective phenomenon rooted in developing trusting relationships. Hence, leadership development relates to the interpersonal domain or skills (for example, social awareness and social skills) required to build and maintain such relationships.

It follows that while leader and leadership development are distinctly different, they are not mutually exclusive. In fact, they are complementary. Leader development is the precursor to and foundation of leadership development. The risk is that many practitioners (and organisations) mistakenly assume that leader development is the same as leadership development and that it leads to the same outcomes and results.

From a more practical perspective, the strategies and interventions used by practitioners are good indicators of the level of development they are working on. The knowledge and skills practitioners require for working at each of these levels are also different.

Leader development typically uses the following tools, processes or strategies:

- assessment tools that focus on competencies, individual/ adult development personality or other types of psychometric assessment (for example, attitudes and values)

- multi-source or 360-degree feedback

- one-to-one coaching

- mentoring.

Practitioners working at this level use their knowledge of and accreditation in psychometric assessment tools, and their coaching and mentoring skills. Most coaching approaches tend to rely on the exchange of information (narratives) between client and practitioner/ coach, without any direct observations of behaviours. The unit of attention and measurement, as also with mentoring, is the individual.

In contrast, leadership development is driven by collective goals, requires shared meaning with others, uses a wide range of methods, and generates collective outcomes and results. Leadership development uses a very different and richer set of processes or practices in addition to coaching. Some examples include:

- action learning

- case-in-point method

- Tavistock-style group relations learning

- open space technology (OST)

- sociometry, sociodrama, and other action methods

- social networks analysis

- creative problem solving

- team coaching

- teaming
- eclectic interventions.

These approaches are discussed in chapter 12.

Most of these methods rely on the direct observations of groups or teams while working together on real-time challenges or projects. The unit of attention and measurement is a collective entity (group, team, organisation or community).

Practitioners working in this domain need:

- knowledge of group dynamics and adult learning principles
- high-level facilitation skills
- awareness and knowledge of social systems theory
- knowledge of and skills in using action methods
- knowledge of game theory
- knowledge of and experience in using the method of choice
- knowledge of and accreditations in using culture and engagement assessment tools of choice.

3. Confusing authority with leadership

Ken Blanchard, author and management expert known for his most successful book, *The One Minute Manager*, which has sold more than 13 million copies and has been translated into many languages, asserts that 'the key to successful leadership today is influence, not authority'.[7]

This point is closely related the previous one. Traditionally, leadership has also been — and sadly for many, still is — mistaken for authority and power. Authority involves exercising conferred and legitimate power to perform a service; people follow those exercising such power because their positions demand authority, irrespective of the ability of the person holding the position to perform their job.

True leadership, on the other hand, involves exercising influence, with or without authority, which creates a following without forcing individuals to accept anything based on positional power. Leadership relies on trust and fairness and, to a large degree, meeting mutual—leaders' and followers'—expectations. Gandhi, for example, did not for the most part hold any official position in India's freedom struggle. He was not followed because he held a position of authority. He became a trusted leader because of his strong vision, judgement, respected expertise and integrity, as well as his ability to provoke others to take action.

Ronald Heifetz and Marty Linsky from the John F. Kennedy School of Government at Harvard University, who are co-founders of global leadership development firm Cambridge Leadership Associates, use the following example to drive this point home in their book *Leadership on the Line: Staying alive through the dangers of leading*. Rosa Parks (1913–2005) was a civil rights activist whom the United States Congress called 'the first lady of civil rights' and 'the mother of the freedom movement'. She went beyond her authority by refusing to move to the back of a bus—the 'colored area' marked to make sure black people 'knew their place' in Montgomery, Alabama. Her behaviour became an act of leadership because civil rights activists used this incident to draw public attention to the need to take responsibility for civil rights issues. This, in turn, provoked a protest that catalysed the civil rights movement of the 1960s.[8]

Being aware of (and responding to) the distinction between leadership and authority matters. It gives organisations a way to assess resources and develop unique leadership development strategies, which has a serious impact on organisational effectiveness and results.

We have all experienced senior managers who display either no leadership, or leadership below the level expected by stakeholders. Yet in the same organisations there are individuals with no formal authority who exercise high levels of leadership, either deliberately or inadvertently. Organisations that miss the distinction between leadership and authority expect leadership to come only from those in positions of authority.

It is also important to realise that leadership occurs in a social context and is governed by psychological and social contracts—implicit, unspoken or unwritten agreements that define and limit the rights and duties of organisational members to cooperate with each other for their mutual benefit.

4. Maintaining a fixation with competency-based models

Richard Bolden, professor of Leadership and Management at University of the West of England, and Jonathan Gosling, Emeritus Professor of Leadership, University of Exeter, asserted back in 2006 that:

> The competency approach to leadership could be conceived of as a repeating refrain that continues to offer an illusory promise to rationalise and simplify the processes of selecting, measuring and developing leaders yet only reflects a fragment of the complexity that is leadership.[9]

They aren't the only ones critiquing competency-based models of leadership.

Keith Grint is professor of Public Leadership and Management at Warwick Business School and worked in industry for ten years before becoming an academic. He stresses that, 'Leadership is fundamentally a relationship; it's not about individual possession of competencies'[10]

Brigid Carroll is an associate professor at the Department of Management and International Business and a senior research fellow for the New Zealand Leadership Institute at the University of Auckland Business School. Lester Levy is an adjunct professor of Leadership at the University of Auckland Business School, and head of the New Zealand Leadership Institute. In their 2008 article 'Leadership as practice: Challenging the competency paradigm', the authors explain:

> While it is not too difficult to call attention to the colonization of leadership by such a distinctly managerial concept and framework as competencies, it certainly is more problematic to depose it.[11]

And they add that accepting competencies 'as a basis for leadership seems particularly problematic, inappropriate and misplaced'.

Furthermore, John Zenger and Joseph Folkman in their 2009 book *The Extraordinary Leader: Turning good managers into great leaders*, explain some of the faulty assumptions about competencies. These include that: 'each organisation has its own unique set of competencies; competencies are distinct and separate from each other within each person; competencies are all roughly equally important; and the best way to develop a competency is to focus on that specific behaviour.'[12]

The Center for Creative Leadership in Greensboro, NC, acknowledged the need to move beyond competencies in its 2014 white paper 'Leadership development beyond competencies: Moving to a holistic approach'. This paragraph captures the essence of its argument:

> **Competency models have taught us a great deal about leadership development, but we believe it is time to question whether we are still focusing on competencies simply because 'the light is better here' and perhaps need to turn on new lights to achieve improved outcomes.**[13]

The expression 'the light is better here'—just in case you're wondering—refers to the streetlight effect, an observational bias where people only search for something where it is easiest to do so.

David Freedman is a journalist specialising in business and technology, and senior editor at Forbes ASAP. In his book *Wrong: Why experts keep failing us—and how to know when not to trust them* he refers to the streetlight effect to explain that 'researchers tend to look for answers where the looking is good, rather than where the answers are likely to be hiding'.[14]

Current models of leadership development mostly focus on competencies. This limits the full picture of leadership as a truly social and relational phenomenon. Leadership development is a much more expansive and relational process than leader development. Competency models are inadequate in today's business context. In practical terms, organisations invest a great deal in individual development and tend to neglect integrated team and broader development as a way to achieve organisational leadership capacity.

While I am not arguing that competencies should be completely abandoned, there is a need to move towards using adaptive or 'meta-competencies' — the sets of knowledge, skills and aptitudes that underpin or allow for the development of other competencies, especially those that people will need in the unpredictable future. Meta-competencies enable learning, adapting, anticipating and creating change. A good example is 'learning agility' — a person's ability to learn quickly by analysing and understanding new situations and business problems.[15]

This capacity to learn quickly and continuously is priceless in the new economic landscape. It enables individuals to assess the limitations and possibilities of their competencies and adapt to new and unfamiliar demands. This may be by learning new competencies or deploying their existing competencies in different contexts. Other examples of meta-competencies include cultural intelligence (CQ) and emotional intelligence (EQ; self-awareness, self-regulation, motivation, empathy and social skills). These are relevant to global contexts and wider settings: they facilitate learning and provide leaders with the flexibility to adapt, anticipate, create and sustain change.

The benefit of using relational measures, as opposed to individual measures, is that they promote collective accountability — not just the leader's — for team performance. Given that leadership is fundamentally a relationship between people, leadership effectiveness is related to everyone's efforts to create positive relationships in the organisation. To this end, direction, alignment, commitment, process orientation, integrity, ethical behaviour and empowering others to achieve purposeful collective action is critical.

5. Underestimating learning agility and adaptation

Anyone who stops learning is old, whether at 20 or 80. Anyone who keeps learning stays young.
— **Henry Ford**

As I hinted in the first chapter, learning agility refers to the ability to learn, adapt and apply knowledge and skills in constantly changing conditions. It is a diverse set of skills that allows leaders to identify complex behavioural cues and patterns in one context and transfer them to a new context. Put another way, learning agility is to know what you should do when you may not know what you should do. Thus, learning agility is a key to adaptation.

Adaptation requires the ability to extrapolate the lessons of the past to new and unfamiliar situations. This involves flexibility, learning from mistakes and rising to a diverse array of challenges with resilience and optimism.

At the organisational level, learning agility refers to the processes and programs that enhance the collective ability to acquire knowledge and skills, and to stay ahead of competitors. Hence, it is also related to competitive advantage.

6. Ignoring relational measures of leadership

Best-selling authors James Kouzes and Barry Posner, in their book *Credibility: How leaders gain and lose it, why people demand it,* explain.

> Leadership is a relationship between those who aspire to lead and those who choose to follow ... and the key to unlocking greater leadership potential can be found when you seek to understand the desires and expectations of your constituents.[16]

Remember Ruben and his Italian team? Both parties had conflicting unspoken and unwritten expectations; these expectations shaped their respective behaviours and caused conflict between the two parties. In fact, they acted as if an invisible or unwritten contract between them — the psychological contract — had been violated.

Psychological contracts cover the reciprocal expectations, obligations, promises or commitments between individuals as they relate to the achievement of collective goals. They are built on mutual trust and respect (the enactment of leadership).

From this perspective, followers play a far more active role in influencing leaders, as well as allowing themselves to be influenced by the leaders — the essence of 'followership'. As a result, organisation-wide stakeholders (traditionally called followers) play far more active roles in influencing organisational outcomes and results. Barbara Kellerman, professor of Leadership at Harvard Kennedy School, says, 'followers are more important to leaders than leaders are to followers'.[17]

As mentioned briefly in chapter 1, the concept of the psychological contract is at the heart of all human relationships. It is like an ocean. We see the explicit, seen or known elements of the relationship floating on the surface, but unless we put on our goggles and swim below the surface, the invisible, unseen elements remain unnoticed and, thus, unexamined. These unspoken aspects of a relationship implicitly determine the quality of interaction and can have detrimental effects if either party fails to meet these perceived expectations. Given the promissory nature of the psychological contract, any violation has a severe impact on the trust in the relationship, which is understandably very difficult to repair. I discuss psychological contracts in more detail in chapter 5.

7. Neglecting global and intercultural dimensions of leadership

> *No culture can live if it attempts to be exclusive.*
> **—Mahatma Gandhi**

In the 1980s, Mountain Bell, a US phone company trying to promote telephone services in Saudi Arabia, released an advertisement featuring a picture of an executive talking on the phone with his feet on his desk; the image showed the soles of his shoes. The advertisement failed miserably because in Saudi Arabia it is considered extremely offensive to show the soles of the shoes.

Demonstrating respect for others is a universal expectation and was something Mountain Bell failed to do. While some leadership characteristics and expectations are universally important, their expression often differs depending on the cultural and social context. As I alluded to in the first chapter, cultural intelligence (CQ) reflects the competence of an individual to deal effectively with those from different cultural backgrounds and includes concepts such as global mindset and cross-cultural competence. Mountain Bell's example, and the story of Ruben and his Italian team, reinforce the need for leaders to develop high levels of CQ if they are to function effectively in today's global and multicultural world.

Most organisations now operate in a global context due to major changes in economies, demographic shifts and advances in technology. Cultural awareness, managing diversity and inclusion, and cross-cultural agility and competence are essential for a global leadership mindset.

Allan Bird is Darla and Frederick Brodsky Trustee Professor in Global Business at the D'Amore-McKim School of Business at Northeastern University. In relation to global leadership competencies, he explains:

> ... [cross-cultural communication] entails a high level of mindfulness, i.e. conscious awareness of contextual, cultural, and individual differences and the way in which these differences influence how messages are encoded, transmitted, received, and interpreted, as well as reciprocal feedback process.[18]

Cultural competence is also relevant for managing multicultural workforces in a leader's own country. In a modern economy such Australia's — one of the most ethnically diverse societies in the world — this is now the norm. Cultural diversity, in fact, is the engine of innovation and the source of the necessary competitive advantage for a twenty-first-century global economy. This explains the increasing number of workplace initiatives aimed at managing and leveraging cultural diversity and inclusion, and at promoting innovation.

Sadly, most current leadership development models are still strongly based on Western principles. Leadership Results (LR), however, incorporates the results of GLOBE (Global Leadership and Organizational Behavior Effectiveness), the largest leadership research program ever conducted. The GLOBE project covers an 11-year period (still in progress) and involves 160 social scientists and management scholars from 62 cultures representing the major regions of the world. These results include the identification of the 22 most universally desired effective leadership attributes across cultures.

8. Being inattentive to creative thinking and innovation

Creativity is now projected to become the third most important skill needed in 2020, according to the 2016 *The Future of Jobs Report: Employment, skills and workforce strategy for the fourth industrial revolution,* published by the World Economic Forum.[19]

Modern organisations need to innovate continuously to improve their products, services and processes to ensure their long-term survival and success. Leadership is a chief predictor of creativity — the precursor of all innovation. Strategically, leaders establish work environments that are conducive to creative thinking and innovation, which in turn leads to a competitive advantage. In doing so, they drive and manage innovation goals.

The behavior of a leader is also an important predictor of innovative workplace behaviour (IWB) — this is what spurs new and useful ideas, procedures, processes or products to be introduced. It has been recognised as paramount in today's uncertain global economy, where organisational renewal has become critical due to the increased competitiveness that accompanies accelerating technological change.

9. Disregarding the measurement of collective outcomes and results

Leadership assessment instruments currently on the market can be classified into four main categories, depending on what they measure:

- competencies or behaviours, such as benchmarks by the Center for Creative Leadership, Korn Ferry, Leadership Practices Inventory and numerous competency-based emotional intelligence instruments

- assumptions or beliefs to promote self-awareness or uncover motivators, such as Hogan, FIRO-B and the Mayer-Salovey-Caruso Emotional Intelligence Test

- style, type and personality assessments, such as DISC, Myers-Briggs Type Indicator, Saville Wave and Occupational Personality Questionnaire

- a combination of these, such as Life Styles Inventory and the Leadership Circle Profile.

These assessment instruments all measure the attributes or competencies of the so-called leaders in an organisation; all have an individual focus. None incorporates relational measures of leadership. This is concerning because, as outlined earlier, leadership is essentially a relationship. None of these instruments measure engagement (the degree of employees' positive or negative emotional attachment to their leader or organisation), performance outcomes or business results.

The Leadership Results survey measures individuals' levels of commitment, satisfaction, discretionary effort and innovative behaviour. These determine how engaged they are and whether or not they intend to stay with an organisation; and so survey results can predict performance, retention and turnover. By measuring engagement, LR provides a more integrated picture of teams and organisations.

10. Failing to conduct impact evaluations

Jennifer Martineau (PhD) is Senior Vice President, Research, Evaluation, and Societal Advancement at the Center for Creative Leadership, and an international authority on evaluation of leadership development initiatives. In her 2014 article 'Laying the groundwork: First steps in evaluating leadership' she explains that 'effective evaluation is an important component of leadership itself'.[20] Impact evaluations are critical but they are—without a doubt—the most neglected aspect of LDPs. This is a major gap and missed opportunity for organisations around the world.

One of the main reasons for this gap is that calculating the return on investment (ROI) of an LDP can be a contentious issue and a challenging task. Most organisations tend to believe that ROI means calculating a financial return that can be easily captured on the balance sheet. Certainly, placing a monetary value on intangible, hard-to-measure qualities such as leadership development, executive coaching or employee engagement can make a good case in a 'show me the money' exercise, but it's not the only way. In fact, ROI can be a poor, unreliable and insufficient measure of demonstrating valuable outcomes and success.

The concept of return on expectations (ROE),[21] for example, is a more holistic measurement and indicator of the value of qualitative (intangible) and quantitative (tangible) benefits. From this perspective, practitioners can use wellbeing and engagement as indicators of improvement—outcomes that are not directly quantifiable but are, nonetheless, real and assessable. This may include indirect returns or financial windfalls from individuals applying new competencies that, for example, attract new clients, build better teams, coordinate actions and execute plans more effectively. Or there may be positive changes in management or leadership styles that result in better handling of conflict, better working relationships, improved quality of work and higher productivity. This may also bring personal benefits to individuals who, in turn, have a positive impact in their workplace. Let me share three good examples.

Example 1: Evaluation of a global leadership development program

I had the privilege in 2015 of conducting a unique evaluation of best practice in a global leadership development (GLD) program that had been implemented for more than ten years.[22]

This program had a very good reputation throughout the company: over the years, anecdotal evidence had been passed via word-of-mouth from one generation of attendees to another. Many of the company's senior managers who had attended then nominated their direct reports for this highly regarded program. So, what made it so successful? What was the actual value? These were the research questions of the evaluation.

When asked about the program's estimated ROI to the business, one participant said:

> The program was a great opportunity to meet people from different geographical locations and cultures. For me, the best takeaway was learning a new negotiation vendor strategy from a European colleague. When I got back home, I applied this new negotiation approach with mobile phone vendors and, in less than a year, I was able to generate savings of just over $100,000.

The interesting thing about this response was that this benefit to the business came about not so much from a direct and specific expected learning outcome of the program, but rather from a broader and subtler one: building networking skills and social capital (the collective value of all the global social networks of the firm). This was simply because this valuable exchange of information occurred during a casual conversation at pre-dinner drinks. The company would have never anticipated this. A practical implication from this finding is that program benefits are not necessarily the result of deliberate attempts to make them happen. This company now encourages program participants to engage in greater networking to build the firm's social and relational capital.

Another participant said, 'This is how the evaluation should be — like this interview. If you send an email survey, nothing happens.' He explained that being invited to participate in the evaluation meant he felt appreciated and valued by his employer, so was willing to reflect on the program. It reinforced what he had learned and how he had been applying it. This response, in fact, emerged as a theme in the evaluation. There were also multiple suggestions from participants on ways to improve the program's content and processes.

Based on this, it became clear that the benefits of evaluation are at least threefold:

1. They extend the reflective dimension of the program by inviting participants to think about the value of the experience and how they apply it. This, in turn, further reinforces the transfer of learning on the job.

2. They gather valuable suggestions for improvements to the program.

3. Evaluations foster employee engagement and loyalty by involving them as the main protagonists.

It is not surprising that following this experience, the company decided to conduct more rigorous evaluations to assess the impact of the projects that emerged from the training, as well to track any business improvements.

Sadly, only 7 per cent of organisations surveyed by Harvard Business School Publishing for its 2016 *The State of Leadership Development* felt they had a best-in-class leadership development program.[22]

Example 2: Evaluation of a coaching assignment

In 2015 I conducted a 12-month coaching assignment with the CEO of a global company. At the end of the assignment, during the evaluation processes, John (not his real name) was asked to 'estimate' the ROI to his business from the coaching he had received. He said, 'The return for the business is a number too large to quantify for the investment of my coach, the program and my time.'

In addition, a post-coaching evaluation comprising 360-degree feedback and interviews with John's stakeholders revealed he had become more assertive, entrepreneurial and strategic. With a reported 50 per cent improvement in John's leadership effectiveness, execution and impact on efficiency, the coaching outcomes identified included making faster and bigger acquisitions, and higher sales for a number of products.

Clearly, these are good indicators of the value delivered — and it is certainly a lot better than having no indicators, for lack of evaluation. If organisations don't ask, because they assume it is too hard to measure, they will never know.

Example 3: Unsolicited feedback from a development program

This final example illustrates the positive impact of providing personal value and benefits to employees, not just managers. I received an unsolicited email following an introductory seminar entitled 'How to Apply Positive Psychology in Your Life' that I delivered in 2015 to a group of employees of a global consumer goods company. The email from one of the employees who attended read:

> **I would like to thank you for the information that you provided us with during the positive psychology seminar. Since then, I have been relating to my six-year-old daughter, with whom I was having some issues, in a very different way. I now feel much more optimistic and confident about myself as a mother. My daughter seems to be happier and we talk and laugh together more often. As a result, I'm also a lot more engaged and productive at work.**

Throughout my career, which spans almost 25 years, I have received many notes of gratitude and testimonials from clients—including employees, middle and senior managers and CEOs—but never one as rewarding as this one. I felt profoundly touched and deeply grateful that I had been able to contribute to this family in such positive way.

This is a good example of how a qualitative response can be a good indicator of the value delivered by the program. Interestingly, it is also a good example of how offering educational and personal development programs (for example, developing self-awareness, positive psychology, strengths development, building resilience, self-empowerment, and managing stress and strong emotions) is one of the most powerful ways organisations can contribute to employee self-engagement and happier families. This is how they become great organisations to work for.

Lessons and benefits of conducting evaluations

These are the eight practical lessons and benefits I have identified from conducting evaluations:

1. There are different ways to demonstrate value.

2. The benefits of LDPs to organisations, including ROI, can derive from the least expected sources.

3. If you don't ask because you assume it is too hard to measure, you will never know.

4. Qualitative responses can be good indicators of intangible benefits that have a very high quantitative numerical value, and which translate into tangible benefits and business results.

5. It is important to conduct evaluations combining self-reported and multi-rater measures by choosing the approach that best suits your program and organisation.

6. The benefits of conducting evaluations extend beyond identifying program improvements. They also reinforce participants' transfer of learning, which is why evaluations are a critical component of the LDP itself.

7. Conducting evaluations fosters employee engagement and loyalty.

8. Keep evaluations as simple as possible.

On this last point, I want to share some tips from management research that can be applied to ensure your organisation conducts effective LDP evaluations.

Simplicity of measures: The principle of parsimony

Simplicity is the ultimate sophistication.
—Leonardo da Vinci

A fundamental aspect of scientific research is the principle, or law, of parsimony. Also known as Ockham's (or Occam's) razor, this principle of problem-solving was devised by William of Ockham—a medieval English Franciscan friar, scholastic philosopher and theologian known for being at the centre of major intellectual and political controversies in the fourteenth century.

'Parsimony' is explaining complex problems simply and generalising solutions to address them, as opposed to using unnecessarily complex models or frameworks. This principle follows the rule that the simplest explanation is often the correct one.

The parsimony principle in applied management and business research translates to achieving economy in developing models by considering fewer variables rather than more, which can lead to less variance or impact.

The parsimony principle is very much like the popular design principle KISS (keep it simple, stupid), which emerged in the United States Navy in 1960. The popular KISS principle advocates that any system will work at its best when kept simple. Both principles are often overlooked by management researchers and practitioners who create new leadership development models. This explains the plethora of complex LDP competency models available today.

The next chapter introduces Leadership Results. As you will see, the model comprises seven fundamental relational variables, or indicators, that have a real impact on leadership results and has the parsimony principle at its core.

Conclusion

Everyone has a view (a set of hidden assumptions) about what leadership is, and how good leaders look, sound and act. Leadership researchers refer to these assumptions as 'naive' or 'implicit leadership theories'. They are mental models initially developed in childhood and carry the beliefs and assumptions of a culture without taking into account current research theories and models of leadership. While naive theories of leadership are anecdotal or based on personal beliefs rather than research, people still accept them as if they were factual. And given they are formed during the early stages of life, they are difficult to change.

Contemporary leadership is not just about enhancing individual effectiveness (in terms of enhancing leader development or human capital). It's also about being able to coordinate actions by building and strengthening relationships, social networks, and social and relational capital. Nevertheless, most organisations keep repeating the same mistakes, which is why they need new lenses.

Insight questions

- When was your implicit model of leadership formed?
- Do you remember how this happened?
- What blind spots about leadership have you uncovered over time and how?
- Which of the ten fundamental and interrelated errors outlined in this chapter sound most familiar?
- How would you describe the leadership model and development practices of your organisation?
- How would describe your current explicit model of leadership?
- Have you conducted an evaluation lately?
- What's the most useful thing you have learned in this chapter?

CHAPTER 5

An integrity model of leadership for our times

An all-in-one solution

A sure-fire way to develop leadership capability in organisations is through a leadership model, a leader development model, an employee engagement model and a leadership development model.

I have distilled these four tools into a single model called Leadership Results (LR).

You may remember Steve Jobs' presentation at the launch of the iPhone at Macworld in the Moscone Center in San Francisco on 9 January 2007. Early in the presentation he said, 'Today we're introducing three revolutionary products. The first one is a widescreen iPod with touch controls. The second is a revolutionary mobile phone. And the third is a breakthrough internet communications device.' Then, while showing the same image revolving on the screen, he said,

'An iPod, a phone, and an internet communicator.' And he repeated it and concluded with: 'This is one device. And we are calling it iPhone!'[1]

The iPhone changed the way smartphones looked and worked forever! It also created a different—more efficient and faster—way to connect. Jobs used the principle of parsimony, which I explain in the previous chapter.

* * *

What if your organisation could build real leadership capacity by developing individual leaders, boosting employee engagement and building collective leadership across the organisation at the same time?

Like the iPhone, Leadership Results has an integration of functions. LR is a pre-eminent research-based model that offers a holistic, relational and innovative approach to leadership development. It was developed in response to the failure of the multibillion-dollar leadership development industry to prepare leaders and build real organisational leadership capacity. LR constitutes the latest leadership development models, provides the mental software needed in the twenty-first century, and offers practices contemporary organisations need to simultaneously develop individual leaders, boost employee engagement and build collective leadership capacity.

How it works: Benefits of the LR model

John Mariotti, president and CEO of the Enterprise Group, once said that, 'In theory, there is very little difference between theory and practice; in practice there's a hell of a lot of difference.'

Learning Results treats leadership and leadership development as both a research discipline and a critical business practice. Research and theory are vital for learning abstract concepts, but nothing is more vital than practice. This model has ten key design features and corresponding benefits:

1. *contemporary*—prepares leaders to deal effectively with current and future challenges

74

2. *integrates leader development and leadership development*—develops individual leaders and an organisational leadership capacity

3. *competencies and relational measures of leadership*—promotes collective accountability for team performance by including everyone's measures, not just the leader's measures or attributes

4. *global and intercultural measures of leadership*—fosters inclusion, cultural diversity and global leadership

5. *creative thinking and innovation*—builds organisational competitive advantages

6. *simplicity through the principle of parsimony*—measures what really matters—the difference that makes the difference

7. *self-leadership, leadership impact, engagement, collective performance, and business results*—integrated picture of current leadership—makes other surveys redundant, which saves time and money

8. *visual representation reflects diagnostic and predictive model capability*—anticipates problems and implements corrective strategies to mitigate risks and ensure successful results

9. *unique scoring system and strengths-based practice*—enables comparisons using team standards and with the expectations of those individuals working together

10. *comprehensive feedback and action planning*—integrates results and comprehensive development action plans.

A holistic and integrated model of leadership development

Learning Results is designed to build organisational leadership capacity by developing self-leadership (individual leadership) and collective leadership (collaborative, shared or emergent leadership). It provides a path out of the current leadership crisis and towards a transformed and strengthened leadership using a holistic and integrated model as depicted in figure 5.1 (see overleaf).

Figure 5.1: collective leadership

By distinguishing and integrating leader development (human capital), leadership development (social capital) and collective or shared leadership, LR enables organisations to develop individual leaders, build organisational leadership capacity and boost employee engagement at all levels simultaneously. To this end, it measures and develops both self-leadership (human capital) and collective, distributed or emergent leadership (social capital) — which, when integrated, enable organisational leadership capacity, as shown in figure 5.2.

Figure 5.2: organisational leadership capacity

Leader Development   **Leadership Development**

SELF-LEADERSHIP
(Human Capital)

COLLECTIVE LEADERSHIP
Collaborative, shared,
distributed or emergent.

(Social Capital)

COLLECTIVE RESULTS
PERFORMANCE
EXTRAORDINARY
OUTCOMES

Leader development is only one aspect of leadership development (a much larger, deeper and expansive process). It focuses on developing an individual's knowledge, skills and abilities or competencies (human capital) using personal goals. When successful, this approach yields individual progress and results. It also focuses on the 'being' dimension of an individual, which encompasses identity, character, principles, morals, ethics and values.

In contrast, leadership development focuses on building relationships (social capital) and wider team and organisational leadership capacity, as well as strengthening employee engagement and shaping culture. It is driven by collective goals. Consequently, when successful, it yields collective outcomes and results.

Leader credibility and leadership impact

The second layer of the model shows two key elements: leader credibility and leadership impact. As leadership is essentially relational, it is important to understand the dynamics of relationships. As shown in figure 5.3 (see overleaf), leadership impact is the link between leader credibility and a cohesive and effective team; between an individual's leadership style and strategies and the collective results.

Figure 5.3: leader credibility and leadership impact

SELF-LEADERSHIP   LEADER CREDIBILITY   LEADERSHIP IMPACT   COLLECTIVE RESULTS
PERFORMANCE
EXTRAORDINARY
OUTCOMES

The link between self-leadership, leader credibility and leadership impact has three functional dimensions:

1. cognitive or rational — thought (head)
2. emotional — feeling (heart)
3. behavioural — action (hands).

These three work in sequence, like a chain reaction that influences team engagement and, ultimately, determines their performance and collective results (see figure 5.4). It is this chain that transforms the leadership practices of individuals and organisations and in this way, LR offers a pathway (a sequence with integrity) to self-leadership, leadership credibility, leadership impact and collective results.

Figure 5.4: functional dimensions of team engagement

HEAD   HEART   HANDS

SELF-LEADERSHIP   COLLECTIVE RESULTS
PERFORMANCE
EXTRAORDINARY
OUTCOMES

The third and final layer of the model displays the seven variables, or indicators, used to measure these three dimensions: fulfilment of expectations, trust and fairness; commitment and satisfaction; and discretionary effort and innovation (see figure 5.5).

Figure 5.5: indicators of leader credibility and leadership impact

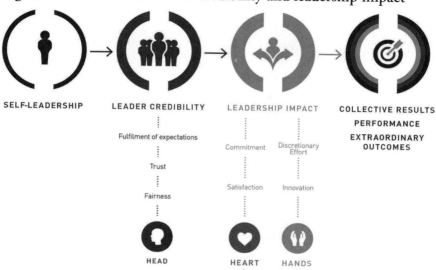

1. *The rational dimension (head)* relates to the credibility of the leader, and comprises fulfilment of expectations, trust and fairness.

2. *The emotional dimension (heart)* of leadership impact comprises commitment and satisfaction.

3. *The behavioural dimension (hands)* of leadership impact comprises discretionary effort and innovation (innovative behaviour).

The combined components of heart and hands comprise the leadership impact — in other words, the team's levels of engagement.

We know that employee engagement is three times greater with higher-quality leaders than with their average counterparts.[2] Lack of engagement in Australia costs the economy A\$54.8 billion. We also know that positive leadership is crucial to employee engagement, effectiveness and overall performance, innovation and results.

Given that engagement is critical to the LR model, it is important to be clear on what the term means.

If disengagement equates to a lack of productivity, having a lack of purpose and fulfilment, and feelings of dissatisfaction, disconnection, stagnation and general unhappiness, surely engagement must be the opposite. When using the word 'engagement', I refer to the degree of employees' positive or negative emotional attachment to their leader and/or the organisation.

Why it works: how the LR model is different

LR has six unique features that distinguish it from other contemporary models.

1. State-of-the-art thinking and practice in leadership

The LR model is the only model that calls upon the latest thinking and practice in leadership and leadership development. This includes the work of 24 leading researchers, authors and prominent practitioners (see table 5.1) — some of whom I have had the privilege of undertaking advanced professional training with.

Table 5.1: leading researchers, authors and practitioners

Expert	Position	Organisation
David Guest	Professor of Organisational Psychology and Human Resource Management	King's College London
David Day	Professor of Psychology, academic director, Steven L. Eggert Professor of Leadership and George R. Roberts Fellow	Kravis Leadership Institute, Claremont McKenna College
Ronald Heifetz	Founding director of the Center for Public Leadership; co-founder	Harvard Kennedy School Cambridge Leadership Associates
Marty Linsky	Adjunct lecturer, co-founder and principal	Harvard Kennedy School Cambridge Leadership Associates

Michael Johnstone	Adjunct lecturer, founder and executive director	Harvard Kennedy School Vantage Point Consulting
Barbara Kellerman	James McGregor Burns Lecturer in Leadership	Harvard Kennedy School
Joseph Raelin	Professor of Management and Organizational Development	Northeastern University
Allan Bird	Professor of Global Business	D'Amore-McKim School of Business, Northeastern University
Gary Latham	Professor of Organizational Behaviour and HR Management	Rotman School of Management, University of Toronto
Gerard Puccio	Chair and professor	International Center for Studies in Creativity, Buffalo State College, SUNY
Richard Bolden	Professor of Leadership and Management	University of the West of England
Jonathan Gosling	Professor of Leadership Studies	Business School, University of Exeter
Jennifer Martineau	Senior Vice President, Research, Evaluation and Societal Advancement	Center for Creative Leadership
Bill Drath	Senior Fellow and faculty	Center for Creative Leadership
Cindy McCauley	Senior Fellow and faculty	Center for Creative Leadership
Marian Ruderman	Senior Fellow and director	Center for Creative Leadership
Mary Uhl-Bien	Professor of Leadership	TCU's Neeley School of Business
Robert House	Professor of Organizational Studies	Wharton Business School at the University of Pennsylvania
Charles Manz	Professor of Business Leadership	Isenberg School of Management, University of Massachusetts
Kim Cameron	Professor of Management and Organizations	Ross School of Business, University of Michigan
Harrison Owen	Creator of Open Space Technology, author and consultant	President of H.H. Owen and Company

(continued)

Table 5.1 (*Cont'd*)

Marshall Goldsmith	#1 coach, leadership thinker and author; professor of Management Practice	Tuck School of Business, Dartmouth College
Martin Seligman	Professor of Psychology, Director of the Positive Psychology Center	University of Pennsylvania
Donald Clifton	Former chairman, creator of the Clifton StrengthsFinder, the father of strengths-based psychology and the grandfather of positive psychology	Gallup

2. Underpinned by the 'relating' leadership capability

LR addresses the long-neglected 'relating' capability of leadership — building trusting relationships. Leadership is fundamentally a process of social influence that entails dynamic and interactive relationships. High-quality relationships are the currency of effective leadership.

Humans crave interpersonal interaction — we seek connectedness and a sense of belonging. We are fundamentally social creatures that exist within relationships with each other. You only need consider the explosion of social networking tools to see this in action. This is almost instinctive, a hangover perhaps from our days of living in the wilderness where being alone could be fatal. Our brains were designed for life as part of the social whole, with the capacity for social cognition, language and both behavioural and emotional regulation. Though we no longer live primitively with our tribe or clan, being a social creature remains central to most of us.

Relating is at the heart of leadership. Yet there is the paradox of the need to relate, to trust, to communicate and to share with, juxtaposed with the urge to complete, to advance the self, to satisfy the ego's need for personal recognition and to be unique. With several current generations touted as being the most selfish (baby boomers have 'benefited from good wages and rising property values before retiring on gold-plated pensions'[3] and the millennials are 'the most self-absorbed one yet, having been shaped by digital technology, overprotective baby boomer parents'[4]), is it any wonder there is an imbalance in the relationship between the individual and the collective? I'm sure you have already worked this out from the TV news.

The leadership model introduced here is designed to fix the current leadership crisis and lack of engagement in organisations, and to prevent future leadership failures.

Malcolm's case

Malcolm was appointed the HR director of a global financial services firm with the CEO's mandate to change the culture from one of working in silos to one of collaboration and high performance. He locked himself in his office for weeks, working out the best strategy.

For Malcolm, building relationships through networking internally was an arduous and unpleasant task that involved talking to strangers. He was not comfortable requesting assistance, nor asking questions about things he didn't know, as would be expected from any new team member. To his mind, this would mean exposing himself and being seen as a weak leader. He felt he had to protect his image as a highly knowledgeable and competent leader, at all costs.

What Malcolm did not realise, because of his lack of self-awareness, was the huge amount of energy it took to keep up this public face. In fact, he was exhausted. Neither did he realise that he was perceived as arrogant and distant by those around him.

In the meantime, day-to-day issues were piling up — recurring conflicts, for example, between marketing and sales, which in turn were undermining production efficiency. Malcolm finally announced a number of changes to policies and procedures, but soon came to realise the big message of reform he had been working for weeks was falling on deaf ears. Most people hardly knew him and the reputation he had among those who did know him — mostly his direct reports — was as an abrupt and pushy

(continued)

character interested only in making a name for himself. When the time came for him to present his progress to the executive, he realised he was completely out of the loop. Most alarmingly, he saw that his future in the firm was at risk.

His experience is not uncommon. I have met many Malcolms in my career, as I'm sure you have. Some managed to change their ways by becoming more relational leaders; others did not.

Executives often talk about the importance of fostering trust, consensus and collaboration but only manage to generate frustration, adversity, cynicism and even anger and conflict. This is because they focus on trying to win their position or argument. They find it difficult to relate to others, especially those who have different views of the world.

In traditional stereotypes of business leadership, relating has seldom been considered necessary, and as leaders were seen to be flawless, it was thought that they should not need to ask for advice outside of their purple circle. A leader was expected to be decisive and in control, with any connection at an emotional level being largely unnecessary. However, in today's world of networks, building trusting relationships has become an absolute must for effective leadership.

Relating doesn't mean avoiding issues or interpersonal conflict, by any means. The relating capability of leadership comprises three key dimensions:

1. *Inquiring* is about genuinely trying to understand the thoughts and feelings of team members or stakeholders. This requires suspending judgement and trying to fully comprehend how and why they have, for example, taken certain views or adopted certain positions on specific issues. This involves exploring their interpretations and conclusions.

2. *Advocating*, in this context, means explaining your point of view and taking a stand on a subject. It is to clearly outline how you reached your interpretations and conclusions, and it serves as the opposite of inquiring. It's important that effective leaders distinguish between observations and opinions and judgements, and detail their rationale without being defensive or aggressive.

3. *Connecting* is about establishing and building strong and durable collaborative relationships with stakeholders with a view to forming alliances that drive change and results.

Janet's case

Janet was the general manager of people and performance at a large bank and was entrusted with a similar mandate to Malcolm's. She started by meeting each of the key stakeholders in the executive team individually, to get their perspective on the firm and the context in which it was operating—market, trends, competitors and so on. She also made it a priority to quickly get to know each of the members of her own new team—their personalities, styles, capabilities, strengths, motivations, challenges and concerns. This enabled her to delegate effectively soon after taking the role, and freed her from the day-to-day tasks while empowering her team by progressively giving them more responsibility. This way she built trust with her team. They recognised Janet as someone who was prepared to trust them and to let go of many issues by taking risks. Janet also made sure she demonstrated the collaboration she expected from her team; she used a consensus-based decision-making style and readily admitted her ignorance by asking a lot of questions.

Janet held regular meetings with her team to observe their interaction, which moulded the strategies she used to build a cohesive team. As the team members progressively bonded, their levels of identification with, goodwill, affection and care for their leader—and each other—grew exponentially. Similarly, their levels of satisfaction rose to new heights. This created the conditions for the team to become more creative than ever and find solutions to old problems, which eventually turned into remarkable innovations.

Janet's efforts paid off. Months later, when the team was under pressure to implement changes, she could make very demanding requests of them to meet urgent deadlines. Given Janet's high

(continued)

levels of credibility and the trust she had with her team, as well as the team's high levels of satisfaction and commitment, each team member was prepared (if not delighted) to contribute by going the extra mile. Not surprisingly, magic happened! Janet's team outperformed all expectations. Not only did they achieve the required system changes under time and budget, but they became innovation award winners of the year.

Needless to say, Janet is a great example of how to use the relating capability of leadership.

3. Grounded in psychological contract theory

It is clear that the quality of the relationships leaders have with followers (team members, stakeholders or associates) is central to effective leadership. And the concept of the psychological contract is central to establishing, building and sustaining successful relationships.

The term 'psychological contract' was coined in 1960 by legendary Harvard Business School professor Chris Argyris to describe the implicit agreements between employers and employees about expectations and perceived obligations beyond those stipulated in a written employment contract. A psychological contract refers to the unspoken and unwritten beliefs and expectations we develop concerning our interaction with other people such as our employer, boss, supervisor, colleague, doctor, partner, spouse or friend. These do not sit idly in our minds but are very active and set the dynamics of our relationships with others. Psychological contracts are the lifeblood of all relationships.

A formal, written contract will never cover everything in a work setting, and it is the psychological contract that fills in the gaps about the reciprocal relationship and obligations between the employee and the organisation. These unwritten, unspoken beliefs and expectations are formed by the contract makers.

Contract makers are any parties or written documents (for example, brochures, mission statements, charters, HR policies, ground rules, principles) that convey expectations, commitments or intentions that can be interpreted as promises or obligations. Managers are the most influential contract makers in any organisation. Even so, given the subjectivity of the psychological contract, it is never possible to address all aspects of all our various relationships.

Angelo's violated psychological contract

Angelo was a hard-working and ambitious executive aspiring to quickly climb the corporate ladder. Even before he joined his new employer, a large telecommunications company, Angelo was told by his recruitment agency that the company rewarded hard workers generously. During his initial interview, he was told that if he was to be offered a position, he would be working for a manager who was extremely demanding, but who also rewarded very generously. Two weeks later, Angelo met someone who had worked for the company—although in a different department—who told him the same thing. 'Boy, they push you hard and expect a lot from you', the person said. 'But you know they also reward you well. Actually, I got promotion within six months!'

In hearing all these comments, and given his ambition and solid work ethic, it was no surprise that Angelo was convinced this was the perfect role for him and accepted the position without hesitation. Twelve months later, Angelo was furious and looking for a new job. Not only was he never offered the early promotion he was expecting, but he was also transferred to another branch twice the distance from his home as the one where he started. All this happened despite the fact that he had been working his hardest since day one! Angelo's psychological contract with this employer had been violated.

In his case, the recruiter, the person who interviewed him, and the individual who had worked for the same company, were the contract makers that had conveyed to Angelo the expectation of an early promotion, which he construed as an implied promise by his employer.

Given that managers are the most influential contract makers in any organisation and 'people leave managers not organisations',[5] the Leadership Psychological Contract (LPC) model, which I conceived in 2014, incorporates the unexpressed beliefs, promises, expectations, responsibilities and perceived obligations between leaders and their followers.[6] The LPC has served as the foundation for the LR model presented in this book.

4. Addresses current deficiencies

Unquestionably, and compared with traditional leadership models, the second most fundamental difference and advantage of LR is that it provides a much more contemporary approach to leadership development by addressing the ten fundamental errors delineated in the previous chapter: (1) using outdated models of leadership; (2) mistaking 'leader' for 'leadership' development; (3) confusing authority with leadership; (4) maintaining a fixation with competency-based models; (5) underestimating learning agility and adaptation; (6) ignoring relational measures of leadership; (7) neglecting global and intercultural dimensions of leadership; (8) being inattentive to creative thinking and innovation; (9) disregarding the measurement of collective outcomes and results; and (10) failing to conduct impact evaluations.

5. Rooted in the concept of positive integrity

The fifth unique quality of the LR model is based on the research and work related to positive integrity. Integrity is defined as the 'state of being whole, unbroken and unimpaired, sound, complete or in perfect condition'. In turn, this condition enables increased performance from individuals, groups, organisations and communities.[7]

The Leadership Results chain

Leadership Results reveals the causal link between the integrity of the various components of the model and extraordinary performance.

In this model, 'integrity' means keeping the link between leaders and their stakeholders unbroken. The causal chain of relationships remains intact to help produce superior value creation by generating unprecedented performance outcomes and business results. Integrity then becomes a factor of production as important as technology, tacit knowledge, creativity, ideas and other critical intangible resources, such as intellectual capital, social capital and relational capital.

Traditionally, integrity has been associated with virtue, morality and ethics, which has seriously diminished its potential power and benefits. This approach to integrity does not in any way ignore, devalue or diminish the paramount importance of virtues, morals and ethics. In fact, it's quite the opposite. This, however, is treated as part of the self-leadership component of the LR model, which I discuss in detail in chapter 7.

Without integrity, nothing works

Richard Buckminster Fuller (1895–1983), architect, systems theorist, author, designer, inventor and visionary, who worked as a 'comprehensive anticipatory design scientist' to solve global problems, said, 'Integrity is the essence of everything successful.'

The Leadership Results chain provides a coherent, logical, sequential and consequential system of leader and leadership development. Integrity is part of the first link of the LR chain. Leading with integrity is fundamental to self-leadership and leads to leader credibility. In turn, leader credibility determines leadership impact. Finally, if the chain remains unbroken (has integrity), this sequence then delivers collective results.

6. Visual representation of diagnostic and predictive capability

The reporting of leadership diagnostic results using the visual representations of a circle graphic referred to as a 'circumplex' has become fashionable in recent years (for example, LSI by Human Synergistics, The Leadership Circle and CLS360). Such images comprise a number of concentric circles. The circle is a common representation of unity, wholeness and infinity. Such representations can look pretty, interesting and even inspiring. From a practical perspective, however, other than sending the message of 'going around in circles', they fail to denote any sense of direction — much less causality (cause–effect) — which is what scientific models do.

Linear models, on the other hand, describe a continuous response variable as a function of one or more predictor variables. This is precisely the case with the LR model.

Linear models have been criticised for being overly simplistic and sequential and not, therefore, depictions of how things really happen. The reality is that all models make assumptions and have limitations. Models cannot scientifically explain every detail of observable phenomena, and no model has ever been totally complete. This is because models are only representations of reality, not realities in themselves: they only approximate natural phenomena and, as such, are inherently inexact.

No model can account for every variable—especially external variables that influence the system under study, which represents a closed system. Consequently, all models need to make assumptions based on a set of observations, circumstances and contextual conditions, otherwise they could not be tested. From this perspective, LR is no exception. A good model, however, must be able to explain as many characteristics as possible, put in the simplest possible way (the principle of parsimony). The LR model represents how humans experience real-life situations in a logical and sequential way over time.

The main benefits of linear models are that they are straightforward; are the least abstract descriptions and representations of a phenomenon; enable the measuring and testing of variables, hypotheses or scenarios; and help to identify and clarify most of the important variables that predict behaviour, even within complex relationships or systems.

The overall graphic design of the LR model is represented by the symbol of an arrow-like shape (which contains four integrated circles representing each of the key components that comprise the model). This arrow-like shape denotes purpose, direction, advancement and causality. It also captures the sequential and progressive nature of LD, which is achieved by advancing through various stages.

How it works: The LR survey

LR uses a 360-degree feedback online survey that captures the indicators of each component of the model. The resulting report contains the results and valuable information to help you better understand your individual leadership credibility and impact so you can take them to the next level.

The LR report also provides information on the levels of engagement of your team and their collective performance. This is a unique feature of this survey. Most leadership 360-degree feedback surveys provide only information related to your personal attributes according to raters' opinions or assessments of you and your performance. The LR survey measures important attributes of your raters. More specifically, it measures their levels of commitment and satisfaction in working with you, and their discretionary effort and innovative behaviour. These are truly 'relational' measures of leadership.

Faced with the results of a large hospital's culture survey several years ago, it became clear to the OD manager and me that there were some concerns at the senior management level. However, neither of us could pinpoint the reasons for the issues as the survey results were mostly figures without many insights.

In contrast, the LR survey collects qualitative information through interviews and/or focus groups. This provides a much more integrated and richer picture that shows 'how' and 'why' things are happening in your team or organisation so the root causes of issues can be isolated and fixed.

Self-leadership

Self-leadership is the process through which you can find the direction and motivation to improve your own performance. This requires self-influence, self-regulation, self-control, self-management and intrinsic motivation.

The LR survey offers the flexibility to accommodate specific competencies or meta-competencies according to your team or organisational needs to measure self-leadership.

Part II of the book is devoted to self-leadership and leader development:

- Chapter 6 explores the concept of the leadership initiation.

- Chapter 7 discusses self-leadership and leader development.

- Chapter 8 reviews character and signature strengths.

- Chapter 9 examines motivation, commitment, goal setting, engagement and self-engagement.

Leader credibility

Credibility—the quality of being deemed trustworthy and believable and, therefore, convincing—is the foundation of effective leadership, as depicted in figure 5.6. Whether you are credible, or the degree to which you are credible, depends on other people's assessment of three key aspects of your behaviour:

- the degree to which your team members or stakeholders believe you have fulfilled their expectations
- how much they trust you
- whether they believe you are fair.

Figure 5.6: leader credibility

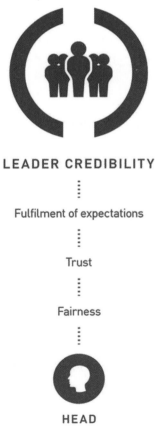

LEADER CREDIBILITY

Fulfilment of expectations

Trust

Fairness

HEAD

There is a detailed discussion of credibility in chapter 13, but suffice to say that leadership credibility arises out of integrity: being true to your word and being open and proactive when you are unable, for whatever reason, to remain true to your word. By acting with integrity you fulfil promises, earn and maintain trust, behave in a way that is reasoned and equitable — and leadership is transformed.

1. Fulfilment of expectations

Fulfilment of expectations measures the degree to which you deliver on your promises, expectations, and/or obligations to others, as they perceive them. Although often implicit and unwritten, expectations have a strong promissory nature, are pervasive and govern the quality of relationships. Perceived breaches or violations of obligations or expectations usually have severe negative consequences on levels of trust and, therefore, credibility.

If you want to be perceived as an extraordinary leader capable of game-changing improvements, you absolutely must be seen as honest. Honesty tops the list of 20 characteristics of admired leaders.[8] The two elements of honesty that really matter in this context are trust and fairness.

2. Trust

Trust is critical to establishing credibility. It measures the level of confidence team members and other stakeholders have in you. Trust involves team members' willingness to make themselves vulnerable and be open, and confidence that you will consider their interests in their absence. It also involves team members' assessment of your intentions, character, integrity and competence. Being trusted by your stakeholders is absolutely critical if you are to lead successfully and deliver extraordinary results.

To measure trust, consider how your team members or stakeholders would respond to the following seven statements.

Our leader:

1. does not blame us when things go wrong

2. communicates openly, honestly and respectfully

3. is competent

4. demonstrates good judgement

5. can be relied upon

6. does/delivers what s/he promises

7. shares important information openly and transparently.

3. Fairness

Fairness indicates how equitable or impartial you are in your team members' or stakeholders' eyes. Whether you are considered fair has a huge impact on what your stakeholders think about you, their willingness to follow you and, ultimately, what they do at work. Perceptions of fairness influence your team members' levels of commitment and discretionary effort.

To measure fairness, consider how your team members or stakeholders would respond to the following six statements.

Our leader:

1. provides opportunities for us to share our views

2. displays consistency in decision-making

3. does not display favouritism

4. does not bully or abuse her/his power or discriminate against us

5. resolves/addresses disputes or conflicts promptly and on a fair basis

6. shares influence and power appropriately.

Leadership impact

Leadership impact describes team members' or stakeholders' levels of commitment, satisfaction, discretionary effort and innovation as a consequence of your leadership, as shown in figure 5.7.

- Commitment and satisfaction are emotional variables (heart).

- Discretionary effort and innovation are behavioural variables (hands).

Combined, these four variables constitute your team's level of engagement.

Figure 5.7: leadership impact

1. Commitment

Commitment refers to your team members' positive emotional attachment, identification and involvement with you in pursuit of common goals. Committed team members identify with your values, principles, purpose and goals. They have a heightened level of engagement, which, in turn, motivates them to exert more effort.

The way you conduct yourself as a leader has a far-reaching impact on your team's level of commitment. To measure commitment, consider how your team members or stakeholders would respond to the following five statements.

1. I am proud to tell others I work for/with our leader.

2. I feel like 'part of the family' with our leader.

3. Our leader has a great deal of personal meaning for me.

4. I really care about our leader's success.

5. My values and the demonstrated values of our leader are very similar.

2. Satisfaction

Satisfaction reflects your team members' emotional response to working with you. There will be varying degrees of satisfaction with your unique leadership style. Satisfaction is both an outcome and motivator.

To measure satisfaction, consider how your team members or stakeholders would respond to the following three statements.

1. I like working with our leader.

2. I am pleased when I see how our leader is progressing.

3. I do not feel frustrated working with our leader.

3. Discretionary effort

Discretionary effort describes performance (behaviour, action or activities) that goes beyond the call of duty (goes the extra mile) or exceeds usual demands, requirements or expectations of the job.

To measure discretionary effort, consider how your team members or stakeholders would respond to the following four statements.

In our team:

1. we really exert ourselves to the full, beyond what is expected

2. we finish a job even if it means sacrificing breaks or lunches

3. we voluntarily put in extra time and effort to achieve better, faster results

4. we persist in overcoming obstacles to complete important tasks.

4. Innovation

Innovation refers to your team members' creative thinking and innovative behaviour. This includes their orientation towards change, as well as the generation and/or adoption of new ideas and/or practices. It also relates to your team members' perseverance with new and promising ideas.

To measure innovation, consider how your team members or stakeholders would respond to the following five statements.

In our team:

1. we look for new ideas, concepts, processes, techniques and/or technologies

2. we produce new and creative ideas

3. we encourage, support, endorse, and reward new ideas from others

4. we implement new, viable, fruitful, promising, and/or commercially profitable ideas

5. we create and advance suitable plans and schedules to implement new and useful ideas.

Collective performance and results

This relates to your team's perceived level of functioning and performance as a team. It also relates to their perceived level of customer service, stakeholder or community impact, and the generation of savings, revenue and profits.

To measure collective performance and results, consider how your team members or stakeholders would describe:

*   team effectiveness (how well the team works together)

*   overall team performance (team output or results)

*   level of responsiveness (internal and external) of your team

*   stakeholder, social or community involvement in planning and design

*   management of budget and resources.

These items can be customised to meet specific team or organisational needs. Similarly, additional items can be added to capture other indicators of performance and results.

Chapter 13 discusses collective performance and results in detail.

Conclusion

Leadership Results is a relational and predictive model of leadership that goes beyond traditional and outdated heroic, competency-only based models of leadership that focus only on developing the individual. LR takes a distributive, or collective, perspective of leadership—which is what leadership really is.

This model is based on the 'relating' capability of leadership, which comprises three dimensions (inquiring, advocating and connecting); positive integrity; and my own original research on the Leadership Psychological Contract. In doing so, LR promotes leader credibility (integrity, trust, fairness and ethical behaviour).

The LR survey results enable leaders to learn 'what' is happening in teams, understand 'how', and explain 'why' it is happening. This enables leaders and teams to effect positive change by developing trust, building strong stakeholder engagement and generating the innovation required to deliver collective and unprecedented outcomes and business results.

A summary of measures and outcomes of the model is captured in table 5.2.

Table 5.2: a summary of measures and outcomes

Function	7 relational variables	Outcomes	Results
The rational (HEAD) element relates to the leader's credibility and comprises 3 variables. **HEAD**	1. Fulfilment of expectations 2. Fairness 3. Trust	Leader credibility	COLLECTIVE RESULTS PERFORMANCE EXTRAORDINARY OUTCOMES
The emotional (HEART) element relates to your leadership impact and comprises 2 variables. **HEART**	4. Commitment 5. Satisfaction	Engagement	
The behavourial (HANDS) element relates to your leadership impact and also comprises 2 variables **HANDS**	6. Discretionary effort 7. Innovation		

Insight questions

- To what degree are you fulfilling the expectations of your team members/stakeholders? What would be their response to this question?

- How much do your team members/stakeholders trust you? What would they say in response to this question?

- How fair are you with your team members/stakeholders? How fair would they say you are with them?

- How committed are your team members/stakeholders to you and your cause/purpose? How proud are they about working with you? What would they say in response to these questions?

- How satisfied are your team members/stakeholders with your leadership style? How satisfied would they say they are?

- How much extra effort are your team members/stakeholders putting into their work? What would they say in response to this question?

- How creative and innovative are your team members/ stakeholders at work? What would they say in response to this question?

- How well is your team working together? How well is it performing? How would your team members respond to these questions?

PART II

SELF-LEADERSHIP AND LEADER DEVELOPMENT

This section explains self-leadership and leader development—the foundation of leadership development—and outlines a range of strategies to develop individual leaders. It comprises four chapters.

- Chapter 6 explains initiation, and why and how leaders need to be initiated.

- Chapter 7 addresses self-leadership and leader development.

- Chapter 8 examines virtues, emotions, and character and signature strengths.

- Chapter 9 covers motivation, commitment and self-engagement.

Self-leadership is the ability to lead ourselves to achieve the direction and motivation necessary to positively influence our own performance. Self-leadership is related to empowering yourself by gaining self-efficacy—the level of belief in your own ability to reach goals and complete tasks.

CHAPTER 6
The initiation to leadership

The debate about whether leaders are born or made has raged for years. But what if this is a dead-end and misleading question that—like most closed-ended questions—not only limits, but actually hides the truth?

What if effective leaders aren't either born or made, but rather 'initiated'? What if leadership requires making a major life transition and is a life-long journey?

The first initiation

A young brother and sister are playing together in the field. They both get highly energised and excited as their game escalates. The boy picks up a fallen branch and threatens the girl with it. Observing from a distance, their parents notice this aggressive behaviour and the father races over and grabs the boy, shouting, 'You must die!' The mother is profoundly shaken and cries, 'No!', but the father drags the boy into a nearby river where he sticks

(continued)

the boy's head under the water and holds it for a long time. The mother and the girl watch in absolute horror until the mother shouts, 'Stop it. You're going to kill him!'

'Yes, that's what I want', responds the father. Finally, he drags the boy out of the water. He's still breathing. The father then shouts, 'My boy is dead and a man is born!' With that, the father has given his son his first initiation.

What is initiation?

Initiation is an anthropological term used to describe the ceremony some societies use to mark the transition from childhood or adolescence to becoming full members of adult society. This usually involves a symbolic rite. The main purpose of any initiation is for the individual to experience a significant change in awareness about the self—their character and their place in the world. Initiations are designed to bring about permanent changes through experiences that are never forgotten. The lessons from the initiation are meant to penetrate the whole person's being (that is, the very nature or essence of the individual) so that the rite becomes a transformative experience.

In the story at the start of the chapter, for example, what would have the longest-lasting effect on the boy in learning that he should not abuse his physical power? A verbal reprimand, or the near-drowning he experiences at the hands of his father?

Leadership initiation

Leadership initiations are specifically designed to ensure leaders won't abuse their power.

To this end, the initiation is an experience of submission where the individual being initiated must surrender to something greater than themselves. This is a reminder that the main duty of leadership is to be of service to others, not self-serving.

This is sometimes at odds with urban myths that portray leadership as the ability to exert power and control, and to achieve success (however that may be defined). In fact, this is pseudo-leadership. True leadership always begins with a 'wake-up call', which entails a transformative and humbling test that can take many shapes and forms, including intense experiences, crises, life-threatening events, uncertainty and self-doubt.

In their September 2002 *Harvard Business Review* article 'Crucibles of Leadership', Warren Bennis (1925–2014), a Distinguished Professor of Business Administration and the founding chairman of the Leadership Institute at the University of Southern California, and Robert Thomas, assert that 'one of the most reliable indicators and predictors of true leadership is an individual's ability to find meaning in negative events and to learn from the most trying circumstances'.[1] Extraordinary leaders conquer adversity and become stronger and more committed as a result of their experiences.

> *Individuals are transformed through initiation, enabling the successful transition from one stage of life to another.*

Dr Robert Moore (1942–2016), Distinguished Professor of Psychology, Psychoanalysis and Spirituality at the Graduate Center of the Chicago Theological Seminary, in talking about 'boy psychology' makes the following comments: 'The devastating fact is that most men are fixated at an immature level of development. These early developmental levels are governed by the inner blueprints appropriate to boyhood.'[2] Interestingly, to compensate for this lack of development, these men seek 'significance' in the world to draw attention to themselves, and the prospect of becoming a 'leader' seems the perfect route. Imagine the impact such driven, yet self-seeking, individuals are likely to have on the world around them. The destructive impact of this boy psychology can be seen in the many abrasive leaders, also called bullies (both men and women), in so many organisations. Workplace bullying has mental, physical and economic costs, which are far from insignificant. In Australia, for example, the Productivity Commission estimates the annual total cost of workplace bullying to be between $6 billion and $36 billion.[3]

Other examples of boy psychology include weakness and passivity, failing to do things effectively and creatively or to encourage creativity both individually or for others, and obsessive and egocentric behaviours. They are all around us. The initiation to leadership through a wake-up call is aimed at preventing this tragedy.

The wake-up call

Wake-up calls, and initiations, are designed to promote sufficient self-awareness to go beyond the cognitive or mental (*knowing*) and behavioural (*doing*) dimension of leadership by tapping into the deeper affective or emotional and attitudinal (*being*) dimension. This develops a leader's identity, values, character, moral potency, ethics, spirituality, and who they are as a human being.

The first two dimensions are pretty straightforward. The *knowing* dimension is developed by acquiring new knowledge. The *doing* dimension is developed by acquiring new skills or competencies. Both are often also referred to as KAS (knowledge, attitudes and skills) or KSAs (knowledge, skills and abilities — the attributes required to perform a job and which help evaluate likely success in a particular job).

Developing the third dimension (*being*), however, is much trickier, because it requires a profound or marked change in nature, form or appearance (hence the use of terms such as 'transformative' or 'transformational'). Not surprisingly, this *being* dimension is usually the most neglected in the development of contemporary leaders.

A wake-up call, in this context, is a symbolic awakening of human consciousness (or awakening to a higher consciousness, as treated in spiritual themes). Thomas Merton (1915–1968), for example, a journalist who left his career to become a monk and student of comparative religions, refers to 'contemplative spirituality' and to the struggle between the 'false self' (sometimes equated with the ego) and the 'true self' (also referred to as 'the self'). By developing our true self, we enter into a relationship, or achieve connectedness or a belonging with who we are. An illusory persona — a false self — shadows our identity if we fail to awaken.

Mircea Eliade (1921–1986), a religious historian, philosopher and professor at the University of Chicago, talks about the split between the 'sacred' and 'profane' worlds. Eliade says that despite the fact many people believe their world is entirely profane (or secular), they are still unconsciously connected to the memory of something sacred or spiritual. From this spiritual perspective, awakening may occur through a divine or supernatural revelation.[4] From a more secular perspective, however, awakening needs to be prompted, or initiated. This requires self-examination or, as Plato put it, 'the life which is not examined is not worth living'.

More often than not, a wake-up call comes from the lessons, insights and/or enlightenment that result from a crisis, failure, painful experience or a stream of bad events. The result can be a deep sense of dissatisfaction and a desire to achieve a new state of being.

A lesson in humility

My first wake-up call was my father's death when I was 13 years old. But there were others. I travelled to South America in my early twenties with my girlfriend at the time, who later became my first wife. The city is the gateway to the Inca Trail, a trek lasting many days that ends at Machu Picchu, the fifteenth-century Inca citadel situated on a 2430-metre-high (7970-foot) mountain ridge. It is one of Peru's most important tourist destinations and one of the world's most-visited sites.

One day we went to the local market in Cusco. I was carrying a cloth bag containing my passport and all my money. Many people had advised me to carry my valuables in a money belt hidden around my waist, because tourist muggings were common. But, of course, I knew better. There was no way this could happen to me. After all, I was very fit physically, full of pride and misguided self-confidence — bordering on arrogance, I'm ashamed to say.

Peruvian mothers carry their babies in traditional blankets, called *aguayos*, or *mantas*, on their backs. The market was extremely

(continued)

crowded, just like peak hour in a Tokyo subway. Suddenly, I felt myself squeezed between two women, both carrying their babies in *aguayos*, moving in opposite directions. I sensed a slight pull on my bag, which I lifted and held firmly against my body. Not long after, when we had moved away from the crowd, I looked at the bag in absolute disbelief. Yes, it was empty!

Within seconds I had lost my passport and all my money. The local police explained that it was a common play. The women use a sharp razor to cut into the bag and take its contents while they distract their target by squeezing up against them. And they are very skilled.

Not only did I not have the humility to listen good advice, I wasn't sufficiently self-aware to realise I was an easy target. I was angry for days and looked at the locals, especially women carrying babies, with scorn and contempt. It took me a long time to get over it. But, in hindsight, it was a lesson I badly needed.

Rites of passage

While life naturally presents us with the challenges and crises that force us to grow up and mature, there are also cultures that have rites of passages to initiate or transition children or adolescents to adulthood.

Rites of passage are rituals aimed at initiating, enabling or facilitating separations, transitions and re-incorporations throughout critical life stages or major life changes. Some of the most common examples include giving birth, transitioning from childhood to puberty or teenage years, from high school to college or university, falling in love, losing your virginity, getting your heart broken, getting married, becoming a parent, getting divorced, losing a loved one, suffering a serious illness, going broke and entering mature age.

Using the wisdom of the ages

We can use the wisdom passed on to us by our ancestors through stories, legends, allegories, fables, myths, metaphors, symbols, archetypes and the so-called great mysteries, to improve our lives. Good myths, like archetypes, are universal. They apply to everyone and appear repeatedly across cultures separated by geographies and thousands of years. They are always relevant, which is why they are immortal and prevail, because they add meaning to our lives.

In the Christian tradition, for example, the opportunity for personal transformation is conveyed in the book of Genesis via the story of the Garden of Eden. The fall (or rise) of humanity, in which Adam (symbol of mankind) gives up to the snake (Satan), symbolises our fantasy of grandiosity by becoming God-like or wise by acquiring knowledge, abundance, and immortality (the temptation to access status, power and greed in modern society) by eating the apple from Tree of Knowledge of Good and Evil.

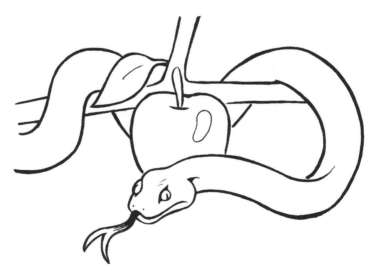

This allegory describes the process that every generation needs to go through to mature into adulthood. It is the transition from a state of innocence to one of becoming responsible through having the freedom to make choices. It also symbolises the dilemmas (temptations) we all face in making ethical choices.

Initiation rites have been enacted differently throughout history, though they all have similarities. Initiation rites for leaders are different in that they have been specifically designed to reduce narcissism, egotistic, self-centred and self-seeking behaviour and the consequent abuse of power. The behaviours that are discouraged include rebelling against or disobeying those who made them their leader (the equivalent of the creator in the Garden of Eden story). To this end, the rites for those marked for leadership put them into a unique place — a 'liminal space' — where their transformative experience was created.

Is initiation exclusive to men?

You may have noticed that most references to initiation relate to men — I did when I started researching this topic. Despite the fact some cultures also have initiation rites for women, the male bias is generally true. This is why: The thinking is that nature takes care of the initiation of women via the menstrual cycle and the pain associated with giving birth, which has been described as 'the worst pain imaginable'. Riane Eisler, cultural historian, systems scientist, educator, attorney, speaker, author of *The Equal Rights Handbook*, and president of the Center for Partnership Studies, refers to giving birth as an experience that alters consciousness — somewhat equivalent to 'the hero's journey'.[5]

It's also reasonable to assume that in patriarchal societies, advancing the rights of manhood has prevailed over the treatment of women. In fact, in looking at the 'glass ceiling effect' (the invisible and unbreakable barrier that keeps minorities and women from climbing the corporate ladder regardless of their achievements or qualifications) it may be argued that the masculine paradigm still prevails.

Liminal space

To imprint the initiation's very important message permanently on a person's psyche requires going beyond just acquiring new information (reading books, for example, or attending training sessions). It has to be in the liminal space—*limina* being the Latin word for 'threshold', or the space between (that is, neither here nor there).

Liminality is an ambiguous and terrifying space where old identities are torn away. It is a unique combination of pain and confusion that's beyond the individual's control and it forces them to experience failure. The experience of not being in control makes it possible to see beyond self-seeking, self-interest and self-will. At this point, the only option is to surrender fully. This allows the boy to die and be reborn as a man (leader). As result, a new consciousness emerges, which is the essence of transformation.

Richard Rohr, in referencing the work of Victor Turner (1920–1983), a British cultural anthropologist known for his work on symbols, rituals and rites of passage, explains that 'Only pain is now strong enough to lead us into this unique place "where all significant transformation happens.".[6] He further notes that 'Everything that is genuinely new emerges in some kind of liminal space.'

Perhaps the way to think about this transformative process is to consider the fables of alchemists in the Middle Ages who reportedly transmuted ordinary metals, or common substances of little value, into substances of great value (such as gold). To do so, they used a 'crucible'—a pot in which the substances were heated to very high temperatures to burn off any impurities, leaving only the precious metals. The crucible, then, is a symbol for a place or situation that forces individuals to change or make tough decisions. It's like a purification rite in which all impurities are purged—or character defects eradicated.

Humility and servitude

Such experiences were designed to teach those being initiated that leadership isn't about a search for significance or grandiosity but rather about surrender, acceptance, humility and servitude. Carl Jung

(1875–1961), a Swiss psychiatrist and psychoanalyst who founded analytical psychology, uses the term 'individuation', which he described as the process of becoming aware of oneself, of one's make-up, and the way to discover one's true, inner self.'

He distinguishes between the 'persona' (or mask) that pretends individuality and the 'collective psyche, or unconscious', which can be accessed through archetypes or universal symbols such as the Great Mother, the Wise Old Man, the Shadow, the Tower, Fire, Water, the Tree of Life and more. Initiations then allow individuals to shift from 'my story' (I) to 'our story' (we), gaining a sense of collective identity, service to others and the desire to achieve higher goals and make a real difference.[6] These themes are captured in Servant Leadership literature.

So, transformation or enlightenment begins with self-understanding. That is, uncovering our blind spots and identifying and dealing with the barriers that preclude every human being from becoming their 'essence', or 'true self', as opposed to their 'false self', or 'conditioned self', the self that others have imposed on us and that, sadly, many have settled for. These themes are embedded in Authentic Leadership literature.

> *Transformation or enlightenment begins with self-understanding.*

Richard Rohr is a globally recognised ecumenical teacher of contemplation and self-emptying, and founder of the Center for Action and Contemplation in Albuquerque, New Mexico, where I spent a couple of weeks doing a retreat internship in 2002. In *On the Threshold of Transformation*, he puts it this way:

> A larger desk, a private office, a bigger house, a newer car, a more expensive vacation—such are the essentially empty rewards men receive for surrendering their freedom and draining their masculinity energy in the service of business as usual …
>
> … When a man is prevented from making any real difference in the world, he creates illusions of difference to protect his self-esteem.[8]

Mythologist, master storyteller and author of *The Power of Myth* Joseph Campbell (1904–1987) explains the 'in search of the promised land' myth as the search for and finding of a 'new self'.[9] The same would apply to the myth of the 'resurrection'—becoming a renewed or 'new self'. He also points out that 'the promised land' is not out there somewhere, but inside of each one of us! This is the essence of self-transformation.

Campbell further explains that most us have misunderstood and underappreciated the power of myth. Rohr expands on this by saying that, when growing up, we were led to believe that myth is something that is untrue. The reality is that there is nothing in the world truer than myth. A myth is something that never was but always is. Myths are pregnant with meaning and connect us with our true essence. Myths are the foundations of moral values.

A new name for a new self

Self-transformation shapes a new self-concept and identity. To anchor and communicate this transformation or new identity, traditionally, once initiated, most leaders change their names. This has been common, for example, among monarchs. Kings and queens adopt 'regnal names', which are different to their original names, when they are crowned. This is a way to symbolise their new role and to acknowledge this new mandate in society.

Taking a new name, however, isn't exclusive to royalty. Many well-known leaders have done it. Nelson Mandela, for example, was known by many names. He was born in the South African village of Mvezo in Umtata, Cape Province, and given the forename Rolihlahla—a Xhosa name meaning 'troublemaker'. Mandela was formally initiated into manhood at 16, like other Xhosa boys, and given the name of Dalibhunga, which means 'creator or founder of the council', or 'convenor of the dialogue'. Later, he was also known as Tata, 'father', and Khulu, 'grandfather'.

Anjezë Gonxha Bojaxhiu (Mother Teresa) was born to Albanian parents in the town of Skopje, Macedonia (formerly Yugoslavia) and changed her name following her decision in 1910 to dedicate herself to God and become a nun. Many other well-known figures changed their names when they joined a religious order or cult, or had a faith conversation. For example, Cassius Clay became Muhammad Ali, and Cat Stevens became Yusuf Islam. These name changes symbolise the death of the 'false self' and birth of the 'true self'.

A key question, of course, is how can we access our true or authentic selves in the modern world?

Follow your bliss

Joseph Campbell said, 'When you follow your bliss...doors will open where you would not have thought there would be doors, and where there wouldn't be a door for anyone else.'[10] His book *The Hero with a Thousand Faces* has inspired many modern writers and artists. Perhaps the best known is filmmaker and entrepreneur George Lucas, the creator of the Star Wars and Indiana Jones franchises.

Following our bliss is like taking 'the hero's journey'. As identified by Campbell, this is the journey taken by 'the hero' as he or she strives to achieve something bigger than themselves, often doing so on behalf of a collective group or civilisation. This myth is evident in many tales in which a hero goes on an adventure, wins a victory in a crisis, and returns changed or transformed. He's now a 'hero' and knows that things will never be the same.

When we follow our bliss, we become creative, new doors open, and unseen possibilities show up. Some refer to this phenomenon as 'miracles happen' or 'magic happens'. In modern life, magic entails identifying your unique talents by deepening your self-awareness. This way you can unleash your ability to perform at your best and deliver extraordinary outcomes and business results by identifying and building on your talents. To get there, however, requires having a clear vision and a strong desire. Multiple award-winner Paulo Coelho reminds us in his book *The Alchemist*—a magical and inspiring fable about listening to your heart and following your dreams—that 'when a person really desires something, all the universe conspires to help that person to realise his dream'.[11]

Pseudo-initiations and phony rituals

The initiation experiences and rituals mentioned in this chapter should not be confused with the many phony, disingenuous, or pseudo-initiations and rituals in the world today. Examples of these include those conducted by gangs, in prisons, or even in some schools, colleges and universities, that involve depraved drinking rituals, bullying and other degrading ceremonies that dehumanise people. Such practices are unacceptable and should be condemned and reported.

The secret initiation rituals conducted at the United States Military Academy at West Point (USMA), commonly known as West Point, are a case in point. The 'silence' was one of the worst aspects of these rituals. 'Silence' is not to be confused with the 'code of silence', which is where someone may opt to keep vital or important information to themselves. The code of silence is often adhered to either because of a threat of force, or the threat of being branded as a traitor or an outcast. The so-called 'silence' ritual at the academy dated back to 1865, soon after the Civil War, when West Point accepted its first African American cadets. As part of this inhumane ritual, no white cadets spoke to black cadets during their entire four years at the academy. These were the times when racism and prejudice was widely accepted in the United States.

General Douglas MacArthur (1880–1964), who became Chief of Staff of the United States Army in the 1930s and played a prominent role in the Pacific in World War II, was a victim of the brutal practices at West Point. He was subjected to hazing — which involves harassment, abuse or humiliation to initiate individuals into a group. He was hospitalised as a result of the injuries he received. This, combined with the death of cadet Oscar Booz from tuberculosis after being hazed, prompted the formation of a congressional committee to examine hazing at West Point. MacArthur was called to testify and the practice was outlawed.

Things do change. In 1976 the academy accepted women for the first time, and supposedly none were forced to endure brutal rituals.

Honour and leadership

*The greatest way to live with honour in this world
is to be what we pretend to be.*
—Socrates

The word 'honour' is no longer in common use, except for in the military. Wikipedia further describes it as 'the perceived worthiness and respectability that affects the social standing and self-evaluation of an individual or corporate body such as a family, school, regiment, or nation.' At West Point, for example, cadets are required to adhere to an honour code as part of their leadership performance. This stipulates that 'a cadet will not lie, cheat, steal, or tolerate those who do'. The academy's cadet leadership development experience rests on three performance pillars: academic results, and physical and military skills.

Warrior cultures throughout history (for example, knights, Vikings, Celts, Spartans, Roman legions, and Samurai) based their codes of behaviour on what their culture perceived to be as the ideal warrior. The codes held warriors to higher ethical standards than ordinary citizens and this kept them from excessive, brutal responses to their enemies. Interestingly, the code was not imposed from the outside. In times of war, a warrior would voluntarily police themselves to keep strict adherence to such standards. Stepping over the line could have serious consequences (such as to be ostracised, shamed, or to be sent to death by their peers).

Professor Shannon French, the director of the Inamori International Center for Ethics and Excellence at Case Western Reserve University, in her book *The Code of the Warrior: Exploring the values of warrior cultures, past and present*, explains true meaning of being a warrior throughout history. First, 'Simply fighting doesn't make a warrior. There are rules a warrior follows.' Second, 'A warrior may be required to kill, but it should be for a purpose or cause greater than his own welfare, for an ideal.' Codes of conduct, French explains, should send an important message to anyone about standards in sports, school, politics or business.[12]

Leadership initiation in the twenty-first century

Initiations in the twenty-first century are very subtle. Carol Gilligan is a feminist, a psychologist known for her work on ethical relationships, a professor at New York University, a visiting professor at the University of Cambridge, and the author of the international bestseller *In a Different Voice*. She notes that boys learn their gender roles very early. In fact, they begin to suppress their emotions and sense of pity, and start adopting competition as their primary cultural value at the age of five.[13]

I suspect that you, like me, heard comments growing up like, 'Be a man! Don't cry like a girl! Don't be a sook! Shake it off! Come on, what are you, a little girl? You need to toughen up little man. Oh no. Don't tell me — are you kidding me? You aren't crying are you?' These comments have a deep and lasting effect. In fact, they have conditioned many males to understand what it means to be, or to act like, a man. The message was clear: boys are not allowed to express emotion. This explains why sacrificing relationships becomes the ritual of initiation into patriarchy for most men. It takes a psychological toll. So, it's not surprising that many men suffer from anxiety and depression. Girls go through a similar process. At the age of 12 or 13 they lose a degree of relational capacity, or 'voice', as a process of initiation. Clearly, this is central to relational leadership and the ability to relate to others.

Anxiety disorders, which interfere with a person's day-to-day experience and bring on depression, or problems with alcohol or drug abuse, for example, are the most common mental illnesses in the United States. The National Institute of Mental Health says they affect 40 million adults aged 18 and over — that is, 12.5 per cent of the population. In Australia, about 3 million people live with depression or anxiety, according to the Australian Bureau of Statistics. On average, one in five women and one in eight men will experience some level of depression. However, only 35 per cent seek treatment. Men, in particular, are reluctant to seek help because they think they're meant to be strong, tough, self-reliant, able to manage pain, and control any situation. Clearly, this is the way men live the initiation script alluded to previously.

In her research, Gilligan asked women, 'How would you describe yourself?', and women described their relationships in response.

In contrast, men defined themselves by separation, or the use of 'I' statements. She also discovered that men thought in more violent terms than women. Gilligan compared her results to the fairy tales in which men fantasise about slaying dragons and women dream about relationships.

Combined with these early life initiation scripts are the negative effects of consumption, materialism and the lack of values in society, according to Tim Kasser, a professor of Psychology at Knox College in Galesburg, Illinois, in his book *Psychology and Consumer Culture: The struggle for a good life in a materialistic world.*[14] The fact is that too many contemporary leaders have been initiated into the quest for power and money at all cost. It's no wonder there are widespread leadership failures, including abuses of power, unethical practices and corruption around the world.

Sadly, many aspiring leaders still hold to the illusion that leadership development is about acquiring knowledge through education (such as by completing an MBA or other degree at a business school, or attending a training program). And this is what they understand by the now-popular expression that 'leadership can be learned'. But this only addresses the KAS, or KSAs. It fails to address the critical leadership initiation. While these individuals may complete their MBAs with distinctions, deep-down they remain uninitiated boys. In fact, most end up claiming centre stage in the corporate world but, regrettably, they miss the grounding, calmness, compassion, clarity of judgement, and inner growth and development that initiation promises.

Having said this, I also acknowledge the advancements that have been made in recent times. One example is the emergence and use of meta-competencies such as emotional and social intelligence, pioneered by Daniel Goleman and his colleagues. This refers to the capacity to recognise our own feelings and those of others, motivate ourselves, and manage our own emotions and those of others to produce effective performance at work. More recently, Susan David, a renowned psychologist and expert on emotions, explains in her book *Emotional Agility: Get unstuck, embrace change, and thrive in work and life* how emotionally agile people can adapt, align their values and actions, and change themselves to bring out their best.[15]

Seeking and realising our true self, however, takes courage and commitment and some form of guidance (such as mentoring, coaching, counselling and sometimes therapy). We all need a mentor/coach, at least at some point, to help us to negotiate the multiple challenges and dilemmas we face. This is particularly relevant for those who prepare themselves for becoming leaders. Successful initiations bring a sense of calmness, serenity and creative energy.

Leadership development in the twenty-first century is more about understanding and looking for 'initiation', through failures and disappointments in particular, to take our leadership capacity to new heights. This is supported through individual coaching or mentoring that focuses on what can be learned from significant failures, as opposed to bragging about success and following the mantra of 'fake it till you make it'. The new mantra I proclaim for leaders of the twenty-first century is 'fake it and you'll never make it'.

* * *

Initiation and transformation begin when we admit our secretly kept failure or brokenness and share our true story without shame or embarrassment—not necessarily publicly, but with at least one other human being. This, of course, requires vulnerability and courage.

While it may sound paradoxical that by making ourselves vulnerable we can become psychologically (emotionally and mentally) stronger, it's actually true. This is how we reclaim our personal integrity and inner authority, which frees us from other people's standards and expectations of who we need to be in the world.

The signs to help us recognise this new state of being are easily identifiable. We experience alertness, clarity, centredness, calmness, serenity and peacefulness. We also feel appreciative and grateful, which in turn impacts on our capacity to have a positive attitude, even in the face of adversity. This results in being able to see new opportunities. In short, we become empowered and develop a new way of relating to ourselves and others. We start telling a different story (our vision). We develop a plan (our mission). We create new possibilities (design the future) and embark on purposeful action in service of that future. This is when the impossible becomes possible. From this place, we commit to act.

From a leadership perspective, we feel grounded, strong, motivated, visionary and purposeful. We command the respect, strength of character and authority that inspires others to act in the same way. This keeps us growing, and connected to others and life.

Sam Keen is a professor and philosopher who is, in his own words, 'overeducated at Harvard and Princeton'. His work explores questions of love, life, spirituality and being a man in contemporary society. In his book *Fire in the Belly: On being a man*, he explains that 'in every society the myths and rites that form our minds, emotions and actions remain largely invisible and unconscious, as water is to a fish'. To discover our living myths we need to examine those things we uncritically accept as the way things are.[16]

To initiate and develop our current and future leaders, and to take our individual and collective leadership to the next level, we need to demystify the myths that inform our lives. We need to question the stories we have been living, tell our true story, and authorise our own life and leadership.

The leadership development industry needs to drop the illusion that we are developing true leaders. Individual practitioners and consumers also should stop their uncritical acceptance of current practices and become far more reflective, discerning, critical and responsible for their work.

Conclusion

No-one is born to effective leadership, any more than great leaders are made. True leadership comes through initiation, which traditionally has involved rites or ceremonies that catapult the individual from one life stage into another. In contemporary society, these transformational rituals are missing, which has contributed to the current leadership crisis.

Leadership candidates need to go through an initiation to properly prepare them for the responsibilities of the roles they face. In the initiation process, individuals move beyond the cognitive (*knowing*) dimension of leadership to learn more about themselves and become more self-assured. They transcend the behavioural (*doing*)

(continued)

dimension to align deeply with their values and, being humbled by the experience, tap into the attitudinal (*being*) dimension of leadership. They emerge more complete into authentic leadership.

Insight questions

- What personal transformational experiences assisted you to make significant life transitions?

- What specific experiences promoted or facilitated you going beyond the acquisition of knowledge or information (*knowing*) and learning new behaviours (*doing*) that developed your self-awareness by tapping into the deeper emotional and attitudinal (*being*) dimension that initiated you to leadership?

- What painful and confusing process or experiences assisted you to emerge with a new consciousness, or perspective of life or leadership?

- In what times of your life you had to surrender to something greater than yourself? (This could include times when you've had to reach out to others for help.)

- In what ways are you a hero by giving your life to something bigger than yourself?

- What myths and rites have informed your story? How are you questioning them?

CHAPTER 7

Self-leadership and leader development

The first and best victory is to conquer self.
— **Plato**

This chapter is the first of three that explain self-leadership — the first component of the Leadership Results (LR) model, and the foundation of leader development. It introduces concepts related to self-leadership and explores each of their capacities and interconnections. It also outlines strategies to build self-leadership.

Bill George is a senior fellow at Harvard Business School, former Medtronic CEO, and author of four best-selling books. In his book *Discover Your True North*, he says that 'the hardest person you will ever have to lead is yourself'.[1]

Understanding self-leadership

Self-leadership is the capability to achieve the direction and motivation to positively influence your own performance. Effective self-leadership entails many capabilities and there are many interrelated terms to describe it:

intrinsic motivation	self-awareness
self-concept	self-confidence
self-control	self-direction
self-efficacy	self-empowerment
self-engagement	self-esteem
self-identity	self-influence
self-management	self-motivation
self-regulation	self-understanding
KAS (knowledge, skills, and abilities or competencies)	
psychological capital: hope, efficiency, self-confidence, resilience, optimism	

The self-leadership approach I present subscribes to the concepts of personal excellence and mastery, and deliberately avoids taking a strong competency-based stand on leader/leadership development. It subscribes to the emergent movement of researchers and practitioners who acknowledge that effective leader and leadership development extends beyond competencies. Representatives of this movement, to name a few, include:

- Craig Pearce, assistant professor of Management at Claremont Graduate University, and Jay Conger, Henry Kravis Research Chair in Leadership Studies at Claremont McKenna College — the authors of *Shared Leadership: Reframing the hows and whys of leading others*

- researchers such as Brigid Carroll, an associate professor of Management, and Lester Levy, an adjunct professor of Leadership, both at the University of Auckland Business School — the authors of the 2008 article 'Leadership as practice: Challenging the competency paradigm'

- authors such as Marian Ruderman, Cathleen Clerkin and Carol Connolly from the Center for Creative Leadership in Greensboro, North Carolina — the authors of the 2014 article 'Leadership development beyond competencies: Moving to a holistic approach'.

In his book *The Fifth Discipline: The art and practice of the learning organization*, Peter Senge, systems scientist and senior lecturer at the MIT Sloan School of Management, points out that 'personal mastery goes beyond competence and skills, though it is grounded in competence and skills'.[2]

Kevin Cashman is a senior partner, CEO & Executive Development at Korn Ferry. He explains that 'competencies get us to the doorway of leadership, but character gets us through the doorway of leadership. Managers tend to control resources to get results, but leaders exert character to build a sustainable future.' Cashman further reminds us:

> ... we need to challenge ourselves to go beyond our competencies. To use our competencies to really make a difference, but make sure that our competencies are balanced with character. Character is that sense of serving others ... to produce enduring results.[3]

Competency models emerged in the 1970s as a way of codifying the required behaviour for particular management positions. They drew on past successes by identifying relevant and effective behaviour, as opposed to examining the mindsets needed for the future (which is today).

Competency-based models are highly structured. Leadership in real life is less clear-cut. It's more dynamic, fluid and often chaotic. To develop contemporary leaders effectively, we need to understand the context in which leadership happens.

To develop contemporary leaders effectively, we need to understand the context in which leadership happens.

We also need to understand people by taking a more holistic and integrated approach to both leader and leadership development. This includes understanding the many (less visible) mental, emotional and psychological processes that drive and often determine behaviour, especially when they are not engaged consciously.

Matt's story

Matt was an intelligent, young up-and-coming executive who graduated from an MBA program with a strong desire to climb the corporate ladder. He came to see me shortly after he was promoted to team leader. At our first coaching session he admitted to feeling swamped by anxiety at the prospect of facing his new responsibilities, which included implementing a large change program. He saw this as a huge challenge.

As our conversation unfolded, mostly driven by questions, it emerged that his internal voice (self-talk) was telling him, 'I'm not good enough for this role', 'I'm out of place here', 'I don't belong here', 'This new role is way too big for me', 'As soon as they find out this is the case, they will get rid of me' and 'Perhaps I should leave before they find out'. Matt was also terrified about making a mistake, because making an error would 'prove' to everyone he was not good enough for the job. So, he kept procrastinating—the best way to avoid making a mistake, of course, is to do nothing at all! It was obvious that Matt lacked the confidence he needed and was terrified of failure.

Matt's self-doubt and lack of self-confidence led him to experience what's known as 'impostor syndrome', which is also referred to as 'fraud syndrome', a term first coined by psychologists Pauline Clance and Suzanne Imes.[4] This term relates to the inability to internalise or acknowledge accomplishments because of a fear of being found out and exposed as an impostor or a fraud. This condition particularly affects high-achieving individuals and tends to emerge following a new appointment, promotion or increase in responsibilities.

There are many Matts. The impostor syndrome affects about 70 per cent of the population worldwide.[5] But true imposters don't suffer from imposter syndrome. We know this because research evidence suggests imposter syndrome correlates with success; those who don't suffer imposter syndrome are far more likely to be the real frauds.

While initially it was thought that impostor syndrome related mostly to women, it is more likely that men won't admit to it to avoid 'stereotype backlash' (punishment in the form of harassment or ostracism for failing to conform to societal expectations).[6] The reality is that even the most successful individuals can struggle with self-doubt.

Many successful people I have worked with are perfectionists. Perfectionism describes a person's refusal to accept any standard short of perfection, and is highly correlated with impostor syndrome. For these people there is no room for mistakes; it's always an all-or-nothing approach, and everything must be done in a very specific way. At the same time, such individuals are extremely hard on themselves, set the highest possible standards, constantly look for errors, and spend a lot of time trying to perfect their work. When they don't achieve what they expect, they become depressed. Clearly this is a recipe for disaster: they keep setting unattainable goals. It doesn't matter how much they try to fill their inner emptiness, it's never enough.

For Matt, deep down, and despite his obvious intelligence and the objective evidence of his competence (for example, his academic achievement and his promotion), he was convinced he was a fraud and didn't deserve success. He dismissed his achievements as luck, good timing and an ability to somehow deceive others thinking he was more intelligent and competent than he believed himself to be. All of this is consistent with imposter symptom. Needless to say, the feelings of inadequacy — and an almost chronic self-doubt and insecurity — were a major source of anxiety for Matt. Especially after he was promoted.

Thinking patterns — locus of control

The term 'locus of control' (LOC) refers to the two contrasting thinking patterns that indicate the degree to which individuals believe they have control over events and outcomes in their lives, versus the degree to which they believe external forces or events beyond their control run their lives.[7]

People with an 'internal' locus of control (ILOC) believe, for the most part, that what happens to them is a direct result of their own actions—they are in the driver's seat. As a result, they tend to take responsibility for their failures and their successes. Contrastingly, individuals who believe their success or failure is outside their influence or control have an 'external' locus of control (ELOC). They tend to blame others when things go wrong, and attribute their achievements and successes to luck or destiny.

Clearly, Matt had an ELOC, as he was convinced his success was due to external circumstances. This wasn't a good sign: research shows that a person's LOC affects their job satisfaction, motivation and performance. ILOC corresponds to greater motivation, commitment, satisfaction, intention to stay in the organisation and favourable work outcomes, while the opposite applies to ELOC. Matt's ELOC led to him relinquishing his control, and the worst part was he wasn't even aware of it. This is why he felt unmotivated, doubtful, gloomy and depressed.

Matt's thinking style also wasn't helping him.

Thinking styles—optimism vs pessimism

The way you mentally explain what happens to you is determined by your thinking or explanatory style. This is a psychological attribute that indicates how we explain to ourselves what we experience in life and decide whether events are either positive or negative. There are two contrasting explanatory styles: optimistic thinking and pessimistic thinking.

The benefits of being optimistic (the belief that we are responsible for our own happiness)—seeing 'the glass half full'—are highly rewarding. Optimists are higher achievers and have better general health. In contrast, pessimists—individuals with the tendency to see 'the glass half empty'—are far more likely to give up in the face of adversity and to suffer from depression.

Matt believed his situation was there to stay. This thinking affected all the other areas of his life. It was also personalised—he believed that the negative things were his fault. These dimensions, referred to as 'the three Ps', distinguish pessimistic thinking styles from optimistic ones.

Martin Seligman, the author of *Learned Optimism*, argues that we each have our own style. He also identifies the three Ps[8]:

1. *Permanence.* Optimists believe bad things are more temporary than permanent. Not only do they see negative events as having temporary causes, they also believe good things happen for reasons that are permanent or durable. As a result, they bounce back quickly from failures or disappointments. Pessimists assume that when things go wrong they will stay wrong for a long time because the causes of such events are permanent, lasting and enduring. They also believe that any good things are only momentary or temporary — so they take much longer to recover from setbacks, or they may never recover.

2. *Pervasiveness.* Optimists compartmentalise or isolate their weaknesses or failures. Pessimists generalise them by assuming that a failure in one area means failure in all — or most — areas of their lives. This leads them to catastrophise. Optimists also allow good events to affect every area of their lives, not just the one in which the event occurred. Pessimists are unable to do this.

3. *Personalisation.* Optimists attribute bad events to causes beyond themselves. Pessimists blame themselves for bad events — they internalise their problems. Optimists internalise positive events and are usually more confident, while pessimists externalise positive events and have nothing to celebrate or feel proud of.

Matt's ELOC thinking pattern and pessimism didn't help him at all. In fact, 'impostor syndrome', if untreated, plays out by causing a very insidious state of affairs — self-sabotage!

Self-sabotage

Self-sabotage is by nature self-defeating. It's the type of behaviour that creates problems and interferes with our long-standing goals. Some of the most common forms include procrastination; comfort (or emotional) eating, especially when trying to lose weight; self-medicating using alcohol or drugs; and, in extreme cases, self-harm.

Self-sabotage works like the programming in your computer; it unconsciously turns our greatest fears into reality using what is called a 'self-fulfilling prophecy'. Matt already had some self-defeating behaviour that was shaping his self-fulfilling prophecy.

Self-fulfilling prophecies

A self-fulfilling prophecy is thinking something will happen, and therefore making it happen. It occurs when a person unknowingly or unintentionally causes a prediction (for example, being found out about something) to come true.[9] This happens because individuals *expect* such predictions to come true. There is no magic about it — this is how it works. As strange and paradoxical as it may sound, self-fulfilling prophecies are our attempts to protect ourselves from failure, pain, grief, disappointment, rejection or any other upsetting outcome.

Matt feared being found deficient or incompetent in his new role, so was preoccupied with this thought and the expectation that he would be caught. He began sabotaging himself by avoiding situations where he could be exposed as incompetent, and he looked for evidence or clues to support and validate his fears.

The first behaviour — avoiding situations — led Matt to procrastinate by avoid decisions, missing deadlines and arriving late to meetings. Obviously, those around him started to notice. The second behaviour led Matt to look for clues that reinforced his own self-defeating belief. He said to me, for example, that he had noticed others were talking about him and avoiding him. Matt's reasoning, of course, was that his peers realised he wasn't up to the task. This was generating a vicious cycle that confirmed all his doubts and fears. Matt was on the track to self-sabotage.

In Matt's case, the three-step process to his self-fulfilling prophecy was:

1. He held a false belief about himself.

2. He treated himself and his situation (work) in a manner that was consistent with his false belief.

3. He confirmed his original false belief ('I'm not good enough for this job') in response to the treatment he received from his co-workers.

Like a chain reaction, Matt was constructing his own reality and further convincing himself about his negative beliefs. This had to stop before he found himself out of a job.

Matt's case, nine months later

I worked with Matt using a combination of strategies, including identifying his core negative assumptions and destructive voices (self-talk), thinking patterns and style, and accepting or challenging them; reframing his thinking, owning his past accomplishments and successes; identifying his talents and strengths, and learning how to apply them; further building his self-esteem; learning to focus more on the present by using mindfulness; journaling; and learning to take things one day at a time.

Matt was gradually able to accept his previous achievements and apply his strengths in specific areas, as well as receive compliments and positive feedback without dismissing them as not genuine. He also learned to stop comparing himself with others and to not over-identify with his work. After six months, his anxiety had decreased dramatically and his self-esteem and confidence had increased.

Above all, Matt learned to genuinely try to help others by contributing through his work, as opposed to trying to prove himself. Today, Matt enjoys work and life more than ever before.

* * *

Striving for success to fulfil or compensate for our own deficiencies is a recipe for disaster. It's not only a selfish goal, because you are striving to be a success for yourself only: it's also unattainable. It doesn't matter what or how much you try to fill this inner emptiness, it's never enough — this is the stereotype of perfectionism. Regrettably, in such circumstances the happiness, contentment and satisfaction that go with success never come.

The key is trying to be of value by helping others. Assisting others to become successful is a sign of true success and is the way to recognise true leaders. These people do not need to try to be successful, because they are already successful and fulfilled. They do not feel the need to prove themselves to, or need approval from, the world. To them success is about contributing and being of value to others. You can easily recognise such individuals by their calm demeanour, selflessness, humbleness and willingness to help.

The best way to deal with the 'impostor syndrome' is by developing humility and courage, and building the self-esteem required to tolerate happiness and success without engaging in self-sabotage.

Leader development strategies

Leader development relates to expanding an individual's capacity to exercise effective leadership.[10] As I highlighted previously, many organisations (and, sadly, practitioners) don't differentiate between leader development and leadership development. To be clear, leader development is about human capital, while leadership development is about social capital.[11] Leader self-development enables individuals to adapt to the continually changing internal organisational environment and to the external context. This individual developmental process serves as the stepping stone or foundation for the organisation's leadership development strategy.

In this section, I outline a range of strategies and practices to strengthen, build and sustain your self-leadership and take it to the next level. In essence, it means developing the self-awareness and understanding of your strengths and weaknesses and your belief in yourself to take control of your life, set goals and make positive choices. This builds your self-confidence and self-esteem.

1. Build and maintain high self-esteem

Self-esteem is our sense of self-worth and confidence in our ability to cope with everyday life. It includes our judgement, attitude or beliefs about ourselves. The term 'self-esteem' comes from a Greek word meaning 'reverence or respect for self'. Our level of self-esteem, then, is determined by the degree to which we accept ourselves for who we are at any point in our life time. This is why self-esteem is associated, and often used interchangeably, with terms such as self-respect, self-regard, pride in one's abilities, self-confidence and confidence, self-assurance and assurance, faith in oneself, pride, dignity and morale.

The relationship between self-esteem and self-leadership becomes obvious from research. Healthy or high self-esteem is correlated with rationality, intuitiveness, creativity, flexibility, inference, benevolence, willingness to admit and correct mistakes, cooperativeness and the ability to manage change. Conversely, low self-esteem is correlated with irrationality denial or blindness of reality, fear, rigidity, defensiveness, hostility, over complaining, too much conformity, too much rebelliousness, and antisocial behaviour.

The higher our self-esteem, the more honest and open we are—we believe in our thinking and don't fear clarity and truth. The lower our self-esteem, the more evasive and muddy we are. We are uncertain about our thinking and fear being wrong. Clearly, then, high self-esteem leads to confidence and self-assurance. People with high self-esteem can make commitments, keep their promises and deliver results. Lower self-esteem, on the other hand, leads to doubt and

The lower our self-esteem, the more evasive and muddy we are.

insecurity, and an inability to make commitments, keep promises or deliver results. Individuals with high self-esteem challenge themselves by setting and achieving demanding goals. In contrast, people with low self-esteem prefer to stay with what's familiar, remain in their comfort zones and avoid risks.

Nathaniel Branden (1930–2014), a psychotherapist and writer known for his work on the psychology of self-esteem, and author of the classic book *The Six Pillars of Self-esteem*, points out that achievements per se are not the source of our self-esteem, but rather our 'internally generated practices that make it possible for us to achieve.' 'Resourcefulness', as he calls it, 'is not an achievement in the world (although it may result in that); it is an action in consciousness—and it is here that self-esteem is generated.' Branden offers the following the six practices to build self-esteem: living consciously; self-acceptance; self-responsibility; self-assertiveness; purposefulness; and integrity.[12]

2. Identify and apply your strengths

Has anybody ever said anything like this to you?

- You need to get better at [this].

- Yes, you have done a good job, BUT you still need to improve on [that].

- The problem with you is that you always ... [a criticism].

How did you feel? Yes, I know!

I once had a boss who loved giving me feedback. When I presented an initial or substantial draft of a project or report, he would glance at it for a few seconds and then pull out his red pen and proceed to explain everything he thought was wrong with it. He would then get a blank sheet of paper and scribble his 'mastermind' plan for the project — which was often his personalised version of my work.

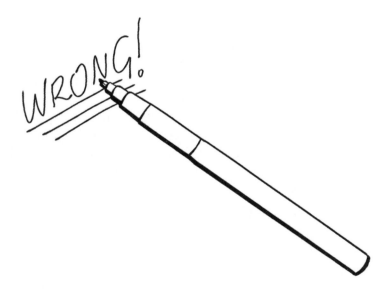

As you can imagine, I used to feel so 'empowered' (I hope the sarcasm is clear) after those sessions that the only thing I wanted to do was to leave my job — which I did. Clearly, he should have been a last-century school teacher.

Does this situation sound familiar? Have you ever worked with someone like this? I sincerely hope not, especially if this is your current boss!

But, this did not only happen at work. I don't particularly recall my parents telling me what my natural gifts or talents were when I was young—perhaps they did, but I honestly don't remember. At school, my teachers were very good at letting me know what I had to change or improve on. In fact, they were absolute masters at it! At university, I'm afraid things weren't that much different.

Years later, I came to realise that my parents, teachers and lecturers probably had the same experiences I had. My parents did to me what had been done to them by their parents, to the parents of their parents, and to the parents of their parents' parents. They didn't know any better, which is why I don't blame any of them—my parents, teachers or educators.

Today, however, we know better and can break this pervasive, generational cycle. This is how.

Donald Clifton (1924–2003), an American psychologist commended by the American Psychological Association as 'the father of strengths-based psychology and the grandfather of positive psychology', asked this very powerful question: 'What would happen if we actually studied what is right with people?'

Clifton was committed to helping people identify and utilise 'their best'. He created the eponymous Clifton StrengthsFinder,© an assessment survey designed to uncover your strengths that was introduced by Gallup in 2001. To date it has been taken by more than 15 million people. In 2008 the book *StrengthsFinder* by Tom Rath, which captured Clifton's work, became a *New York Times* bestseller.

Positive psychology uses evidence-based interventions such as scientific research, understanding, and effective interventions (unlike positive thinking, pop-psychology or happyology) to help people achieve satisfaction and wellbeing. By scientifically studying strengths, positive psychology focuses on personal growth rather than on pathology, enabling individuals and communities to thrive. It studies the processes and conditions that contribute to optimal performance and helps individuals, groups and organisations flourish.[13]

Strengths blindness

Peter Drucker (1909–2005) was a business visionary and management consultant who has been described as 'the founder of modern management' and a forerunner of the 'strengths movement'. He advocated focusing more on developing our strengths than on fixing our weaknesses, and for people to take advantage of their fundamental strengths in order to achieve the best results.

> Most people know what they are good at. They are usually wrong. More often, people know what they are not good at—and even then more people are wrong than right. And yet … One cannot build performance on weaknesses, let alone on something one cannot do at all.[14]

I have posed this question to many people around the world, and very few can clearly tell me without hesitation what their strengths are. This is quite normal. It is estimated that most people (up to two-thirds) do not have a meaningful awareness of their strengths. Everyone has some degree of strengths blindness. People who know and apply their strengths have greater success in life, so I strongly recommend you identify yours using the Clifton StrengthsFinder. Once you have completed the assessment and downloaded your report, find a Gallup-certified strengths coach to help you make sense of your results and build on your strengths in all areas of your life. (There are many Gallup qualified coaches around the world.)

Why shifting mindsets is so challenging

The business case for strengths-based leadership and wider organisational practices is a simple, clear and compelling one, yet it seems to be falling on deaf ears. Many organisations keep using old ways. Why? Well, it's like the question of whether the glass is half full or half empty: it's a matter of perspective.

Which one are you?

We have all been conditioned to focus on what's missing, what's wrong, what doesn't work or what we don't have as opposed to identifying what our strengths are, how to apply and benefit from them, and how to exploit them for ourselves and the common good.

In some contexts and professions, a focus on the glass as half-empty is relevant and even desirable. Consider, for example, the case of accountants, engineers and other technical and risk-averse professions where practitioners have been trained to find and fix errors. They are paid to prevent and mitigate risk—perfectly understandable. In the case of leadership, however, this is far from desirable. Leadership is not a 'technical profession'—it's not a profession at all. Neither is it about being 'well-rounded'.

The myth of the 'well-rounded' leader

Tom Rath, co-author of *Strengths Based Leadership: Great leaders, teams, and why people follow*, says, 'Being well-rounded is the antithesis of great leadership.'[15] When you are 'well-rounded', it simply means you are a jack-of-all-trades (and master of none)—someone who can do a lot of different things without being competent at any of them.

Yes, it means you're a generalist, but it also means you're not known for anything in particular. It means you don't have a personal brand, trademark, uniqueness or differentiation, and consequently no competitive advantage in a highly competitive market.

How useful is being a jack-of-all-trades? Let me tell you, it is a set-up for failure! What would you prefer—to be known as a well-rounded executive, or as exceptionally brilliant at a few things?

Clifton said:

> …a leader needs to know his strengths as a carpenter knows his tools, or as a physician knows the instruments at her disposal. What great leaders have in common is that each truly knows his or her strengths—and can call on the right strength at the right time.[16]

The same applies to great athletes. Footballers such as Lionel Messi, Cristiano Ronaldo and Luis Suarez are not good at goalkeeping or defending—they are brilliant at scoring goals. That's why they are the top strikers in the world. Being aware of your strengths also has important implications if you are a team leader: leaders who know the value of their unique strengths are, in turn, appreciative and willing to develop the unique strengths of others.

A caveat about weakness

A weakness is any personal attribute that gets in the way of your success. From a strengths-based perspective, this includes the misapplication of a strength, knowledge or skill that causes problems for you or others. Let me share a personal example.

One of my top strengths is that of being an 'activator'. We — activators — are impatient for action. We know we are judged by what we get done, not by what we think. As an activator, I can make things happen by turning ideas into action. I'm a self-starter and I'm not afraid to take risks. Nothing slows me down. I'm sure you get the picture.

Balconies and basements

When I operate with this strength from my 'balcony', I'm fired up and bold, and I spark energy in others. However, when I operate with this strength from my 'basement', I leave others behind and they feel lost. I come across as not thinking things through and, at its worst — like when I was a much younger man — as a loose cannon, or pushy.

Even your greatest strength can become your worst weakness if you deploy it without taking the context into consideration — at the wrong time and in the wrong place.

Eccentricity and unconventional behaviour

Great leaders honour, cherish, cultivate, practise and develop their unique talents and strengths. Such strengths are often eccentricities (which could be easily mistaken for weaknesses). Interestingly, research shows that leaders can promote creativity and innovation by leading through unconventional behaviour.[17] Jaussi and Dionne note that when leaders demonstrate unconventional or counterintuitive behaviour (such as 'standing on furniture', 'hanging ideas on clotheslines or sticking' out their tongues), they are creating an expectation about creative behaviour. Leaders who take risks by acting outside the norms make statements to team members that risk-taking is acceptable and encouraged.

Steve Jobs, Richard Branson and Warren Buffet are good examples. Their eccentric leadership, and their passion for their work and innovation, has left a profound legacy. They had to break boundaries, challenge the rules and status quo and, most importantly, they had to leverage their unique strengths. This is consistent with role-modelling theory, whereby a person learns by emulating a demonstrated behaviour. Somehow, it is like leaders giving permission to others to be creative, with their unconventional behaviour offering a guide to what 'outside the box' looks like in the organisation.

Richard Branson once appeared in public dressed as a flight attendant in the bright-red Virgin Airlines uniform, wearing matching lipstick, a wig and makeup. His leadership style encourages employees to have fun at work and make their own decisions, and it takes failure as proof that people are stretching themselves.

Another example is Don Winkler, former CEO of Ford Motor Credit (FMC), who demonstrated unconventional behaviour while increasing group cohesion and stimulating creative thinking. When car sales were poor at the beginning of 2000, Winkler gathered a task force together at an off-site location. When the group arrived, they discovered a 2002 reunion party, complete with horns and banners, to celebrate the success of the task force — a celebration of the future. The meeting began with Winkler praising the achievements of the task force's 2000 meeting, and this future thinking went on to inspire employees to innovate in new ways, leading FMC to be startlingly successful for the first half of that year.

It is undeniable that unconventional leader behaviour can lead to greater group cohesion. Further, when team members witness unconventional behaviour from their leader it becomes a powerful shared experience and a common referential and mental model. In turn, it helps bond team members and increase the team's cohesion.

What unconventional behaviour have you demonstrated lately to promote your team's creative thinking and innovation?

How to set your team on fire

Team diversity, as opposed to sameness, is the key to building high-performing and innovative teams. To achieve this, leaders need to know their team members' unique strengths intimately, and the team members need to know each other's strengths. This allows them to use their complementary strengths to build a robust and high-performing team. Not surprisingly, this triggers the following unstoppable ripple effect: individual engagement → team engagement → low staff turnover → high collaboration → high performance → outstanding results (such as excellence in customer service, increased sales and profits) → enhanced company brand and reputation. (Part III of this book deals with building and working with your teams and stakeholders.)

Applying your strengths not only improves team function from a structural or architectural perspective; it also greatly enriches your life by allowing you to be in 'flow', or 'in the zone'.

3. Experience flow as often as possible

Mihaly Csikszentmihalyi, Distinguished Professor of Psychology and Management at Claremont Graduate University, former head of the University of Chicago's psychology department, and a pioneer of the positive psychology movement, coined the term 'flow' in his book *Flow: The psychology of optimal experience.*

When I work on something (such as facilitating a group, or writing an interesting piece on leadership), I really enjoy applying my signature strengths — the character strengths most essential to who I am. Time flies. I experience such a flow of inspiration, energy and creativity, I could go forever (hours and hours). I get so absorbed and engrossed in what I'm doing I can even forget to eat. I'm in flow, or in the zone. In this mental state, I am immersed in a feeling of energised focus, full involvement and enjoyment. If you have experienced this, you'll know exactly what I'm talking about.

If you have not experienced flow yet, or you wish to experience it more often and more intensely, I urge you to spend more time working on activities in which you must use your signature strengths. In addition to finding the strengths that derive from using your natural talents, you can identify your signature strengths by taking the free VIA Survey (www.viacharacter.org/www/Character-Strengths-Survey). This is a simple self-assessment that helps you identify your virtues—the foundations of your core value system. Practising those builds character.

4. Build character

Character is like a tree and reputation is like its shadow. The shadow is what we think of it; the tree is the real thing.
—Abraham Lincoln

Character is the unique combination of mental characteristics and behaviour that distinguishes individuals. It demonstrates your moral potency and its three components: moral ownership, moral courage and moral efficacy.

James Sarros is a professor in the Department of Management at Monash University, and an expert in leadership, corporate culture, values and character. In his book *The Character of Leadership: What works for Australian leaders—making it work for you*, he explains that 'character is revealed in the moral and ethical choices we make. To act with character means to show virtue, and virtues are central to character.'[18]

In case you're wondering, personality and character are also independent from each other. It is possible, for example, for someone to be shy, introverted, nervous and personable, and not interact with a lot of people. However, their character may be positive and they may do positive things for many people. Other individuals may have very outgoing and friendly personalities but may have a character that makes them disappoint, cheat or deceive others.

Character defines your integrity—a firm adherence to a code of moral principles or values. Integrity refers to a set of characteristics through which you build trustworthiness and generate trust. Leaders with integrity live their principles and motivate their teams through ethical behaviour. Integrity creates conditions in which your teams/ organisations will resist corruption and be more trusted and efficient. Integrity, as opposed to personality, is a personal choice to hold ourselves to consistent moral and ethical standards that are based on beliefs about the right thing to do.

Henry David Thoreau (1817–1862), an American essayist, poet, philosopher and historian, said, 'You cannot dream yourself into a character; you must hammer and forge yourself one.' Winston Churchill (1874–1965), British prime minister from 1940 to 1945 and again from 1951 to 1955, reminded us, 'You can measure a man's character by the choices he makes under pressure.'

Character is what differentiates true leaders from pseudo-leaders, and it is character, as opposed to competencies, that is the foundation for success. Fred Kiel is Executive Director at the KRW Research Institute. In his 2015 Harvard Business Review Press article 'Return on character: The real reason leaders and their companies win', he identified two types of CEOs: 'self-focused CEOs' (those with low character ratings) and 'virtuoso CEOs' (those with top character scores). Companies led by virtuoso CEOs had an 9.35 per cent average return on assets (ROA) over a two-year period. This was almost five times that of companies led by self-focused CEOs – ROA averaged was only 1.93 per cent.[19] James Toner, professor of international relations and military ethics at the Air War College, Maxwell AFB, Alabama, wrote in the article 'Mistakes in teaching ethics' that 'competence without character is perversion and our greatest threat'.[20]

Examples that illustrate this threat of character and ethics violations are Kenneth Lay at Enron, Bernard Ebbers at WorldCom, Conrad Black at Hollinger International, and Lee Farkas at Taylor, Bean & Whitaker. There are many others.

> *Character is what differentiates true leaders from pseudo-leaders...*

Research results published in a *Harvard Business Review* article titled 'The most important leadership competencies, according to leaders around the world' show that 'having high ethical and moral standards' was rated the highest of 74 attributes.

The second was 'communicating clear expectations'.[21] The interesting thing about this study is that the question leaders were asked was 'What makes an effective leader?' Despite the title of the article, this open question didn't make any mention of competencies or character—but the results speak for themselves.

Relational leadership, which underpins the LR model, entails creating safe and trusting relationships not only by having high ethical standards, but also by fulfilling expectations, and acting with fairness—which directly relates to organisational justice. A meta-analysis of 413 research studies investigating employees' perceptions of justice in managerial behaviour found a positive correlation between organisational justice and higher employee performance.[22]

The third construct that constitutes the leader credibility (head) component of the LR model is trust (a construct that measures competence as well as elements of character—in this case, for example, 'communicates openly, honestly and respectfully'; 'shares important information openly and transparently'; 'does/delivers what they promise'). This, in turn, elicits positive emotions (heart) and engagement. Next, this chain triggers creativity, innovation and discretionary effort (hands), which culminates in collective performance and extraordinary results.

Reputation

Your character, as leader, also determines your reputation.

Wayne Dyer (1940–2015), a philosopher, self-help author and motivational speaker whose first book, *Your Erroneous Zones,* is one of the all-time bestsellers, said, 'Your reputation is in the hands of others. That's what the reputation is. You can't control that. The only thing you can control is your character.'[23]

Reputation is the estimation in which you are held by others, so can be considered a component of your identity as defined by other people. Reputation, then, is the basis of good leadership. It is among one of the most treasured and powerful assets a leader can have and is usually built over a long time, one deed at a time.

Leaders without character and integrity erode their personal reputations. A good example is what happened to Richard Nixon as a result of the Watergate scandal. As Warren Buffett, business magnate and philanthropist, said, 'It takes 20 years to build a reputation and five minutes to ruin it. If you think about that, you'll do things differently.'

5. Always act ethically and with integrity

> *Be as you wish to be seen.*
> — Socrates

Ethical behaviour is one of the least appreciated sources of self-empowerment, and it is also an effective way to empower and engage others.

Nathaniel Branden talks about the challenge of keeping our integrity in a corrupt world. He says, 'The challenge for people today, and it is not an easy one, is to maintain high personal standards while feeling that one is living in a moral sewer.'

Ethical leadership and moral potency

Credibility and reputational capital are bound to provide a competitive advantage in the context of leadership crisis and confidence of leadership. Your ethics should never be left to chance. Ethical leadership requires more than values, as it relates to the moral dimension of leadership. While values such as respect, justice and integrity can be considered the raw material of ethical leadership, leaders have to create effective action in complex and ambiguous situations. This requires ethical reasoning. Without it, values can be used to rationalise unethical behaviour. But reasoning alone is not enough. Many leaders know the right ethical decisions and actions, yet still fail to take them. Moral potency is also needed.

Sean Hannah, executive director of the Center for Leadership and Character at Wake Forest University School of Business, and Bruce Avolio, executive director at the University of Washington Center for Leadership and Strategic Thinking, define moral potency as:

... a psychological state marked by an experienced sense of ownership over the moral aspects of one's environment, reinforced by efficacy beliefs in the capabilities to act to achieve moral purpose in that

145

domain, and the courage to perform in the face of adversity and persevere through challenges.[24]

Ethics is a common theme in all forms of positive leadership, including Servant Leadership, Authentic Leadership and Ethical Leadership. Servant Leadership, for example, emphasises service to others and is linked to ethics, virtues and morality. The core characteristic relates to 'going beyond one's self-interest'. Authentic Leadership advocates setting high moral and ethical standards.

Myths surround ethics and ethical leadership

Ethics is one of the most misunderstood topics in management and business in general. Often, the word 'ethics' evokes seriousness, boredom and/or a perception of incompatibility with organisational effectiveness and achieving of business goals. But nothing is further from the truth. Ethics—derived from the Greek word *ethos* (custom or habit), relates to defining the 'right conduct' and pursuing a good life worth living. That is, a happy and satisfying life. True wellbeing, joy and contentment (happiness) derive from applying virtues—traits or qualities deemed to be morally good (such as gratitude, courage, humility, kindness and justice). Clearly, this understanding of happiness differs significantly from popular views that seek happiness through power, status or material wealth. These goals are driven by the need to fill an existential vacuum, and bring only a temporary sense of satisfaction.

> *Applied ethics relates to the treatment of moral problems, practices and policies in either our personal or professional life.*

Ethical behaviour refers to actions judged by, and consistent with, one's personal principles and the commonly held values of the group, organisation or society. It requires that we take responsibility for the consequences of our ethical or unethical behaviours. Applied ethics relates to the treatment of moral problems, practices and policies in either our personal or professional life. Ethical codes (such as corporate or professional codes of practice) help us understand the difference between right and wrong, and to apply that understanding to the decisions we make.

6. Build your psychological capital

Positive psychological capital (PsyCap) relates to your state of development, and it influences your satisfaction levels and your performance. It comprises your internal resources for dealing with challenges at work.

Fred Luthans, Distinguished Professor of Management at the University of Nebraska, who coined the PsyCap term and pioneers its research, maintains that PsyCap predicts performance and satisfaction better than any individual strengths.

He defines PsyCap as the powerful synergistic effect (that which is greater than the sum its individual effects) of four components:

1. *hope*—your desire, ambition or expectations to persevere and, when necessary, to change direction to reach goals

2. *confidence (self-efficacy or efficacy)*—your belief or confidence in your ability to take on and succeed at challenging tasks

3. *resilience*—your ability to cope positively and bounce back from adversity to succeed

4. *optimism*—your ability to make positive attributions about success now and in the future.[25]

The acronym HERO (hope, efficacy, resilience and optimism) is sometimes used. These dimensions also meet the criteria for positive organisational behaviour (POB), which Luthans defines as 'the study and application of positively oriented human resource strengths and psychological capacities that can be measured, developed, and effectively managed for performance improvement in today's workplace'.[26]

A good example of how PsyCap relates to self-leadership is the story of Nelson Mandela. His 27 years of imprisonment didn't compromise his resolution to unite his country. Neither did the apartheid government. He said, 'When I walked out of prison, that was my mission, to liberate the oppressed and the oppressor both.'

Rene Van Wyk, an associate professor in the Department of Industrial Psychology and People Management at the University of Johannesburg, investigated Nelson Mandela's leadership style by conducting a documentary analysis using the lens of PsyCap. Her main findings portray Mandela's pursuit of a non-racial South Africa and his aim to foster political and economic rights for all through peaceful negotiation as the embodiment of PsyCap characteristics. Van Wyk says Mandela viewed himself as an ordinary leader exposed to extraordinary circumstances, but that he used extraordinary PsyCap in conquering the most challenging political obstacles. Robben Island, where he spent 18 years imprisoned, later became a symbol of the victory of the human spirit over adversity.

Wayne Cascio, Distinguished University Professor at the University of Colorado and Chair in Global Leadership at the University of Colorado Denver, and Luthans, also reference Mandela's PsyCap (hope, efficacy, resilience and optimism) to explain how he survived the abuse and appalling conditions at Robben Island. Cascio and Luthans say Mandela's collective forgiveness was critical in changing the attitude of the guards. The authors say the change from an oppressive culture, to one with a climate of learning, to the eventual end of apartheid and to freedom, was one of the greatest societal transformations in modern history.[27]

In a business context, a study that investigated the financial impact and return on investment of developing employees' PsyCap estimated that small increases in PsyCap could lead to large increases in revenue.[28] This is because PsyCap predicts multiple organisational outcomes at the individual level, including satisfaction, commitment and employees' intentions to leave or to stay.

Conclusion

Self-leadership is the capacity to achieve direction and motivation and positively influence your own performance. Self-leadership is achieved through consciously and purposefully building and maintaining high self-esteem, identifying and applying your strengths, experiencing 'flow' regularly, building character, acting ethically and with integrity, and building your psychological capital.

The next chapter explores virtues, emotions, and signature strengths as components of self-leadership.

Insight questions

- How would you rate your current level of self-esteem? If your self-esteem diminished, how would you recognise it? And what would you do?

- What are you really good at? What makes you unique?

- What are your top five strengths? How well can you articulate them? And how present are they in your everyday life?

- Are your team members aware of their strengths?

- Do you have any eccentricities? If so, how do you use them to your advantage?

- When do you experience flow? What can you do to experience more of it?

- What has, or how have you, built your character? How can you keep building it?

- How would those who know you well describe your reputation?

- How often do you discuss issues related to integrity and/or ethics with your people?

- How would you rate your PsyCap (hope, efficacy, resilience and optimism)? How would those who know you well rate it?

CHAPTER 8

Virtues, emotions and signature strengths

Jean-Pierre

Jean-Pierre was the son of a billionaire. As he approached his twenty-first birthday, he told his father that he would really like a small penthouse in Paris that he had admired for many months. He wanted to move out of the family home and start living an independent life.

On his birthday, his father called him into his office and expressed how much he loved him before giving his son a beautifully wrapped package. With a mix of curiosity, anticipation and excitement, Jean-Pierre tore away the packaging, but to his surprise, found only a leather-bound holy book. In bitter disappointment, he shouted at his father, 'With all your wealth, all you can give me for

(continued)

151

my twenty-first birthday is a holy book?'. Fuming, he slammed the book on the desk and angrily left the house, never to return again.

Many years later, Jean-Pierre had become a prominent businessman with a beautiful family. Unexpectedly, one day he received a call from an inheritance lawyer who told him his father had passed away and Jean-Pierre had to take care of his father's estate immediately.

When he arrived at his father's house, he was filled with sorrow and sadness and as he searched through his father's documents, he came across the holy book. It was exactly where he had left it years before. Tears rolled down his face as he opened the book, only to realise that it contained a hidden compartment containing a small envelope. Jean-Pierre took the envelope from the book and on opening it, found a set of keys on a tag with the address of the penthouse he had wanted so much. The tag carried the date of his birthday and the words: 'Paid in full and ready to move in tomorrow.' The following note was also in the envelope:

> Dear Jean-Pierre,
> You are my beloved, and I'm very proud of you.
> On your 21st birthday, I want to give you a very special gift –
> the penthouse you always wanted.
> With all my love, your father Joseph

This story reminds me of the many times I have judged books (situations and people) by their covers—and the many opportunities I have missed as a result. When we judge others, we not only push them away from us and engender a bad image and reputation, we also miss great opportunities—some of which we'll never even know about.

I now make a great effort not to judge others, and I regularly look for things I'm grateful for—and I always find them. You should try it.

Jean-Pierre's story also helped me become aware of other valuable things. For example, the fact that the key to the car he so badly wanted was always within his reach makes me wonder how many great opportunities we cannot see, even when they are possibly within our reach.

***

This chapter builds on the themes in the previous chapter and explores how virtues, emotions and signature strengths can boost self-leadership.

Emotions are experiences that, while short-lived, produce changes in our actions, thoughts and physiological responses. Positive emotions lack negativity, pain or discomfort. Barbara Fredrickson, Kenan Distinguished Professor of Psychology at the University of North Carolina at Chapel Hill and principal investigator at the Positive Emotions and Psychophysiology Lab at the same university, identifies the following ten general positive emotions: joy, gratitude, serenity, interest, hope, pride, amusement, inspiration, awe and love. Fredrickson explains her 'broaden-and-build theory of positive emotion' like this: Positive emotions fuel psychological resilience, trigger wellbeing, and broaden what's called our 'momentary thought–action repertoire'. That is, specific emotions prompt thoughts and actions. For example, '… joy sparks the urge to play … and love sparks a recurring cycle of each of these urges within safe, close relationships.' Conversely, negative emotions narrow our 'momentary thought–action repertoire'. At the extreme, they call for a fight or flight response to protect ourselves.[1]

Sonja Lyubomirsky, professor of Psychology at the University of California, Riverside, and author of the bestseller *The How of Happiness: A scientific approach to getting the life you want,* has written about strategies to increase happiness. She explains how positive emotions broaden our attention and mental activity and boost our physical, intellectual and social inner resources, which are all the requirements for general wellbeing and high performance.[2]

Have you ever been judged or stereotyped? We all have, of course. It's an awful feeling. Have you ever met someone who is ungrateful? Worse, have you ever worked with someone who is ungrateful? Even worse, have you ever had an ungrateful boss? Worst of all, have you ever felt ungrateful? It's a bad feeling, isn't it?

We all have been judged, stereotyped and unappreciated, and we know how bad it feels. And we all have done so to others — have we not? What we rarely consider is that we miss things when we judge and stereotype others, and we also miss out on the benefits of positive emotions such as gratefulness.

Gratitude

Gratitude is not only the greatest of virtues,
but the parent of all others.
— Marcus Tullius Cicero

Gratitude is a virtue and though it is arguably the most powerful emotion, it is one of the most neglected. Gratefulness is the emotional state and attitude to life that strengthens and enhances our personal and relational wellbeing. We feel grateful, thankful, glad or appreciative when someone does something for us that we value, enjoy or appreciate. Consequently, we feel indebted (owing gratitude or recognition) for what they have done for us.

It's a great emotion to experience. And the good news is that it can be learned and cultivated.

Benefits of gratitude

Gratitude is an amplifier of positive emotion, and it heals, energises and changes our lives. It is a great motivator and leads to action. Grateful people are excellent at setting goals, making progress towards them despite obstacles, and achieving them.

Research by Robert Emmons, professor of Psychology at the University of California at Davis and the world's leading scientific expert on gratitude, indicates that grateful people:

• have much higher levels of wellbeing

• experience lower levels of anxiety and depression

• have higher self-esteem

- experience higher levels of satisfaction
- are more optimistic
- reframe disaster and adversity better
- are more socially connected
- are less likely to be sensitive about rejection
- are much less likely to get angry
- have lower blood pressure
- are more successful at achieving their goals.[3]

Gratitude can be learned through practice and is especially powerful when it's expressed directly to others. Practising gratitude is essential to building self-leadership, self-confidence, effective teamwork and high-performing organisations. Conversely, being ungrateful and not showing appreciation to others is a recipe for isolating yourself and gaining a negative reputation. Needless to say, this is particularly relevant to team leaders.

Barriers to gratitude

The fact that gratitude can be learned doesn't make it easy to learn. In fact, it rarely happens by default, and it requires a conscious effort. While it may sound counterintuitive, being grateful requires acceptance and surrender. That's why 'control freaks' find it very difficult to be grateful, or to show appreciation—they micromanage, need to be on stage all the time and feel that they make everything happen. If you have ever had a boss like this, you will know exactly what I'm talking about.

> *Practising gratitude is essential to building self-leadership, self-confidence, effective teamwork and high-performing organisations.*

Some of the most common obstacles to developing gratitude include the following.

- *Conditioning.* Culture and consumerism have conditioned us to focus on what we don't have, as opposed to developing appreciation for what we already have. Like trust, gratitude requires vulnerability and being indebted to others. It's easier, of course, to believe we have done it all by ourselves.

- *Lack of maturity.* Children want just about everything under the sun and throw tantrums when they don't get it or when others don't meet their demands. Maturity brings a realisation that this is unrealistic and that we are not the centre of the universe. Most people learn to delay gratification and consider the needs of others, but not everyone learns this by the time they are adults. In the extreme, this is narcissism and borderline personality disorder. Perhaps you know someone like this? Hopefully, it wasn't your boss.

- *Entitlement.* Believing we deserve more than we have, or more than has been given to us—having a sense of entitlement—also leads to ingratitude.

- *Suffering.* This is possibly the greatest barrier to gratitude, as it can be used to legitimise unhappiness and ungratefulness. This doesn't mean suffering and gratefulness cannot coexist. (Read Viktor Frankl's classic *Man's Search for Meaning*. As an Austrian psychiatrist and Holocaust survivor, his experiences in a concentration camp led him to discover the importance of finding meaning in even the most brutal conditions, and thus continue living.)

Some of the most powerful strategies for building and sustaining gratefulness include keeping a gratitude journal and saying 'thank you'. Gratitude is especially powerful when it's expressed directly. It's essential for building self-leadership and self-confidence.

Why character strength and virtues matter

Character refers to qualities that lead individuals to desire to do good. As shown in the previous chapter, and expertly noted in *Character strengths in organizations* by Peterson and Park, 'character matters because it leads people to do the right thing, and the right thing can be productive and profitable'.

No doubt the fallout of the 2008 global financial crisis and the subsequent disregard for labour, environmental and social standards have put a greater emphasis on the study and practices of ethics and virtues. This is of paramount importance.

In their article 'The bored self in knowledge work', Jana Costas, Chair in Business Administration at the European University Viadrina in Frankfurt, and Dan Kärreman, professor at Copenhagen Business School, highlight how boredom in contemporary knowledge professions includes a combination of unfulfilled aspirations and a sense of stagnation. There is a clear need to address integrity and truthfulness, along with the intellectual virtues and practical wisdom of responsibility, courage and cooperation to revitalise knowledge workers.[4] As noted by Álvaro Turriago-Hoyos from Universidad de La Sabana in Colombia, this is in line with the virtues outlined in Peter Drucker's management theory. This theory focuses on the knowledge worker as the main unit of our contemporary information- and knowledge-based society, where intellectual virtues are the foundation of critical and creative thinking and innovation.

> *Character strengths require us to exercise judgement, and lead to recognisable excellence.*

In their book *Character Strengths and Virtues: A handbook and classification*, Christopher Peterson (1950–2012), professor of Psychology at the University of Michigan, and Marty Seligman, professor of Psychology at the University of Pennsylvania, the define character strengths as 'the psychological ingredients—processes or mechanisms— that define the virtues and dispositions to act'. They require us to exercise judgement, and lead to recognisable excellence. They can be distinguished from individual differences such as abilities and talents. The authors also present a measure of virtues that has been empirically and scientific investigated with their research identifying 24 character strengths that can be classified into six categories: wisdom, courage, humanity, justice, temperance and transcendence. These strengths are universally valued and encompass the capacity for helping ourselves and others, with positive effect.[6] The VIA Survey is an online survey designed to highlight your character strengths. It produces a personalised report with exercises and resources to help you realise your potential.

Are values a trap or overrated?

What happens when you ask people about their organisational values? Unless you live on a different planet from the one I live on, or you're asking people who work in an organisation that is the exception to the rule, the responses will range from disillusionment and cynicism to sarcasm, irony, mockery, banter and gobbledygook. We all know why. Don't we? The organisation's senior and middle managers talk the talk, but don't walk the walk. They don't put their money where their mouth is.

Many individuals and organisations set themselves up for scrutiny. The fact is that the more you proclaim your values, the more closely you will be watched to see how well your behaviour reflects them.

Espoused (or aspirational) values—the values an organisation says it values (such as integrity, collaboration, teamwork, customer focus, diversity, quality, innovation, blah, blah, blah...) are simply—sadly—'wallpaper rhetoric'. This is what the organisation desires and aspires to, and how it would like to be seen. Enacted values (or values in action), on the other hand, are the values actually being exhibited by the organisation's members—the reality.

With the backdrop of recent economic scandals, corruption, greed and unethical practices, and the consequent general disillusionment, it's not much of surprise that organisational values and authenticity are being questioned. Look at Enron, for example. Its stated values were 'communication', 'respect', 'integrity' and 'excellence'. Enron's may be at the extreme of meaningless value statements, but are these statements more than just a 'nice to have' thing for most organisations?

Charles Galunic, professor of Organisational Behaviour and professor in Leadership and Responsibility at Insead, Paris, says values are a way to shape internal stakeholders' understanding of the firm and an attempt to influence their behaviour. To this end, the company produces a wish list of cultural values. However, Galunic asks, 'Does it really matter what list of values a company ends up with as long as they can present "something" to the world?'[7]

The popular management literature (for example, works by Peters and Waterman, Collins and Porras, and Richard Barrett) turned values and culture into the new 'corporate speech' during the 1980s and 1990s. They insisted (and some of us believed it) that certain leadership styles, and formal management systems, could foster shared values to create high-performing cultures. As a result, nearly every CEO and senior manager who attended training or leadership development at that time embraced a single mantra: 'We are a values-driven organisation.' Yet by 2002, Patrick Lencioni, author of team management books and best known for the popular business fable *The Five Dysfunctions of a Team*, in his *Harvard Business Review* article 'Make your values mean something', says:

> … most values statements are bland, toothless, or just plain dishonest. And far from being harmless, as some executives assume, they're often highly destructive. Empty values statements create cynical and dispirited employees, alienate customers, and undermine managerial credibility.[8]

In the same article, he warns about the 'values management fad sweeping through organisations around the globe'.

Is it really a fad? I'll let you answer this question.

But wait! There is much more to it.

Mistaking values for principles, morality, virtues and ethics

The difference between values, principles, virtues and ethics can be a little confusing for many people as they are often used interchangeably. I'm going beyond semantics here. Insights from neuroscience and psychology shed some light on this.

Robert Wood is a professor at the Australian Graduate School of Management at the University of New South Wales, and director of the Centre for Ethical Leadership at the University of Melbourne. In his paper 'Ethical leadership framework', he explains:

> Ethical leadership requires more than values. Values such as care, justice, integrity and respect are the raw material of ethical leadership, but they require a production process to convert them into effective actions in complex and dynamic situations.[9]

Values relate to personal and/or organisational 'preferences'. Morality, on the other hand, requires more complex cognitive and emotional processes. You can read more about this in *The Moral Brain: Essays on the evolutionary and neuroscientific aspects of morality* by Dr Amir Muzur, a cognitive neuroscience researcher at University of Rijeka in Croatia.

The moral brain

It appears that despite the fact that people (and authors) claim values are enduring and stable over time, they actually are not. Values are subjective and changeable. We shift our values (such as from material things—salary, car or house—to a good education or professional development).

Morality, on the other hand, requires our brain to work more intensely. Making moral choices requires effort to deal with rational and explicit demands, as well as emotional, quick and intuitive ones. Morality, then, overlaps with other complex processes (highly complex neural circuitry) in the brain. From a neuroscience perspective, morality works by simultaneously engaging multiple areas of the brain, such as the frontal and parietal lobes, temporal lobe and insula, and subcortical structures. This is why morality is far more enduring than values.

Principles

Principles, such as honesty, compassion and fairness—as opposed to values—are more stable, consistent, objective and universal (transcultural). They are rules or beliefs that govern morally correct behaviour and attitudes.

Principles are personal convictions and commitments to what is true to our hearts. They become a 'code of ethics'; guiding principles that stem from the virtues we value most are never compromised or abandoned. A well-known example is the conviction and adherence to the golden rule of 'do unto others as you would have them do unto you'. The main difference between values and principles, then, is that values (preferences) are something nice 'to have', 'to talk about' and 'show'. Principles are something 'to be', and are acquired through virtues.

Conclusion

Positive emotions are conducive to wellbeing and more productive work. In the context of developing effective and ethical leaders — as well as engaging employees — organisations should consider whether the time has come to replace values with virtues, principles, ethics and character strengths. They seem to connect more deeply both intellectually and emotionally, offering richer human and financial benefits for employees and organisations.

Insight questions

- How do you cultivate positive emotions?

- How grateful is your team?

- How do they express gratitude to each other and their customers and stakeholders?

- How do you express gratitude to them?

- Are you, or is your team, experiencing any barrier to gratitude?

- What are your character strengths?

- How do you cultivate your character strengths and virtues?

- How about your team?

- Do you and your team discuss and practise a common set of values?

- How often do you discuss principles, morality, virtues and ethics with your team?

- Does your team understand the differences and links between values, principles, morality, virtues and ethics?

CHAPTER 9
Motivation and self-engagement

Two happy frogs were playing and hopping around a farm when suddenly they fell into a big vat of milk. Desperately, they puddled as they tried to climb out but after a while, one of the frogs lost motivation, stopped swimming, and drowned in the milk. However, undiscouraged by her friend's fate, the second frog stayed motivated and continued to swim, her movements eventually churning the milk into butter. She then found herself on solid footing again and leaped out of the vat.

Yes, I'm afraid that the moral of this short story is something many people don't like to hear: Motivation is overrated!

Motivation is always necessary to start anything. It's about desire. But motivation alone won't get results, especially if what you are trying to achieve is difficult or challenging. This is because motivation is often short-lived or temporary. How many times have you heard the expression, 'they lost motivation', or have lost motivation yourself?

This explains, for example, why most people never achieve their New Year's resolutions—such as losing weight by joining a health club and adopting a healthy diet. They go to the gym regularly for the first few weeks, then lose interest and motivation. A similar thing tends to happen when people listen to stories about heroic leaders or inspirational tales (for example, seminars or TED talks). They feel inspired at the time, temporarily uplifted and motivated; but does much change in the workplace a few days or months later?

The reality is that no-one lives in a constant state of motivation. We all experience ups and downs and moments when we don't feel like doing what needs to be done—just like one of the frogs in the urn.

So, if motivation doesn't cut it, what does?

Commitment—not motivation—leads to results. The two frogs were motivated to get out of the urn, but only one was committed to keep going.

In this chapter I explore four very important and interrelated concepts associated with self-leadership—motivation, goal setting, commitment and self-engagement.

Motivation

Motivation is about having the psychological force, drive or reason to initiate something. Motivation can be triggered externally (extrinsic) or internally (intrinsic).[1] Intrinsic motivation is when we do something because we find it interesting and enjoyable. In other words, we do it for its own sake for personal reward and a sense of satisfaction. Extrinsic motivation is when we do something because of external pressures or tangible rewards, such as for financial compensation, as opposed to doing it for fun or intellectual stimulation.

The girl and the precious stone

A young woman who was feeling dissatisfied and confused decided to travel the world in search of meaning and purpose. One night, in one of the many villages she encountered, she heard of a poor old woman who helped young people to find purpose and success in life.

The next morning she visited the old woman, who lived very simply in a clean but humble house. The old woman listened to the young woman's story of her quest for understanding, wisdom and happiness, then gave her a precious stone and said: 'This is a very valuable stone that was once given to me by a person very dear to me. It has brought me good luck ever since. Now it is yours. Do whatever you want with it. You can either keep it or sell it — it's worth a lot of money!'

The young woman left, thoughtful and puzzled. After a few days she returned to the old woman and said: 'I came back because what I would really like from you is whatever it is that prompted you to give me the precious stone.'

The young woman clearly wasn't extrinsically motivated by money, otherwise she would have sold the stone. She knew deep down that some things are more precious than material wealth. She was motivated by her desire (intrinsic motivation) to find meaning and purpose in her life. Her motivation was to learn, grow and develop. The old woman's act of unconditional generosity had a profound impact on the young woman, who learned from the experience what it was that she really wanted.

Different people have different motivations. What motivates you? What motivates your team?

At work, the following factors increase intrinsic motivation:

- *Challenge* — pursuing goals that have personal meaning and that enhance self-esteem.

- *Curiosity* — doing something that attracts attention by stimulating curiosity and a willingness to learn.

- *Autonomy*—having control of what to do and how to do it.

- *Cooperation and competition*—helping others and being able to compare personal performance with others.

- *Recognition*—being recognised for accomplishments.

Extrinsic motivators include higher pay or promotion. These are important, but only to a point. Once these motivations have satisfied some basic needs, their power tends to diminish.

This relates directly to research by Frederick Herzberg (1923–2000), a psychologist who became one of the most influential names in business management by introducing the concept of job enrichment and the motivator-hygiene theory of motivation (also known as Herzberg's dual-factor theory, or two-factor theory of motivation). His 1968 publication *One More Time, How Do You Motivate Employees?* had sold 1.2 million copies by 1987 and it became one of the most requested articles from the *Harvard Business Review*.

Two factors: motivators and KITA (kick in the ass)

Certain factors in the workplace create job satisfaction, while others cause dissatisfaction. Intrinsic things, such as recognition, achievement and personal growth, increase motivation. Herzberg's so-called 'hygiene' factors do not provide satisfaction or increase motivation. However, their absence creates dissatisfaction. Examples of hygiene factors include job security, status, salary, fringe benefits, working conditions, good pay, and holidays. The term 'hygiene' is used to indicate that these are maintenance factors and are external to the role.

Herzberg refers to hygiene as a KITA (kick in the ass) factor. That is, to motivate people through either incentives or the risk of punishment. Herzberg says you don't motivate people by offering inducements, or what's commonly known as the 'carrot and stick' approach. Instead, you motivate people by giving them recognition, responsibility and the opportunity to achieve through job enrichment.

Let me reinforce this point by explaining the motivation 'threshold', using money as an example.

Money as a threshold motivator

An 'equity threshold' is the point at which an employee's salary is high enough to remove their financial concerns. Employees below the equity threshold can feel they are being paid unfairly, which can demotivate them. However, paying above the equity threshold does not significantly increase motivation.

Based on this premise, there are four possible scenarios:

1. *High hygiene and high motivation* is the ideal situation; the basics are covered so employees will be highly motivated are unlikely complaints.

2. *High hygiene and low motivation* results in few employee complaints, but the job is viewed as just a pay cheque. This tends to burn people out. The people I met over the years working under fly-in, fly-out conditions in the mining industry are good examples. They made very good money but paid a high price. Their personal lives suffered to the point where would they often end up facing divorce or separation. It's unsustainable in the long term.

3. *Low hygiene and high motivation* produces a lot of complaints from motivated employees. This is when the job is challenging and exciting, but with poor pay and work conditions.

4. *Low hygiene and low motivation* is the worst possible scenario. Employees have little motivation and a lot of complaints.

In contrast to Maslow, where little data was provided to back his theory, Herzberg and other researchers have published considerable empirical evidence on the motivation-hygiene theory. However, the methods of this research have been questioned. Having said this, in their book *First, Break All the Rules: What the world's greatest managers do differently* best-selling authors Marcus Buckingham and Curt Coffman provide strong support for Herzberg's research. Their book details the Gallup organisation's research that identified 12 questions for identifying high-performing individuals and organisations.[2] However, while the questions are correlated with Herzberg's motivation factors, the hygiene factors did little to motivate high performance.[3]

Herzberg's theory was further discredited by academics for positing two continua (job satisfaction and job dissatisfaction)—the methodological artefact of using the critical incident technique rather than a continuum. This criticism, however, does not detract from the practical significance of his research findings on ways to enrich a job.

Visioning

A youngster approached an old man and asked him, 'What's the secret to staying motivated in life to become successful and achieve real results?'

The old man looked the youngster in the eyes and replied, 'The secret is to have a big vision that you really want. Dare to dream and to make your dreams become reality: vision, dare, dream and believe.'

* * *

Paulo Coelho de Souza is a Brazilian novelist and the winner of several international awards such as the Crystal Award by the World Economic Forum. In his 1993 book *The Alchemist*, when referring to the principle that governs all things, he says, 'When you want something, all the universe conspires in helping you to achieve it.'[4]

Visioning is creating a future positive scenario with you in it. It entails developing a vivid mental image of what could be in the long-term future. This is important as it can motivate us to move beyond our existing perspectives to give us a genuine sense of meaning about both our present and our future.

> *Crafting your personal mission statement will illuminate and pull you towards your desired future.*

Visions are conceptual and provide us with meaning. They motivate and assist us to have a clear purpose, which in turn we use to develop plans and formulate goals and objectives, and activities to achieve them. Effective leaders are able to create and frame visions first for themselves, and then for others using the language of possibility, as we see in chapter 3 with the examples of John F. Kennedy, Martin Luther King Jr and Winston Churchill.

Organisations use visions to produce mission statements—clear and succinct descriptions of what the organisation should look like (its preferred future) once it achieves its full potential. Crafting your personal mission statement will act as a shining light that will illuminate and pull you towards your desired future. It will provide you the direction necessary to plan and prioritise personal and career choices. Write your personal mission statement, and treat it as a living document that changes over time, depending on what is going on in your life.

Here are two examples of personal mission statements:

- 'To serve as a leader, live a balanced life, and apply ethical principles to make a significant difference.'—Denise Morrison, CEO of Campbell Soup Company

- 'To have fun in [my] journey through life and learn from [my] mistakes.'—Sir Richard Branson, founder of The Virgin Group

Goal setting

Goal setting relates to formulating action plans to motivate and guide individuals and groups to achieve goals. It has been the subject of extensive research.

Gary Latham, Secretary of State Professor of Organizational Effectiveness and professor of Organizational Behaviour and HR Management at the University of Toronto, has extensively researched the benefits of goal setting in organisations. He explains that goal setting increases employee motivation and organisational commitment and is most effective when organisations are ethical and supportive, not punitive when individuals fail to reach their intended goals.

Latham says goal setting affects outcomes in four ways:

1. *Choice.* Goals can focus an individuals' attention and keep them away from irrelevant tasks.

2. *Effort.* Goals can encourage an individual to make a bigger effort and to work more intensely.

3. *Persistence.* Individuals become more likely to work through setbacks to achieve goals.

4. *Cognition.* Goals can spur individual development and create behavioural changes.

Latham further highlights that:

> Motivation of oneself is arguably as important as, if not more important than, motivating the behaviour of others. Goal-setting is a key mechanism for self-management... When people discover that they are below their goal, they typically increase their effort and/or modify their strategy.[5]

Motivation can be overestimated. Take, for example, the performance equation (Performance = Ability × Motivation) — initially formulated by psychologist Norman Maier in the 1950s. If either ability or motivation is zero, there goes performance out the window. This is why commitment to goals is the sine qua non of goal setting. Without commitment it's all pie in the sky! (Commitment is covered in detail later in this chapter).

Anthony Grant, associate professor and director of the Coaching Psychology Unit at the University of Sydney, explains that goal setting needs to support the creation and application of an action plan.

> The action plan should be designed to motivate the individual into action, and should also incorporate means of monitoring and evaluating performance, thus providing information on which to base follow-up coaching sessions.[6]

The acronym SMART (specific, measurable, attainable, relevant and time-bound) is used extensively in management and coaching literature as it relates to goal setting for personal development.

Feedback and feedforward

Feedback is a necessary condition for effective goal setting and goal attainment, and extensive research confirms it produces significant performance improvements. In the words of Ken Blanchard, author, speaker, management expert and business consultant, 'Feedback is the breakfast of champions.'

Dr Marshall Goldsmith is one of the world's most recognised and well-respected leadership and business thinkers and the author or editor of 35 books, including the bestselling *MOJO* and *What Got You Here Won't Get You There: How successful people become even more successful*. One of Goldsmith's most valuable pearls of wisdom relates to providing leaders with 'feedforward' instead of feedback. Goldsmith talks about the miracle of feedforward by referring to it as his 'special sauce' methodology to assist leaders to become better in the future. In essence, feedforward involves offering suggestions to another party for them to consider incorporating into their future behaviour.[7]

Think about driving a car. How much time do you spend looking in the rear-view mirror as opposed to looking forward? How difficult do you think it would be to drive if you relied on directional information gathered mostly from your mirrors? (Difficult!—even without the blind spots in the rear-view mirror.)

It's simple, isn't it?

Well, the same applies when providing feedback to others, especially to leaders. Feedback relates to the past—what they did or didn't do. In contrast, providing someone with feedforward is about clarifying expectations with the intention of genuinely helping them. It's more like a using GPS navigator—it clearly paves the way ahead.

More often than not, senior leaders tend to take feedback as a criticism. (A CEO said to me once, 'Believe me, I get a lot of flak!') Yet they're far more receptive to receiving feedforward, especially if their permission is sought first and the intention for doing so is clearly stated upfront. Feedforward, then, is often a far more useful motivational, goal setting and attainment device than feedback.

Employee engagement

Employee engagement (EE) has four commonalities with leadership.

1. It doesn't have a universally agreed definition.

2. Most authors and practitioners tend to agree that it is a source of competitive advantage for organisations.

3. It's a hot topic.

4. Despite investing heavily in efforts to make it happen, most organisations don't reap the expected or desired results.

According to the Gallup organisation, 'The world has an employee engagement crisis, with serious and potentially lasting repercussions for the global economy' — with only 13 per cent of employees engaged worldwide.[8] Gallup estimates the annual economic costs associated with disengagement are extremely high, costing £32 billion in the UK, €100 billion in France, US$370 billion in the United States, and $54.8 billion in Australia in lost productivity. Not surprisingly, Bersin by Deloitte predicted that in 2016 culture and engagement and leadership were the most pressing challenges for organisations.[9]

Jack Welch, retired business executive, author, chemical engineer, and chairman and CEO of General Electric between 1981 and 2000, said that employee engagement, customer satisfaction and cash flow are the only three measurements needed to understand the performance of an organisation:

It goes without saying that no company, small or large, can win over the long run without energised employees who believe in the mission and understand how to achieve it.[10]

Alan Saks, professor of Organizational Behaviour and HR Management at University of Toronto Scarborough, explains that most writing about employee engagement is from a practitioner perspective and is based in practice rather than in science. 'As a result, employee engagement has the appearance of being somewhat faddish or what some might call, "old wine in a new bottle".'[11]

To make things even more confusing, EE—like leadership—has been defined in many ways.

Broadly, EE is 'a positive attitude held by the employee towards the organisation and its values. An engaged employee is aware of the business context and works with employees to improve performance'.[12]

William Kahn, from the Questrom School of Business at Boston University, was the first author to introduce the concept of EE. He explained it in terms of two extremes—engagement and disengagement—in relation to the behaviour of people at work. He defined engagement as 'the harnessing of organisation members' selves to their work roles; in engagement, people employ and express themselves physically, cognitively, and emotionally during role performances'. Disengagement he defined as 'the uncoupling of selves from work roles; in disengagement, people withdraw and defend themselves physically, cognitively, or emotionally during role performances'.[13]

The Gallup organisation later developed a model that explains three levels of engaged employees:[14]

1. 'Engaged' employees are passionate, consistently show commitment and innovation, and exert discretionary effort. They are the most desired employees.

2. 'Not engaged' are sleepwalkers and their contribution is minimal. They act as if they are working, but actually are not.

3. 'The disengaged' are the unhappiest and they spread their unhappiness, causing dissatisfaction and lack of contribution. They are the biggest liabilities for the organisation.

Gallup defines employee engagement as happening when individuals are emotionally connected to others, satisfied, as well as enthusiastic for work. The Gallup Workplace Audit measures employees' attitudes including: their intention towards customer service and to stay with the organisation; and how loyal, satisfied and proud they are to be there. These are then weighed against what employee attitudes are in a manager's control.[15]

Authors Marcus Buckingham and Curt Coffman in their book *First, Break All the Rules: What the world's greatest managers do differently* popularised Gallup's definition of engagement: 'work with a passion and feel a profound connection to their company' and 'drive innovation and move the organisation forward'. Gallup says, 'A highly engaged workforce means the difference between a company that outperforms its competitors and one that fails to grow.'

Gallup suggests the following five best practices that improve engagement and performance:

1. Make engagement an integral part of the organisation's people strategy.

2. Ensure engagement measures use psychometrically valid and reliable instruments.

3. Clarify the organisation's current situation and its desired future state.

4. Keep in mind that engagement is a multidimensional construct.

5. Integrate engagement into the organisation's objectives and values.

Aon Hewitt Corporation defines EE as 'the level of an employee's psychological investment in their organisation' and warns about confusing EE with satisfaction or happiness.[16] Its research indicates only about 50 per cent of employees know what employee engagement is; it's suggested that a critical initial step in creating a culture of engagement is ensuring that employees have an understanding of the concept of engagement and that it is their own responsibility.

The Aon Hewitt approach is referred to as the 'say, stay, strive' model, where employees are asked:

- if they speak positively about, and stand for, their employer
- if they plan to stay as long as possible with their employer
- if they strive for success with their very best.

The Aon Hewitt model also measures the following 15 dimensions that are key to an effective workplace: 'employee value proposition (EVP); reputation; career opportunities; collaboration; diversity and inclusion; empowerment/autonomy; enabling infrastructure; learning and development; manager; performance management; rewards and recognition; senior leadership; talent and staffing; work fulfillment; and work–life balance'.

Engaged employees are passionate, consistently show commitment and innovation, and exert discretionary effort.

Aon Hewitt recommends four principles for measuring engagement and deriving insights to help you achieve breakthrough impact:

1. Align the measurement process to business goals and talent challenges.
2. Empower key stakeholders who affect engagement.
3. Take an outside–in view to build meaningful insights.
4. Create a continuously engaging work experience.

Wilmar Schaufeli, professor of work and organizational psychology at Utrecht University (Netherlands) and distinguished research professor at Leuven University (Belgium), and his colleagues define these constructs as follows:[17]

- *Vigour*—experiencing high levels of energy and mental resilience while working ... and persistence even in the face of difficulties.

- *Dedication*—being strongly involved in one's work and experiencing a sense of significance, enthusiasm, inspiration, pride and challenge.

- *Absorption*—being fully concentrated and happily engrossed in one's work...

(Notice the similarity with 'flow', which is discussed in chapter 7.)

All approaches, however, are in agreement that employee engagement is a predictor of performance.

Engagement is an inside job

'You can lead a horse to water, but you can't make it drink.' People cannot become fully engaged unless they really want to. Real motivation comes from within.

But the story of the two frogs shows that motivation is not enough. Commitment is a must.

Commitment

Commitment is about determination and dedication. It's the state or quality of being dedicated to another person, group, cause, goal or activity. As opposed to motivation, commitment is enduring, or long-term. It doesn't vanish over time, so it leads to sustained action and results — like in the case of the second frog.

Individuals who are committed have an allegiance, fidelity or adherence to someone or something. They are also devoted, loyal and faithful to a cause. As a leader, you should also know that there are different kinds of commitment.

Three types of commitment

There are three types of commitment: normative, continuance and affective.

Normative commitment stems from having a sense of duty, such as feeling obliged to remain with a team or organisation. This sense of obligation could come from multiple places. For example, some employees may feel obliged to stay in a role if an organisation has invested in training them. In this case, the employee stays because they 'ought to'.

Continuance commitment occurs when an employee commits to the organisation because they perceive a high cost of losing something, such as organisational membership, economic benefits such as superannuation or pension accruals, or friendships with co-workers. In this case, the employee remains because they 'have to'.

Affective commitment relates to employees' positive emotional attachment to the team or organisation. Affectively committed employees are those who chose to stay in the organisation because they strongly identify with the goals and values of their employer. Such employees commit to the organisation because they 'want to'.

Affective commitment is the type of commitment that matters when it comes to EE. It means loyalty or allegiance from employees who are satisfied and proud of their work. These people exert discretionary effort — they are willing to go 'above and beyond' the call of duty — which includes making sacrifices to get things done, helping others with heavy workloads, looking for opportunities to perform more effectively and volunteering for additional duties.

Computer maker Dell views EE like this: 'To compete today, companies need to win over the minds (rational commitment) and the hearts (emotional commitment) of employees in ways that lead to extraordinary effort.'[18]

Innovative behaviour

High levels of satisfaction and commitment stimulate the creative thinking that leads to innovative behaviour. This relates to having a positive orientation towards change, generating and adopting new ideas and/or practices, and persevering when implementing new and promising ideas.

Self-engagement

Self-engagement relates to the sustained capacity to be able to generate motivation, passion, satisfaction and commitment. This, in turn, leads to self-leadership through which individuals can influence their performance to achieve goal-directed behaviour and success.

The self-engagement and self-leadership value model depicted in table 9.1 is based on data from the Human Capital Institute.[19]

Table 9.1: six levels of self-engagement and self-leadership value model — six levels

Level	Mindset/focus	Indicators		Outcomes	Benefits/Results
4. Impact	Self-engagement and self-leadership	- Satisfaction/joy - Gratefulness - Serenity - Commitment	- Increased capacity - High energy/vigour - Discretionary effort - Flow	Spectacular or extraordinary performance 90% to 100%	Return 120% of their salary in value
3. Deploy	Self-development	- Self-responsibility - Motivation - Optimism	- Self-confidence - Conviction - Resilience	High performance 70% to 80%	Return 100% of their salary in value
2. Activate	'Light bulb moment' Turning point	- Self-awareness - Self-acceptance - Curiosity - Interest - Hope	- Exploration - Learning possibility - Options - Action - Relating	Medium performance 50% to 60%	Return 80% of their salary in value
1. Initiate	Reclaim (Crossing the threshold)	- Struggle - Encounter - Confrontation	- Submission - Surrender - Transformation	Low or mediocre performance 30% to 40%	Return ranges from 50% to 60% of their salary in value
0. Survival	Blind spots (Don't know what I don't know)	- Lack of self-awareness - Confusion - Disinterest	- Apathy - Indifference - Self-doubt - Procrastination		Return ranges from 10% to 30% of their salary in value, or no return (costs −10%)
−1. Distress	Survival	- Worry - Detachment	- Depression - Anxiety	Negative performance −20% to −10%	
		— Needs help right now (duty of care) —			

Level −1 and level 0: Distress and survival

At these levels, individuals have significant blind spots, lack self-awareness, and have limited or no sense of identity, purpose and direction. They feel confused, apathetic, indifferent, detached, disinterested and doubtful. In the worst case (level −1), they may be in distress or just surviving, and feeling detached, worried, anxious or depressed. This may be due to a range of reasons, such as personal issues; high levels of work-related stress; or conflict at work, including harassment, discrimination or bullying. Employees at this level can meet their performance goals intermittently or occasionally, or in the worst cases cost their organisations money.

Moving to the next level requires professional help or initiation. This may take different forms, from addressing the current problems to creating enough dissonance or discomfort to change the status quo. Individuals at level 0 return between 50 and 60 per cent of their salaries in value. Those at level −1 return between 10 and 30 per cent of their salaries in value, or cost −10 per cent.

Level 1: Initiate

Initiation means making a life transition by confronting life events; in particular, unpleasant or painful experiences from which we derive meaningful learnings. This can include forgotten or unattended experiences that have shaped individuals' negative assumptions or core beliefs about themselves.

Level 1 symbolises the crossing of a threshold, or a rite of passage to a higher level of development. This is a life-defining moment in which people make a decision to take responsibility and gain independence. Initiation indicates a commitment to change, renewal, rebirth or transformation by leaving behind the old and accepting the new. Individuals at this level still return between 50 and 60 per cent of their salaries in value.

Level 2: Activate

Activation at this level is characterised by a 'light bulb moment'. Individuals experience a turning point as a result of acquiring new knowledge, higher self-esteem and self-confidence. This awareness triggers interest and curiosity. It also offers hope of new possibilities, which can expand self-awareness and willingness to explore options to change. The critical outcome is that people display initiative by taking action.

Employees at this level are likely to begin meeting their performance goals consistently. They return up to 80 per cent of their salaries in value.

Level 3: Deploy

Employees at this level begin to deploy their inner resources and feel motivated, confident and optimistic. They take responsibility for their own development, which gives them greater self-confidence, conviction and resilience. Most individuals at this point experience peace, serenity, joy or even elation. Most importantly, however, they continue to take decisive action that leads them to true self-engagement.

Employees at this level consistently deliver high performance by meeting or exceeding their goals. These individuals return 100 per cent of their salary in value.

Level 4: Impact

Individuals at this level have achieved self-engagement and self-leadership. They feel high levels of gratefulness, serenity, satisfaction, joy or even elation. In turn, this generates abundant levels of vitality, discretionary effort and innovative behaviour. They experience flow regularly and consistently deliver high performance and exceed their goals. And they keep getting better by maximising their performance and coaching others. They return up to 120 per cent of their salary in value to their organisations.

* * *

Moving from one level to the next involves hard work and you cannot do it alone. It requires you to work with a suitable professional you trust.

Conclusion

Motivation is an important force we all need in life. Intrinsic motivation (when we do something because we find it interesting, enjoyable or intellectually stimulating) is far more enduring than extrinsic motivation (when we do something because of external pressures or tangible rewards or compensation). Creating a personal vision, writing a personal mission statement and setting goals are effective ways to motivate yourself to take action. However, while motivation is important in initiating action, it's not enough to create sustained effort and get to completion.

Commitment is also required, and it has to be emotional—not rational—commitment. This is relevant to employee engagement because, above all, engagement is an inside job and a predictor of performance. This is despite the fact employee engagement means different things to different researchers, consultants and organisations. There are six levels of self-engagement and self-leadership: levels −1 and level 0 (distress and survival); level 1 (initiate); level 2 (active); level; 3 (deploy); and level 4 (impact). Moving from one level to the next requires working with a suitable professional you trust.

Insight questions

- What motivates you? What motivates your team/ stakeholders?
- What's your vision? Do you have a written personal mission statement?
- What's your team's vision?
- How committed is your team?
- How self-engaged are your people?
- Does your organisation offer self-engagement programs to employees?

- At what level of the self-engagement/self-leadership model are you?

- How about your team?

- How might you/they reach the next level and stay there or move higher?

PART III

COLLECTIVE LEADERSHIP DEVELOPMENT

This section deals with collective leadership development, including case examples of collective leadership and various approaches or methodologies for developing leadership capacity within teams and organisations.

- Chapter 10 explains collective leadership, the barriers in achieving it, and presents five real case examples.

- Chapter 11 discusses leadership development best practices.

- Chapter 12 reviews ten approaches to leadership development.

- Chapter 13 examines spectacular performance.

- Chapter 14 prepares you for action.

CHAPTER 10

Collective leadership

What is collective leadership? This is invariably the first question people ask when I talk about the subject, and in response I tell them this short story.

The orphanage

Jasmine was an obese girl who lived in an orphanage and was very much disliked by all the other children. They were always playing pranks on her and insulting her. This made her feel very distressed, lonely and miserable. And to add to her misery, she was also bullied and victimised by an influential staff member — the deputy principal — who was very close to the principal.

One day, all of the orphanage children and the deputy principal met to plan a strategy to get rid of the 'fat cow', as they called her, forever. The group put forth a few ideas, until the deputy said, 'I've got it! I have been watching the fat cow and every day just before midnight she gets up and goes out into the bushes. I propose that

(continued)

one night we wait for her to get up in the middle of the night and follow her to see what she does. We will then ambush her and will have an excuse to get rid of her.'

The group agreed and asked the principal and members of the management committee to join them to witness a transgression they hoped would get Jasmine expelled. The following night, they waited until Jasmine got up and went into the bushes as expected. She walked a short distance from the orphanage to a large tree. The group hid silently behind bushes, ready to switch on their torches as soon as the girl did something suspicious.

At the tree, Jasmine reached up and put a folded piece of white paper in the fork between two branches. At that point, the deputy signalled to the group to switch on their torches and they caught Jasmine in a pool of light.

The principal walked over and took the note from the tree. The group waited anxiously while he unfolded the note and read it to himself. As he did so, the group saw tears running from his eyes. He then read the note aloud:

Whoever you are, wherever you are, whatever you do,

I just want you to know one thing: I love you!

You may think this story is fiction. But in the light of the widespread institutional abuse recently revealed by the royal commission in Australia, it's obvious that the story may in fact be close to the truth.

As you can imagine, the reactions I get in response to Jasmine's story vary, but it's not uncommon for people to cry, or express their anger or even rage. Occasionally, some will choose to disengage by saying they feel nothing.

Once my audience has had the opportunity to vent their emotions, I ask the following questions:

- If you had been part of that group in the orphanage, what would you have done?

- What do you think would have been the right thing to do?
- What would have been the ideal response from anyone in such a situation?
- If you were ever part of a group in a situation like the one described where someone is victimised or taken advantage of, at work or elsewhere, what would you do?

The reality is that there are many Jasmines who, whether because of their looks, disability, shape, race or cultural background, gender or sexual orientation, lack of competence or above average success, are unfairly targeted by others.

This is how Jasmine's story relates to collective leadership.

Collective leadership is one of the many descriptors used by researchers when referring to 'pluralistic leadership'[1]—an umbrella term that encompasses collective, collaborative, shared, distributed and emergent leadership. Collective leadership involves all employees and means that everyone is responsible for the team or organisation's success and not just for their individual role. This means leadership is distributed, rather than being centred on a few individuals in formal positions of authority. The broad distribution of responsibilities is naturally more inclusive, as it involves all participants, which makes collective leadership more effective than individual leadership.

Collective leadership means each individual has a voice in the organisation, and power and voice is distributed according to the capabilities and motivations in the group, team or organisation. This, in turn, empowers people, who then feel more valued, trusted and heard. In this way, everyone's interaction and effort at every level drives performance and shapes the culture of the organisation.

> *Collective leadership ... empowers people, who then feel more valued, trusted and heard.*

Collective leadership is relational rather than hierarchical. It enables everyone to be active in leadership roles as it flattens hierarchical workplace structures. Giving people more responsibility also means allowing them to be more accountable, take risks, make mistakes and learn from them. This can allow individuals to be more accountable and empowered, making them more committed, engaged, creative and innovative. In this context, leaders become mentors, supporting each other to achieve an organisation's collective goals and outcomes.

Years of traditional leadership have resulted in systems that value hierarchy, status, authority and control. The move to collective leadership requires change not only at a leadership and cultural level, but also at an individual level. The challenge in shifting to collective leadership is that people are not used to having a voice. Instead, they are used to a dependency created by the pervasive 'leader–follower' paradigm. This is clearly reflected in Jasmine's story: no-one dared to challenge the situation, even though some of them surely knew that something was wrong. They were not empowered to speak up.

Leadership dependency vs empowerment

Dependence on a leader does have some clear implications, even though influential leadership can wean followers off their dependence.

First, it implies that the followers or subordinates have limited ability to make decisions and get work done without guidance or permission. This results in hesitation, employees who feel vulnerable and threatened by change, and substandard decision making and, therefore, less than desirable results and decreased productivity. Psychologically, this means the subordinates' self-esteem and motivation depends on receiving recognition and approval from their leader. William James (1842–1910), an original thinker and philosopher considered one of the fathers of psychology, said, 'The deepest principle of human nature is the craving to be appreciated.'[2] Leadership dependency creates this craving and keeps individuals in a cycle of looking for recognition from places beyond their control. This often leads to dissatisfaction, powerlessness and anxiety.

> Empowerment is about providing others with autonomy and independence.

Second, it means that for leadership to succeed, the followers must idolise their leaders, often as authority figures, attribute to them unrealistic qualities and create unrealistic expectations of them. In turn, leaders on pedestals can be pressured by the need to always be correct and can become overly defensive to criticism.

Finally, dependence stifles followers' creativity and kills any chance of them offering innovations. Traditional leadership paradigms rely on control, obedience and conformity. Followers who dare not depart from their leader's ideas are not engaged in their own creative processes.

Empowerment, on the other hand, is about providing others with autonomy and independence. This occurs when people feel valued for their experience, potential and contribution. Empowered individuals are motivated, believe in their ability to perform successfully and are also more creative. Collective leadership allows individuals to develop their own abilities and independent thinking skills, which builds collective social identification and self-efficacy—a shared belief in the ability to accomplish tasks and achieve common goals. This in turn fosters team creative thinking and innovation, which creates an environment rich with job satisfaction and improved results.

The bystander effect

There is another psychological phenomenon playing out in Jasmine's story—the bystander effect.

A bystander is present at an event, but does not take part. The bystander effect (also known as bystander apathy) is a social psychological phenomenon in which people do not help victims when in the presence of others. In fact, the likelihood of a victim receiving help can be directly contrasted to the number of bystanders—the more witnesses or bystanders to a situation in which a victim requires assistance, the less likely it is that assistance will be offered. Being part of the group absolves the individual from the sole responsibility of doing something that may be right or wrong. There are three main reasons this happens: ambiguity, cohesiveness and diffusion of responsibility.[3]

Ambiguity means that people are unsure whether someone needs help. This ambiguity, of course, can be high or low, which in turn determines bystanders' reaction times. For example, hearing someone yelling for help is a less ambiguous situation than witnessing a person fall and then slowly stand up. In a high ambiguity situation it can take an individual or group up to five times as long to take helpful action, according to research. In such cases, bystanders assess their own safety first. Bystanders are more likely to help in low ambiguity or insignificant and inconsequential situations than in situations with high ambiguity or potentially significant consequences.

Group cohesiveness refers to the way 'norms' of social responsibility affect helping behaviour. This unwritten norm says, 'We should help others who need it and who depend on us for it.' This means that others not taking action can establish a 'normal' response, a belief that help is not needed or is not 'socially appropriate' in the situation. Any decision to help others depends on whether there is an established relationship (for example, family, friend, acquaintance or stranger) with the person requiring or asking for help. As you would expect, generally speaking, the more cohesive a group (for example, family), the more likely it is that individuals or groups will offer help.

Diffusion of responsibility, according to Wikipedia, refers to where 'a person is less likely to take responsibility for action or inaction when others are present.' In other words, a person assumes that other bystanders are either responsible for taking action or have already done so; at the very least they feel the burden of action is shared and therefore that there is a lesser need to act alone. This often depends on the context. A person may assume, for example, that other bystanders, such as doctors or police officers, are more qualified to help. In Jasmine's case, the other children would have reasonably expected some of the adults at the scene to have stepped in. Similarly, the members of the management committee would have expected the principal or deputy principal to act. All of which led to a diffusion of responsibility by all of the people present.

Another reason for diffusion of responsibility is that people may fear that they will be superseded by another, superior bystander (for example, the principal), that they will offer assistance that is unwanted, or that they will need to face the repercussions of giving unwarranted assistance. In Jasmine's case, the other children, and perhaps even some of the management committee members, may have feared being reprimanded or punished by the principal had they gone to Jasmine's assistance.

Collective leadership averts situations like Jasmine's because it means that everyone takes responsibility for the success of a team or organisation, not just for their individual responsibilities or jobs. In this case, success for the team would also mean success for Jasmine. Collective leadership values innovation, and people are therefore free to act independently, to question and seek refined solutions — and consequently feel good about themselves and each other. This sense of buoyed self-esteem and social connectedness inhibits the likelihood of bystander behaviour.

There is another concept that affects people's performance in groups or teams: social loafing.

Social loafing

Social loafing means that people tend to exert less effort, or fail to shoulder their fair share of the load, in a group. As a result, members working individually in a group are often more productive than when members contribute as a group. This happens because individuals know their contributions to the team can easily go unnoticed, and perhaps consider they have little incentive to contribute. Consequently, they 'loaf' without fear of consequences.[4]

Social loafing is a big trigger for team stress as it builds resentment towards perceived 'free-riders' and discontent among hard workers who see little consequence for not trying. Social loafing occurs when people are disengaged and not held accountable for their actions (or inactions), in low performing teams where it is the norm, when evaluation and review are absent, when there is a lack of cohesion and when staff have low motivation.

Social loafing can be extremely disruptive in terms of output, satisfaction and connectedness. Fostering collective leadership is a way to deal with it. This means clarifying roles and responsibilities, and tracking the progress of projects using metrics that link individual contributions to collective goals. Given collective leadership is relational, team networks and connections are built on open communication, which creates cohesion and support. Above all, it fosters transparency of individual tasks and goals, and ensures accountability among team members. This is the true culture of collective leadership.

Psychological safety

Amy Edmondson is Novartis Professor of Leadership and Management at Harvard Business School, and has been recognised by the biannual Thinkers50 global ranking of management thinkers since 2011. She coined the term 'psychological safety'—the 'shared belief held by members of a team that the team is safe for interpersonal risk taking'.[5] This concept has great relevance not only to collective leadership, but also to high-performing teams.

The co-pilot

A young co-pilot working for a large commercial airline notices that his pilot-in-command might have made a crucial mistake just before taking off on a long international flight. He's thinking about alerting his superior, but then he remembers the unfavourable comments he received the last time he asked something related to the navigation instruments in the cockpit.

Just under an hour after take-off, the aircraft disappears from air traffic controllers' radar screens. Three years later, the plane is still to be found. It was carrying 12 crew members and 227 passengers from 15 nations.

The story about the co-pilot was inspired by the various scenarios Edmondson shares at the opening of her 'Building a psychologically safe workplace' talk at TEDxHGSE.[6] I would like to propose the lack of psychological safety experienced by the co-pilot (while making clear that Edmondson is not saying this at all in her talk) as a plausible hypothetical explanation for the disappearance of Malaysia Airlines Flight 370 on 8 March 2014.

Edmondson investigated the rates of medication errors made among physicians using the research question: Do better teams make fewer mistakes? Her study yielded unexpected results. While the data made it appear that better teams made more mistakes than other teams, it was more likely that better teams' willingness to discuss mistakes meant they were making fewer mistakes or the same level of mistakes. However, they learned faster and improved their performance by reducing future error rates.

Successful teams have a climate of openness and trust that enables them to talk openly about their mistakes. This allows them to learn more and solve problems better. In a climate of psychological safety team members are willing to discuss errors, because they realise that everyone's voice is necessary if the team is to learn and succeed. Teams operating in environments without psychological safety are motivated by fear, self-protection and managing the impression of competence — like the young pilot in the story.

Research evidence documenting human error resulting from failures in interpersonal communication (such as a breakdown in communication between a captain, co-pilot and air traffic control) reveals it to be one of the main causes of aircraft fatalities.[7, 8, 9] This is despite the last three decades of training aimed at encouraging crew members to speak up.

More than likely, this is a legacy of the 'single-pilot tradition' in aviation. The days of pilot as single, fearless males, white scarves trailing, challenging the elements in an open cockpit, are well and truly gone! But, like heroic leadership, this stereotype of independence, masculinity, bravery and control still lives on as a pervasive myth.

The reality is that, as with leadership, the aviation context has changed dramatically. Aircrafts are more complex, and the limitations and fallibility of pilots has become more evident. Today, effective flight crew performance requires teamwork. In the broader context this involves aircraft maintenance crews, air traffic control and so on. From this perspective, the aviation industry is a microcosm for collective leadership, where everyone has an active voice and takes responsibility for success.

High-performing teams have the collective understanding (psychological safety) that allows them to feel comfortable being themselves — without fear of being punished, rejected or embarrassed when they do so. This enables their members to voice their mistakes and concerns, ask stupid questions and volunteer new ideas.

Edmondson offers three tips for bringing everyone's brains and voices into play to create a work climate where catastrophes are less likely:

1. Frame work as learning opportunity, not an execution problem.

2. Acknowledge your fallibility ('I might be missing something here that I need from you').

3. Model curiosity by asking a lot questions. This creates a necessity for voice.

These practices acknowledge the uncertainties faced by teams, recognise the interdependence of team members, and provide the rationale and safety for people to speak up. Edmondson refers to such practice as 'inclusive leadership'.

Psychological safety also enables learning from failures or mistakes,[10] and promotes creativity[11] and innovation.[12]

Project Aristotle

In 2012 Google conducted Project Aristotle to investigate a very important question: Why do some Google teams shine while others stumble?

Google studied hundreds of teams in a quest to understand what makes or breaks a successful team. Their research revealed that psychological safety was the factor that makes the real difference when it comes to teamwork.[13]

* * *

A collective focus or orientation puts group goals and combined action before self-interest, reinforcing the desire to help the team. It also provides satisfaction and feelings of achievement from team successes. Additionally, collective leadership sets an expectation that all group members will contribute, which becomes a far more likely outcome. This is particularly relevant to global virtual teams, which include members from multiple cultures who must work together while being separated by time and space.

The case for collective leadership is compelling and justified, as the following ten benefits to organisations show:

1. It breaks down the silos created by organic growth or acquisitions.
2. It increases the social capital and knowledge sharing across the organisation.
3. It dissolves power structures and bureaucracies that obstruct change.
4. It creates stronger identification with the team/organisation, and more collective responsibility and mutual accountability.
5. It makes greater use of people's knowledge, skills and expertise.
6. It creates higher levels of commitment and engagement.
7. It improves inclusion, the acceptance of multiple voices, and celebrates diversity.
8. Change and innovation are accepted and implemented more quickly.
9. It ensures superior coordination of action (execution) and performance.
10. It produces unprecedented levels of performance and business or community results.

Five real-life examples

Collective, collaborative or shared leadership is more likely to emerge in health care and knowledge-intensive industries, or in sports teams and community-based organisations. Here are five real-life examples that illustrate the benefits of collective leadership.

Example 1: Cisco's C-LEAD

Under the C-LEAD (collaborate, learn, execute, accelerate, disrupt) model, innovation is an absolute imperative and the focus is on 'super teams' not 'superstars'.[14] Cisco claims to have made millions of dollars of savings and generated billions of dollars of new businesses as a result.

In 2008 Cisco was one of the largest technology companies in the world, with about 73 000 employees in 83 countries and revenue of more than $40 billion. However, the company's growth began to decline as other technology giants matured, and it pursued higher revenue outside its core market with mixed results. In response, Cisco decided to abandon its traditional top-down leadership structure for a collaborative model built on a series of boards and councils. Annmarie Neal, the chief talent officer at the time, says it wasn't an easy transition but that eventually, competition for power and resources was replaced by shared responsibility for success.[15]

Example 2: The King's Fund

The King's Fund is a think tank and policy and research institute that was engaged to help reform national health and social care in the UK.[16] The institute has helped shape policy and practice with the vision that 'the best possible care is available to all'. It used 'research and analysis', developed 'individuals, teams and organisations', promoted 'understanding of the health and social care system', and brought 'people together to learn, share knowledge and debate'.[17]

The project was the biggest shake-up of the National Health Service (NHS) since it was established in 1948. NHS providers and commissioners ended the 2015-16 tax year with the highest cumulative in NHS deficit on record: £1.85 billion. The required efficiency savings totalled £22 billion. The King's Fund subsequently adopted a collective leadership approach, with the conviction that this was the only way high-quality, compassionate and continually improving care would develop and thrive. This entailed interacting with everyone and exercising leadership at every level by shaping the emerging culture of the organisation.

Example 3: The All Blacks

The All Blacks (the New Zealand national men's rugby team) has, over a 100-year period, an extraordinary 75 per cent test match winning record. An evaluation of the collective leadership approach used by the All Blacks management shows that the club's winning ethos is embodied in its organisational culture. Remarkably, this was established when the first national team was formed in 1903 and has been nurtured, developed, and sustained ever since.[18]

Leading from 'the back seat of the bus', as they put it, the original senior players proved extremely effective in keeping their winning culture intact as the organisational and socio-cultural environment evolved around them. The key finding of the study was the presence of a strong senior collective leadership in the team. It also provided evidence that the collective leadership model of the All Blacks instilled a commitment to honesty, team evaluation, and reflection. The following narratives that emerged from the study illuminate this.

As noted by Johnson and others in 'Collective Leadership: A Case Study of the All Blacks', in instances where leadership was not visible in key roles:

> ...then another part of the All Black organization assumed leadership responsibility. If the coaching was poor, for instance, the players stepped up. Alternatively, when there were player misdemeanours, the coach stood up and when hard decisions had to be made, the administrators/board made them.

The bottom line was that in the All Blacks organisation, at any time, there was someone ready and willing to step up for the collective benefit of the club. Arguably, such findings can be transferable to other sports teams, businesses, and communal contexts in assisting their organisational development.

Example 4: IDEO

IDEO is a global design company that helps organisations innovate by building learning platforms and tools to unlock creativity and empower people. IDEO, founded in Palo Alto, California, in 1991, has the philosophy that innovation in public life starts with people, creates human-centred products, services, spaces and organisations that empower communities, cities and even countries.

John Foster, IDEO's former head of Talent and Organization, described the firm as a leaderful organisation made up of a flat hierarchy, with project teams that support individual autonomy, creativity, and the socialisation of recruits and engineers. In the foreword to Joseph Raelin's book *The Leaderful Fieldbook: Strategies and activities for developing leadership in everyone*, Foster explains that 'collaborative leadership is a very effective model for creating breakthrough results in very challenging circumstances'.[19]

David Kelley is the founder, chairman and managing partner of IDEO, and professor at Stanford University, where he teaches design thinking. This is a creative problem-solving approach any business or profession can use to tackle complex challenges and achieve extraordinary results. It is now used by leading world brands such as Apple, Google, GE and Samsung. Kelley states:

> … the main tenet of design thinking is empathy for the people you're trying to design for. Leadership is exactly the same thing — building empathy for the people that you're entrusted to help.[20]

This statement articulates relational and collective leadership: relational leadership occurs beyond hierarchies, position or roles.

Example 5: Alcoholics Anonymous

Alcoholics Anonymous (AA) is an international fellowship founded in 1935 by Bill Wilson and Dr Bob Smith in Akron, Ohio, with the purpose to assist alcoholics to achieve sobriety and stay sober. In his book *The Different Drum: Community making and peace*, psychiatrist and bestselling author Scott Peck (1936–2005) refers to AA as the most successful community organisation in the world.

The first principle of AA states that '…the ultimate authority for AA world services should always reside in the collective conscience of our whole fellowship'. Its first tradition reads: 'Each member…is but a small part of a great whole. AA must continue to live or most of us will surely die. Hence our common welfare comes first.'[21] These declarations are testimony to its collective culture of leadership and egalitarian relations.[22]

There are many who have publicly spoken about the benefits they derived from attending AA. Some examples include Al Pacino, who confessed, 'I had to go to Alcoholics Anonymous. I am not ashamed of that.' Alec Baldwin admitted that AA had helped him for more than 30 years. Bradley Cooper spoke openly about how his addiction had negatively affected the amount of work he was offered. Anthony

Hopkins, Liza Minnelli, Mel Gibson, Lindsay Lohan, Demi Moore, Kate Moss and Samuel L. Jackson are other examples.[23]

* * *

Clearly, collective leadership is a relational, fluid and evolving approach where multiple (if not all) employees or individuals assume leadership roles in a group or organisation in response to specific situations, settings or contexts. It means everyone takes responsibility for the success of the organisation as a whole. With everyone taking responsibility for the organisation's success, power needs to be distributed to where the right capabilities, expertise, and passion exist.

Collective leadership, therefore, requires networking and collaboration across organisational boundaries. It draws on a firm's social capital and builds on the knowledge, skills and abilities of all employees. It requires individuals to engage in high levels of communication and to work openly and interdependently to share ideas and have a joint vision and common goals. When done successfully, collective leadership benefits everyone, allows for more innovation, allows organisations to adapt to change quickly, and delivers outstanding performance and results.

The next chapter explores leadership development.

Conclusion

Collective leadership reduces followers' dependency on their leaders and increases the performance of teams and organisations. It also diminishes or eliminates the diffusion of responsibility and social loafing among team members. This is because collective leadership empowers people by providing them with a voice and enhancing their belief in their own abilities to cope, perform successfully and be more creative. Psychological safety is critical to achieve collective leadership, teamwork and high performance.

Collective leadership helps organisations become more collaborative and innovative and to mobilise towards collective action and change. Individuals feel valued and respected in a

(continued)

---

collective leadership paradigm. They are motivated by a common purpose and work across boundaries to use collective knowledge and skills to achieve common goals. Furthermore, as shown in the examples, collective leadership can lead to breakthrough results, and transform the lives of individuals, organisations and entire social systems.

Insight questions

- Have you ever experienced leadership dependency, diffusion of responsibility or social loafing in a group or team environment?

- How did it look?

- How did it feel?

- How would you describe the current degree of empowerment in your team?

- What behaviours do you see that reflect psychological safety in your team?

- What behaviours may indicate that psychological safety is missing in your team?

- Are your team members able to raise problems and tough issues to the team?

- Do your team members speak openly about their concerns?

- It is safe to take risks in your team?

- Are the unique talents and skills of your team members valued and utilised?

- What benefits could be achieved within your team/ organisation by fostering a culture of true collective leadership?

- How might you achieve this?

CHAPTER 11
Leadership development

Letting go of the ball

In 2010 I had the privilege of working with a multiple-premiership-winning Australian Football League club in Victoria — the heartland of the sport and a place where winning, and leading a team to success, resonates deeply. The club was not going well, which is why I was asked to come in.

The club's premier side had an inconsistent track record, with an unpredictable pattern of wins and losses, uneven gamesmanship and players facing media scrutiny. The player leadership group told me that before each game they put a strategy in place — how they would play to win, according to their strengths, and the strengths and failings of the opposing team. Every player understood it and knew their role on the field. But on the day, the strategy was forgotten and the players didn't stick to the plan. We circled

(continued)

around this for a while and explanations were put forward, none of which rang true. Finally, the captain fronted up to the issue. With a wry smile, he cut to the chase. 'What it comes down to is that we all like to have possession of the ball', he said.

A few of the group shifted in their seats uncomfortably. Others chuckled in acknowledgement. Everyone knew he had nailed it. With the ball came the chance of glory, of wresting control and taking the team to a win in front of the crowd and the television-watching nation. For young men in a testosterone-driven environment, competing for their place in the team and a sense of their own identity as elite sportsmen, the temptation to emerge as the maverick game-changer who would ditch the strategy, break the rules and emerge as a star player was too much. When I had asked them individually on previous occasions about the most important thing for them in the context of the game, they all said the same thing: 'Don't let the team down.' Yet, this was exactly what they were doing.

What these young players were striving to come to terms with was the difference between understanding leadership, and enacting it. As we worked together to develop the club's leadership capacity across the board, it emerged that their success depended on the players finding the trust, maturity and inner strength to relinquish their chance of personal glory for the sake of the team. They would still get a win, but they would get it together.

For some, it took a painful initiation to come to terms with the idea. When one young player was sanctioned for disgraceful behaviour in a nightclub and bringing the club's name into disrepute, he was suspended indefinitely. Not only did he not have the ball, he was no longer even on the field. He had really let the team down. What he came to recognise was that had he behaved in a manner the club required, he would have exhibited the leadership qualities it expected of every player, in every circumstance on and off the field.

The embodiment of leadership lies in the collective game. Only then does the magic begin, because all members truly exercise leadership.

Leadership development relates to the collective capability of teams and organisations to produce direction, alignment and commitment.[1] This collective capability is developed by focusing on the processes of leadership rather than the attributes or properties of individual leaders. It means treating the collective entity (team, organisation or community) as a single unit of focus and measurement. Let's first look at the various forms of leadership that have emerged in recent times, then the different approaches to developing and building this capability.

Most recent forms of leadership

To fully understand the latest advancements in leadership development, it is critical to first understand the most advanced forms of leadership. Collective leadership practices have emerged in recent years in response to the increasingly complex contexts in which teams and organisations now operate. Effective teams, for example, usually have multiple individuals leading (exercising influence), depending on the situation. This way of leading is rarely learned in leadership development programs. Most teams learn it as they do their everyday work, which applies especially to the geographically dispersed teams that are now the norm for many organisations. This form of mutual influence is the essence of distributed leadership. Central to this is the concept of 'pluralistic leadership', which is an umbrella term used by researchers to label various forms of leadership (for example, collective, collaborative, shared, distributive and emergent).[2] I will use these terms interchangeably.

Collective leadership means several things and has various implications. First, it means abandoning the view that properties or attributes (for example, traits, personality or competencies) belong only to certain individuals traditionally called leaders. Second, it means that everyone in a team or organisation takes responsibility for the progress and success of the unit, not just their own jobs or roles. This implies the teams/organisations distribute the leadership capability to the most suitable expertise, capability, motivation or voice. This type of leadership emerges (hence the term 'emergent' leadership) through the social/relational practice as the team works on a project. This contrasts with, for example, assigning a formal leader before a project begins, which is known as 'leadership-as-practice' (L-A-P).[3] The priority, focus and unit of analysis becomes the actual 'practice of leadership', which is referred to as 'leaderful practice'.[4]

Leaderful practices are collective, concurrent, collaborative and compassionate — attributes called the four Cs.

- *Collective.* Any member in the team/organisation can provide leadership at any given time to mobilise action or make decisions on behalf of others.

- *Concurrent.* Leadership emerges from everywhere, and at any time, as important issues arise; no-one depends on one individual or authority.

- *Collaborative.* Anyone can speak for the whole team/ organisation, and advocate a point of view they believe can contribute to the common good.

- *Compassionate.* Everyone is committed to preserving each other's dignity, regardless of background, social status or point of view.

As you can imagine, in practice, transitioning from traditional conditioned and constrained mindsets of current organisational and managerial conventions can be extremely challenging. In fact, one of the most common questions I am asked on this topic is how to make this transition.

> Collective leadership means everyone takes responsibility for the progress and success of the unit, not just their own jobs or roles.

In the example of the AFL club, the 'team' (unit of focus) had to learn how to best play the ball by using the players on the field (the practice of leadership). Their real challenge is not knowing what to do, but actually getting themselves to do it. This is leaderful practice. In this chapter we'll explore the most effective methods of making the transition.

What is leadership development?

First let me clarify some of the often-confusing terminology by reinforcing the distinctions between 'management development' and 'leadership development', and between 'leader development' and 'leadership development'. While these activities complement each other, and often even overlap, they are actually different beyond pure semantics. From a practical perspective, these differences matter because they determine the choices leadership development practitioners make in using the multiple approaches (methods, strategies and techniques) available to affect organisational goals, outcomes and results.

Management vs leadership development

Management development or education relates broadly to literacy (education and training). This includes the curriculum and various processes by which managers learn and improve their management skills.[5] The emphasis is on managers changing or acquiring specific types of knowledge, skills and abilities (KSA) to enhance their performance. (Most recently KSA has expanded to include 'other attributes' — KSAOs.)[6] Managers, however, may exercise leadership some of the time, most of the time or never.

Traditional MBA programs, for example, provide management education by covering a wide range of topics such as finance, accounting, strategy, marketing, human resources, entrepreneurship and so on. Many contemporary MBAs also offer 'leadership skills'. The goal is to prepare a generalist or well-rounded professional who is ready to manage any business or organisation. It's important to remember, however, that an effective leader is more than just an effective manager. Anyone in a management position is often assumed to be a leader. In reality, however, not all managers provide leadership. Conversely, not all leaders manage. Leadership can also come from people not in management positions (informal leaders).

John Kotter, professor of Leadership at the Harvard Business School, talks about the distinction between managing and leading. While this distinction has been done to death in text books, business magazines and blogs, it is still falling on deaf ears. This is obvious when people in organisations say 'our leaders' in reference to their senior managers.

In a nutshell, managing is about improving the status quo by setting and consolidating the efficiency of processes and systems that produce a well-oiled machine. Leadership, in contrast, is concerned with the future, people, and driving change. This includes what's often called 'softer skills', such as providing a vision, generating values, inspiring people and setting the right culture. This thinking is in line with one of the most prominent pioneers of contemporary leadership studies, Warren Bennis (1925–2014), who saw the writing on the wall as far back as 1989: 'To survive in the twenty-first century, we are going to need a new generation of leaders—leaders, not managers.'[7]

Leader vs leadership development

Leader development entails developing individual leaders (human capital). Another way to put it is that leader development focuses solely on expanding an individual's capacity.

Leadership development, on the other hand, relates to extracting the potential benefits inherent in relationships (social and relational capital). Social capital (SC) relates to the benefits derived from the strength of connections among individuals within an organisation.[8] Relational capital (RC) relates to the benefits derived from external relationships (for example, those between firms, suppliers, and other institutions and people).[9] From this perspective, the popular dictum of 'it is not what you know but who you know' holds true. Clearly, in looking at these critical dimensions of leadership development, the relevance of relational leadership (RL) becomes critical.

> Leadership, in contrast, is concerned with the future, people, and driving change.

RL focuses on achieving effective interpersonal relationships as a social process of mutual influence and collective endeavour. It also covers the communication and relational dynamics that occur during the collaborative achievement of organisational goals, as opposed to focusing on the attributes or behaviour of individuals.[10]

While leader and leadership development are different, they do complement each other. Leader development is one of the foundations of leadership development. It is driven by personal goals, uses coaching as the main method, and yields individual outcomes and results. It does not necessarily build teams or leadership capacity in organisations. In contrast, leadership development is driven by collective goals, requires shared meaning with others, uses a wide range of methods, and generates collective outcomes and results. They each use different processes and require different knowledge and skills from leadership development practitioners.

The shift in focus from behaviours or competencies to leadership as a relational process poses a challenge for designing and delivering leadership development programs (LDPs). This is because developing individuals is markedly different from developing teams and organisations. It is critical to link individual development objectives with an organisation's strategic goals to achieve a collective impact and results. Hence, the design and selection of suitable learning strategies is paramount.

Leadership development best practices

A global study my colleagues and I conducted in 2015 identified 14 best-practice principles of LDPs.[11] The study involved analysing primary data (interviews, direct observations and an online survey) and secondary data (documentary analysis, analysis of archival records and end-of-program participant evaluations). It also incorporated an extensive review of the extant literature and external benchmarking of current industry best practices used in 18 global companies: AT&T, BP, Boeing, Cisco, Citibank, Colgate-Palmolive, Dell, Ericsson, FedEx, GE, HP, IBM, Johnson & Johnson, Motorola, PepsiCo, Prudential, Shell and Vodafone.

The following principles are common to the successful design and delivery of LDPs.

1. CEO's commitment

Top management commitment emphasises the importance of equipping participants with the leadership capability to achieve the organisation's long-term goals. The strategy needs to be supported by a strong commitment from the CEO and other senior managers. It is consistent with the message that top management needs to communicate clearly and allow people to tackle strategic challenges.

2. Strategic orientation, alignment and scope

Program participants are grouped across organisational levels, divisions, departments and geographical regions to work on strategic projects that address some of the organisation's current challenges. Strong strategic orientation, alignment and scope come through integrating the program's curriculum with a subset of features and activities aligned with business goals, and the development of leaders capable of developing the business. Examples of such projects include finding ways to reduce costs, attract clients, improve quality or innovate.

In our study, for example, the organisation under investigation during its journey of 181 years had grown significantly in the most recent decade, and survived major challenges such as financial crises, fierce competition and incorporation of great technological advancements while meeting socio-ecological requirements, and mergers, acquisitions and joint ventures. A critical challenge was to generate and maintain a healthy pipeline of leaders with strategic thinking, global business acumen and intercultural competence. With 55 per cent of its business in emerging markets such as China, the firm needed leaders able to adapt to cultural and market needs, and progressively shift to decentralised and collaborative decision making, while promoting and preserving the company's unique culture, values and behaviour.

3. Senior management's involvement

The active involvement of senior managers in the program delivery usually entails the CEO, vice-president or member of the executive management team being guest speakers at team-based strategic project presentations. Senior executives should consider implementing projects that can add value to the business.

There are many organisations that have used senior leaders in their leadership development initiatives. At PepsiCo, for example, former CEO Roger Enrico spent 100 days a year running development programs for top executives. General Electric (GE) has a leadership centre, where executives at all levels are largely responsible for running activities. At Dell, former vice chairman Mort Topfer was a sponsor and coach of the leadership development program. Compaq, Hewlett-Packard, Johnson & Johnson, Shell, ServiceMaster and McKesson have adopted similar initiatives.

4. Clear and relevant program goals and objectives

The goals of leadership development programs need to be specific to each organisation. Some examples include:

- to contribute to creating a common understanding of the group's values, vision, strategy and way of working

- to develop people and their leadership capabilities

- to help participants be aware of how their actions and decisions affect the group's results.

These goals help turn individual technical experts or contributors (professional groups) into leaders of teams, and strategy implementers (middle and senior managers) into strategic thinkers. The goals and objectives should follow the best-practice principles in that they are tied to specific business imperatives.

Leaders must develop a global mindset to face complex challenges, innovate and inspire others, and acquire self-reliant leadership development. This is also consistent with the notion that there is a key competitive advantage in attracting and developing leaders who not only operate effectively across cultures but also influence and motivate people at a global level.

5. Careful selection and mix of participants

Candidates should not necessarily come from the same organisational levels, types of roles or geographical regions. In fact, the aim should be to seek diversity. This supports a matrix structure that encourages collaboration and decentralised decision making, despite the inevitable hierarchical managerial structures, roles and responsibilities. This mix helps participants gain new perspectives and learn from meeting and working with employees outside their peer groups. Further, it promotes cultural diversity and shared organisational values, and promotes a common language and consistent meaning across the organisation. Finally, this approach aims to break down silos or barriers between divisions and teams by promoting cooperation and collaboration. This is reinforced as groups of participants work together on the projects mentioned in principle 2.

6. Comprehensive and integrated assessment

A comprehensive and integrated pre-assessment process should include two key components:

1. individual assessment (for example, personality assessment or strengths finder)

2. an integrated 360-degree feedback assessment using leadership competencies clustered in core meta-competencies (for example, leading people, leading business, delivering results). Ideally, it also includes dimensions such as the level of pressure participants are working under to deliver results; the degree to which their teams have the capabilities, resources, systems and processes to achieve their objectives; and items related to the degree and pace at which changes are taking place.

Using adaptive or meta-competencies, rather than the many common complex competency models of leadership development, is highly desirable. Our research found that the Chase Manhattan Bank's competency models comprised 250 competencies. In contrast, the frameworks of companies such IBM and 3M comprised 11 and 12 competencies respectively.

7. Thorough preparation process

This includes three components:

1. a goal-setting discussion with line managers
2. initial development of a personal development plan (PDP) or personal action plan (PAP)
3. strategic project preparations.

This last feature allows participants to get to know each other by engaging as a virtual team. Virtual teams are critical for global organisations. Cisco's C-LEAD model and Executive Action Learning Forum are examples of how a company has successfully used work projects to uncover strategic opportunities.

8. Pre-entry feedback/coaching sessions

Participants should receive feedback on their assessments during a one-to-one pre-entry feedback/coaching session at least one week before their immersion in a one-week intensive residential program. While this format may vary, live-in experience is highly desirable; it allows participants to bond so they can together deal with the inevitable obstacles and challenges during the experience.

Ideally, the feedback sessions should be conducted by the same facilitators—usually two—that deliver the program. This allows the facilitators get to know each participant's specific issues and challenges, and so enables better coaching.

9. Coaching and peer coaching

Facilitators then are in an ideal position to provide coaching or feedback to individuals and to the group. Coaching is an effective short-term leadership development activity with a strong focus on goal setting, feedback and performance, and it is designed to highlight strengths and skills gaps.

It's important to point out here that this setting is very different from traditional one-to-one coaching, in that the actual coaching process (questioning and feedback) takes place throughout the experience of the group interacting, as opposed to relying on the narratives between a coach and participant (or counterpart) in closed-door conversations. In other words, coaches can witness how each group member behaves in the group. Facilitators/coaches have the unique opportunity to coach the group at any moment by stopping the 'action' and inviting the group as a unit to observe, reflect on and discuss the group dynamics and immediate consequences. The skill of knowing how to bring this direct and instant awareness to groups while they are working is called 'immediacy'. It is one of the most valuable skills any facilitator can have and it is an absolute requirement for some of the most effective and state-of-the-art leadership development approaches.

It is good practice to also integrate peer coaching in LDPs. Peer coaching entails arranging performance partners to achieve new behaviour, increase organisational effectiveness, and improve personal and team productivity. It aims at enhancing personal and professional development, as well as team development. To this end, participants are paired with a coaching counterpart and introduced to a suitable coaching model or approach that they can use during and after the program. Vodafone, Dell and PricewaterhouseCoopers have used this type of coaching to accelerate learning and culture change.

Interestingly, the evaluation results of our study found that several individuals had kept up the coaching relationships they had formed years before. These relationships had usually been formed with employees in other countries with whom they had established regular contact.

10. Highly experiential approach

Perhaps one of the strongest features we identified in our research via documentary analysis, direct observations and interviews is the fact that LDPs need an experiential approach. The practice of experience-driven leadership development entails driving learning through working collaboratively on projects and challenges that address the program goals and objectives. This should be achieved through a progressive escalation in intensity and complexity of activities. In this way, participants acquire knowledge and perspectives by working together, reflecting and collectively debriefing.

This process should be driven by the experiential learning cycle, which includes the following key stages: concrete experience, abstract conceptualisation, reflective observation and active experimentation. This is a powerful way to contextualise the training and enhance the transfer of knowledge and skills.[12]

Active learning involves emotionally intense, team-focused experiences that directly address the immediate needs of the organisation. In this way, it encourages participants to learn with and from each other, while finding solutions to immediate real problems. This links leadership development to business problems. AT&T, Boeing, Cisco, Citibank, GE, Johnson & Johnson, Motorola, Prudential Insurance and Shell use this approach.

11. Reflective learning and journaling

Reflective learning and journaling expand on the approach. At the end of each activity participants gather to debrief. During these small group sessions, team members learn about group processes and dynamics and the impact their individual communication styles have on the group. This process should be followed by participants taking the time to record their reflections, which provides gains in self-efficacy, changes in interpersonal behaviour and improves performance.[13]

12. Building social capital through networking

Networking is a strong feature of contemporary organisations. The coming together of participants from different geographical regions, cultures and levels of the organisation generates a unique social networking experience that creates strong emotional bonds. The quality of these relationships is at the heart of social capital — the benefits created by leveraging networks to achieve positive business results. Such benefits include the informal relationships that promote cooperation between individuals, as well as the reciprocity and reliability that comes from such relationships. The strength of these ties is very similar to those between immediate family members, close friends or good neighbours, and is called 'bonding capital'.

Interestingly, but not surprising, this is what a program facilitator said during an interview as part of the evaluation component of the study we conducted:

> **It is not uncommon for participants to declare at the end of the program that they got to know some of the members of their working teams better than some of their closest friends or family members.**

From this perspective, social capital is an extremely valuable resource that can be converted into economic capital. The response by this research participant is a good example:

> **For me, the best takeaway was learning a new negotiation vendor strategy from a European colleague. When I got back home, I applied this new negotiation approach and, in less than a year, I was able to generate savings of just over $100 000.**

A lack of social capital can reinforce company silos and delay coordinating action across the organisation, due to impoverished decision-making. On the other hand, strong social capital breaks organisational silos, establishes more cohesive teams, and facilitates the flow of information and resources. As result, organisations can better identify and react to threats and opportunities.

Ericsson is good an example of an organisation we found through our research that makes extensive use of social networks, as part of its Excellerate Global Leadership Program.

13. Program follow-up

It is important that participants reinforce their learnings after completing a leadership development program, including implementing action plans through:

- a follow-up discussion with their line manager to review how their personal development plans will be implemented, how the expected changes will be demonstrated in their leadership behaviour, and to ascertain the support and resources they will require

- completing at least two e-learning modules related to the content of the program.

In addition, it is highly recommended that participants:

- seek coaching from their line managers on actions defined in their personal development plans so the follow-up becomes a continuous process rather than a one-off review

- seek a mentor and become a mentor for someone else within the company

- consider continuing the peer-coaching relationships initiated during the program. As I mentioned previously, this often happens by default, which indicates how valuable these relationships can be.

14. Evaluation

Evaluation is a critical component of LDPs. Regrettably, while 86 per cent of organisations evaluate at the level of participants' reactions (satisfaction) immediately after their executive programs, only 11 per cent evaluate the impact of their programs at the organisational level, and only 3 per cent assess the ROI of the initiatives.[14]

The case for more LDP evaluations is compelling. PricewaterhouseCooper's 2015 Global CEO survey shows 81 per cent of CEOs rate their LDPs as less than highly effective. Korn Ferry Institute's 2015 'Real world leadership' survey indicates that less than 20 per cent of respondents say they have the leaders they need to deliver on strategic priorities.[15] Deloitte's 2015 *Global Human Capital Trends Report* surveyed 2200 global HR leaders and found that 86 per cent believed their organisation's future depended on the effectiveness of their leadership pipelines. However, only 13 per cent were confident about their succession plans, and 54 per cent reported damage to their businesses due to talent shortages.[16] The 2016 Harvard *State of Leadership Development* research report surveyed more than 700 individuals from companies around the world, 56 per cent of which were line managers and 44 per cent were learning and development managers working with companies with more than 10 000 people. Not surprisingly, it identified the following results:

- only 7 per cent of respondents believed their programs were best in class (these were twice as likely to drive the firm's financial and competitive performance)

- 50 per cent of best-in-class organisations considered leadership development a strategic priority compared with 28 per cent of respondents from all other groups

- three-quarters of best-in-class programs had strong CEO support, compared with half of all companies

- only 26 per cent of respondents acknowledged having a way to measure the impact of their leadership development programs.[17]

In our research, we found that best-practice organisations are committed to evaluating the effectiveness of their LDPs. This entails considering the evaluation process at all phases of program design and implementation.

There are three main approaches that can be used to evaluate the impact of LDPs.

Kirkpatrick model

The Kirkpatrick model has a strong legacy over 55 years and comprises four levels of evaluation.[18]

Level 1 (reaction) represents 'the degree to which participants find the program favourable, engaging and relevant to their jobs'. The methods used to measure these outcomes are end-of-program evaluations — commonly referred to as 'happy sheets', and participants' verbal comments at the end, or soon after the completion, of the program.

In our study, for example, we analysed a total of 335 participants' end-of-program evaluation responses from a period of four years and five months. This was done using a standardised questionnaire that included rating scales, closed-ended items and open-ended items to accommodate free-text responses. We also used an online questionnaire that was sent a few days after the end of the program and covered the following seven dimensions:

1. general impression of the program

2. materials received

3. exercises

4. extent to which the course met expectations

5. knowledge, insights and information acquired

6. whether the training had well-defined objectives

7. whether they would recommend the program to others.

Participants reported satisfaction rates between 'excellent' and 'good', averaging 93.5 per cent upon completion of the program. This information was used to make future versions of the program better (for example, to correct what participants disliked in the program and add what they felt was absent).

Level 2 (learning) represents 'the degree to which participants acquire the intended knowledge, skills, attitude, confidence and commitment'. This is measured through observations, interviews and participant self-assessment conducted months after the end of the program. In our study, the five most common areas in which participants reported advancing their knowledge, skills or attitudes were self-awareness, team building, listening, coaching, and being able to see the 'big picture'. These results were consistent with achievement of the learning objectives and the acquisition of knowledge relating to the company's core leadership competencies. By and large, this indicated that participants acquired the intended knowledge.

Level 3 (behaviour) measures participants' transfer of learning. It addresses questions such as whether the participants' learning affected their behaviour, and to what degree participants applied what they had learned to their jobs. The methods used to assess these behavioural outcomes are observations from line managers and senior managers, and interviews over time, including years after the end of the program.

The following statements are from people who had completed the program two years before our evaluation:

It was very useful getting a better picture of myself—a critique, and to see and accept. I'm now pacing myself more. I used to have a more confrontational style. During the training, I became cognizant of my own pushing style with others in the room. The syndicate room discussions were also very useful, with very interesting dynamics.

The last day's exercise was the most confronting. I learnt to listen, be quite and receive feedback from others. It was humbling and confronting, but I enjoyed it.

Now, I'm less of a control freak.

Level 4 (results) measures the impact on the business. It addresses questions such as whether participants' behavioural changes have affected the business. The measures of these outcomes are usually quantitative (for example, reduced costs, savings, improved quality, increased in productivity, or higher revenue).

In our study, respondents were asked to indicate their answers using a five-point scale (low–slightly–moderate–significant–high). In response to the question, 'To what degree would you say you're able to have a greater impact on the business today (either directly or indirectly), as result of having attended the program?', almost 67 per cent answered that they had had a significant to high impact after the program, and close to 21 per cent believed they were having a moderate impact on the business. Interestingly, the average across the four regions (Americas, Middle East and Asia, North Central Europe, and South Europe and Africa) was remarkably similar, indicating the that program was being implemented consistently. One participant commented:

> I now feel I lead the team whereas before I was managing the team. The team own the product, where 12 months ago I owned the product and the team followed my every decision/command. Last year my team produced $6 million of product, this year we are heading towards $17.5 million.

Return on investment (ROI) is a common term used to refer to outcomes at this level. ROI, however, can be a contentious issue as it can be measured using a wide range of indicators that reflect whether a leadership program has delivered value. It may not necessarily mean a financial return that can be easily captured on the balance sheet. It may include, for example, indirect returns or financial windfalls as individuals apply new skills, such as attracting new clients, building better teams, coordinating actions/executing more effectively, or positive changes in management/leadership style, improved quality of work and higher productivity.

In fact, it may be argued that financial ROI is a poor, unreliable and insufficient measure of outcomes and success. One potential approach to evaluating the impact of leadership development is to use measures of wellbeing and engagement as indicators of improvement; these outcomes that are not directly quantifiable but are nonetheless real and assessable. An alternative approach would be to use return on expectations (ROE).[19] This would represent a comprehensive measurement of all the benefits (quantitative and qualitative) of a program.

Anecdotally, the term 'value for money' (VfM) is sometimes used in certain industries, such as large infrastructure projects and government agencies. Although its definition may differ each time, value for money commonly refers to measuring the quality and benefits of a purchase against the purchase's monetary cost. This term can cover many diverse factors such as plant costs and maintenance.

ROI methodology

The second evaluation approach for measuring the success of leadership development programs is the ROI methodology used by the ROI Institute.[20] This is similar to the previous method and comprises a process model with a framework and operating standards. It captures performance metrics from simple satisfaction scores to financial impact. The most difference is that there are six levels: 0 (inputs or indicators), 1 (reaction and planned action); 2 (learning); 3 (application and implementation); 4 (impact); 5 (ROI).

Level 5 (ROI) has a strong financial benefits focus and compares monetary benefits from the program with program costs. This is calculated using three key measures: benefit–cost ratio (BCR), ROI (percentage), and payback period.

The model also collects the appropriate (qualitative and quantitative) data on the performance of a variety of initiatives and program types, which can allow practitioners to isolate the effects of the program from other influences. The evaluation results aim to provide metrics and ROI reports acceptable to financial executives and stakeholders. This methodology is reportedly being used by more than 5000 organisations.

Customised systems

The third evaluation approach is to design a customised evaluation system or approach by integrating elements of the Kirkpatrick model and the ROI methodology. Best-practice organisations that have done so include BP, Colgate-Palmolive and IBM.

Mixed-method triangulation design

Regardless of your approach to evaluating LDPs, I strongly recommend using a mixed-method triangulation design.[21] 'Triangulation' means using two or more methods of collecting data to check the results from more than one perspective. The rationale for using triangulation is to show that different methods lead to the same result—which demonstrates confidence. A mixed-method entails evaluating a program by collecting and analysing both quantitative and qualitative data, which is integrated or mixed.

Triangulation not only applies to data collection and analysis techniques, but also to data sources. In our study, for example, we collected quantitative and qualitative data via a survey and interviews respectively. However, we also use three sources of data collection: primary data, secondary data and a comprehensive review of the relevant literature.

Primary data refers to that observed or collected directly. Secondary data includes that collected in the past or by other parties. Our primary data included interviews, direct observations and an online survey with program participants. Our secondary data comprised a documentary analysis (for example, program materials used over the past ten years for the same program), and analysis of end-of-program participant evaluations collected by other parties over ten years. It also included interviews with senior company executives, most of whom were the managers of participants and had nominated their direct reports to attend the program. Feedback from a company vice-president, for example, included that some of the participants he worked with were displaying 'less hiding behaviour'. By this, he meant that the individuals were more transparent in talking to him when something went wrong, as opposed to covering up their actions to avoid accountability (as they had done in the past).

Various managers reported that some of their direct reports had become team players after previously working as loners. They promoted teamwork a lot more and took less individual credit for successes. Other feedback from senior managers was that some of the participants had concluded that they did not want to become leaders and had decided to remain individual contributors or technician experts. This was very valuable information not only for the company, but also for the individuals.

We also interviewed the facilitators, which added another dimension to the feedback. This was particularly useful in that it enabled us to have very detailed technical conversations relating to the design and delivery of the program. This assisted greatly in addressing some of our 'how' or 'why' research questions, cross-checking data, and in forming our final recommendations to the organisation. It also assisted us to better understand the causal link between observations during the program, participants' feedback and their managers' feedback. This was very useful in making recommendations for practitioners who design and deliver LDPs, which I cover in the next section.

Practical implications for OD practitioners and using the findings

The responses of the lead facilitator, combined with the evidence-based practices found in the relevant literature, offered some of the most relevant practical implications of the findings from our study for practitioners who design, implement and evaluate leadership development programs.

These findings helped shed light on two key research questions: what features of the program help produce the results achieved, and how did this happen?

The sequence of activities during the week-long residential program was found to be critical. More specifically, a three-stage process was identified: entry, learning from experience, and integration. These are best represented by a 'U' shape as participants go through various psychological states, depicted in figure 11.1.

Figure 11.1: delivery sequence

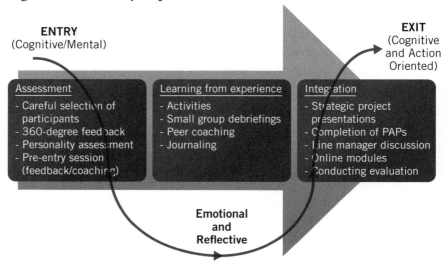

During the entry stage, participants were taken through an 'assessment' phase, which is cognitive in nature. This included 360-degree feedback, personality assessment and a pre-entry feedback/coaching session. The 'learning from experience' stage followed, characterised by exposing participants to activities grounded in experiential methods and action learning principles, followed by debriefing. Participants progressively transitioned from a surface-type of mental labour to a much deeper emotional and reflective psychological state, culminating at the inflection point at the bottom of the U-shape.

During the 'integration' or exit stage, participants progressively emerged at the end of the U shape. Psychologically they emerged in a more cognitive state, where they integrate their experiences and plan for action. This stage includes presenting the strategic projects, completing their personal action plans, having a follow-up discussion with their line manager, and completing the online modules.

The integration of the 14 principles described earlier in this chapter is critical. It requires a progressive sequencing of the content features that enable the delivery of the intended results. This finding addressed our first research question. From this perspective, practitioners who wish to achieve the desired results from their LDPs should carefully follow four key practices:

1. Design a range of progressive experiences, bearing in mind their duration and intensity, that will take participants through an increasingly challenging sequence of rich development exercises and balance three key elements: assessment, challenge and support (for example, strategic scope, high-level sponsorship, careful selection of participants, 360 feedback and personality assessment).

2. Create psychological safety — the belief help by all group or team members that it is psychologically safe for them to take interpersonal risks in that particular group or team. This is critical to giving a voice to the learning group for teamwork, team learning and organisational learning. This stage should never be undermined or rushed, and skipping it could easily compromise the entire learning experience.

3. Deliver the program as a well-integrated developmental experience, using not only the prepared content and process but, most importantly, weaving into it the emerging issue the group brings. This includes recognising the unique group dynamics, parallel processes, and the emergence or replication of here-and-now dynamics, communication patterns or leadership styles that reflect their unique organisational culture, and how those are likely to affect the business as a whole (for example, teamwork, overall execution of the company strategy, productivity, customer service, adaptability to change, capacity to innovate, degree of shared leadership and so on).

4. Facilitate participants' ability to make sense of, and learn from, their own experiences and each other. Participants should have ample opportunities to debrief and reflect on each program phase. This is where 'here and now' mind/paradigm-shifting learning experiences occur; these enable participants to create

a new narrative of who they are as leaders and what it means to exercise leadership. This should be done while carefully monitoring participants' reactions to the chain of psychological dimensions (namely, cognitive/mental, emotional and behavioural) that comprise each of the elements in the previous three stages.

Additional unsolicited feedback

Finally, it is important to highlight that many of the individuals interviewed as part of the evaluation provided unsolicited feedback in relation to the evaluation itself. They stated that the evaluation helped them to reflect on the program and it reinforced what they had learned and how they had applied it. This is represented in this participant's response: 'This is how the evaluation should be. Like this interview. If you send an email nothing happens.' This response, like others to this effect, reinforces two key points.

First, conducting evaluations is an important component of leadership development. It reinforces reflection on the experience and extends the life of the program and the impact it has on participants and their organisations.

Second, the evaluation process boosts employee engagement and loyalty to the organisation by inviting participants to tell their stories.

Benefits of conducting evaluations

The benefits of LDP evaluations, then, include being able to ascertain the value of the organisation's current LDP, including its ROI or ROE, and improving the program using the evaluation results as well as benchmarking current practices against world's best practice.

Additional, often unseen, benefits are that evaluation creates opportunities to recognise the contribution of specific departments and/ or professional groups (such as learning and organisational development) that provide such services. Furthermore, when completed, evaluations can be written and published as case studies. They can then be used to position the organisation as an industry leader, as was the case in the study we conducted.

Insights from the AFL team

Like most sports teams, the AFL team I mentioned at the opening of this chapter placed great importance on evaluating their performance. In fact, evaluating performance was a natural and constant practice, as you would expect from any elite team. As I have explained, most teams evaluate performance using a combination of measures: score (of course), feedback from the players and perceptions provided by the coaches. The role of the coaches and players was to improve the team's performance. To this end, the head coach was evaluated separately.

I gained three valuable insights from that AFL team that organisations can apply to improve the evaluation of their LDPs.

Having only a single and short-term focus on the scoreboard can be dangerous. It's just as futile as a business pursuing quarterly revenue goals to the detriment of long-term financial success, or becoming obsessed with quantifying every dollar spent on developing people. In fact, in some instances, this focus can do harm in the long term and be an inaccurate reflection of what is being achieved. The key is to balance the focus on the scoreboard and the game with an understanding of what's really happening, how it is happening, and why it is happening. Let's remember that improving performance is one of the main reasons, if not *the* main reason, for conducting impact evaluations.

The back-and-forth flow of feedback between players and the coach was critical to the high performance of the AFL team. This offered players insights, ideas and strategies to improve their game. In a similar way, program evaluations provide key stakeholders with valuable feedback on performance targets and company goals. But the AFL team was using even more sophisticated and powerful evaluation techniques than the ones I have explained in this chapter. I recall how the players watched endless videos of their games and their competing teams. Among other things, they were able to evaluate their own performances using objective and

(continued)

unbiased feedback. This feedback was combined with quantifiable indicators such as the number of ball possessions by each player.

Finally, the AFL team always evaluated what they did well (their strengths and successes) as emphatically as what they did wrong (their weakness and failures). Understanding what they were doing well was arguably more critical than understanding what they could improve.

Evaluation of strengths is ignored in too many organisations. Our conditioning allows us to identify weakness more easily than strengths when we're evaluating performance. It's much easier to become excellent at something the team is doing well than it is to become good at something the team is doing not so well. This, of course, is not to say that serious deficiencies should be ignored.

Focusing on strengths and successes serves two very important purposes. First, it provides self-belief, self-assurance and confidence. Second, it enables team members to identify, appreciate and celebrate progress. The accumulation of progress eventually produces a tsunami of success. Critical to this, then, is not so much the actual results of an evaluation, but rather the way in which they are used.

Conclusion

Organisations will benefit from assessing their LDPs against the best practices presented here. They will also benefit from ensuring their initiatives have a significant impact on the business and that their leadership pipeline is ready and able to execute the strategies critical for long-term success.

There are 12 important lessons, which I'm tuning into recommendations, for OD and L&D practitioners in conducting evaluations of leadership development programs:

1. Design your LDP by building evaluation into the program.

2. Find different ways to demonstrate the value of LDPs.

3. Don't be afraid to ask. If organisations don't ask, because they assume it's too difficult to measure value, they will never know how to improve their programs.

4. Formulate clear and relevant research questions (What? Who? When? How? Why?).

5. Use an overarching model or framework.

6. Use a mixed-method design by combining quantitative and qualitative measures.

7. Qualitative responses can be good indicators of value that can be translated into figures.

8. Keep it simple. However, always use triangulation to combine objective, self-reported (subjective) and multi-rater measures to capture different perspectives.

9. Make sure you identify and involve key stakeholders.

10. Value (ROI, ROE or VfM) can emerge from the least expected sources.

11. Conduct follow-ups to ascertain long-term benefits.

12. Document the evaluation by writing a case study whenever possible.

Insight questions

- Is your organisation responsive to the distinction between leaders and leadership development?

- To what extent does your organisation use leadership development best practices?

- Does your organisation conduct leadership development evaluations?

- If not, is your organisation fully aware of the benefits of conducting leadership development evaluations?

CHAPTER 12

Leadership development methods

Putting the cat on the table

I learned a new expression — 'putting the cat on the table' — while running a leadership development program with a group of 25 executives from a global company in Finland in 2013. The 'cat' appeared over dinner at the end of the third day of a five-day residential program. One of the Finnish executives sitting next to me commented on a critical insight that had come up for him during the day. This was the importance of having tough, or difficult, conversations to produce effective and high-performing teams. He explained that there is a popular Finnish saying that translates to 'putting the cat on the table'. This expression means to speak frankly and honestly to others about difficult subjects. It is used when there is an issue that needs to be discussed but that

(continued)

may be uncomfortable to talk about. He said it was important to do this with all valued human relationships. As the discussion unfolded, and two others joined the conversation, it emerged that when 'putting the cat on the table' it was important to be direct, honest, open and respectful. They also commented on the need to be courageous in standing up for one's beliefs even if this meant voicing unpopular views. They said it generated greater accountability and real teamwork.

This dinner conversation and the expression that sparked it reminds me of what I have observed over and over again about what it takes to bring groups of individuals together to accomplish great and meaningful things. (And what it takes to turn low-performing or mediocre teams into high-performing teams for large, complex and high-value collaborative projects.) One of the main barriers is an inability (a reluctance due to fear) to 'tell their truth', become vulnerable with each other, and trust each other.

Once everyone's truth has been told, listened to, honoured and respected—once the cat has been put on the table—contrary to what many people think or expect, tensions diffuse and relationships improve. If done effectively, the rules of the game change. Transformation has taken place and there is only *one* perspective. What a great example of the value of so-called soft skills with a hard edge! The impossible is seen to be possible, then becomes possible, and the team is ready to move mountains. I don't want to make it sound easy, but it is doable.

* * *

I mentioned earlier that the first thing people ask when I talk about collective leadership is 'What is it?' Not surprisingly, once I have explained it, the next question is, 'How do organisations transition from traditional leadership practices to a more collective form of leadership?' My answer is, by *doing*. How, for example, did you learn to ride a bicycle if not by getting on it until you got the hang of it? This exemplifies the nature of the methodologies and approaches I explain in this chapter.

Joseph Raelin is Knowles Chair of Practice-Oriented Education, and professor of Management in the D'Amore-McKim School of Business at Northeastern University. In his paper 'It's not about the leaders: It's about the practice of leadership', he puts it this way: 'Leadership development … requires an acute immersion into the practices that are embedded within the lived experience of the participants.'[1] This means that the engagement needs to occur within a group while working on their routine issues, but using new approaches in their interactions.

I will outline some of the most prominent methodologies that are used to build leadership capability within organisations. While these methods are unique in their assumptions and theoretical foundations, they have two main commonalities: their purpose and focus, and the mechanisms, or processes and techniques.

Broadly speaking, their purpose is to help organisations build leadership capacity. They do so by using the organisation's social and relational capital to establish the direction, alignment and commitment required to coordinate the necessary action to achieve its goals. Therefore, the focus, unit of analysis and measurement of any leadership development approach covers the collective entity — the group, team, organisation or community. Such methods use facilitation and group work — and arguably training — as their modus operandi.

Facilitation

The word 'facilitation' comes from the Latin *facilis*, which means 'easy', an adjective formed from the verb *facere* (to do). It literally means make something (an action or process) easy or easier.

Roger Schwarz is president and CEO of Roger Schwarz & Associates, and adjunct professor at American University in Washington, DC. In his book *The Skilled Facilitator*, he defines group facilitation as:

> …a process in which a person whose selection is acceptable to all members of the group, is substantively neutral, and has no substantive decision-making authority diagnoses and intervenes to help a group improve how it identifies and solves problems and makes decisions

to increase the group's effectiveness. The facilitator's main task is to help the group increase its effectiveness by improving its process and structure.[2]

Facilitation, like leadership, is about relationships. At the most basic level, facilitation covers four dimensions.

The first is the content or the task (the 'what'). This includes what the group is trying to achieve, and its associated components (for example, data, products, services, plans and decisions).

The second relates to the processes the group uses to achieve what it's supposed to achieve (the 'how'), which is also referred to as the 'maintenance' function of the group. This includes communication patterns, group dynamics and group cohesion.

The third dimension relates to the way participants react to the agenda, activities and each other. This includes the interpersonal or social dimension of the group. For example, it may cover issues related to communication, such as the language being used, the feelings of group members, and the levels of trust and openness.

> Facilitation, like leadership, is about relationships.

The fourth dimension relates to the intra-personal psychological reactions of participants — for example, how individuals' self-esteem or self-efficacy is affected by being part of the group.

Facilitators require self-awareness, self-management, social awareness and relationship management skills (those relating to emotional intelligence as a meta-competency) to achieve results. Effective facilitation also requires conducting multiple activities before, during and after working with groups.

John Heron is founder and director of the Human Potential Research Project, director of the International Centre for Co-operative Inquiry, and a group facilitator and author. In his book *The Complete Facilitator's Handbook*, he notes there are 'six dimensions of facilitation: planning, meaning, confronting, feeling, structuring and valuing. And three modes of facilitation: hierarchical, cooperative and autonomous.'[3]

Facilitating leadership involves enabling the group to adapt, solve problems and improve performance collectively, while learning by often creating or inventing new ways of relating. The key words are 'collectively' and 'learning'.

Leadership facilitation aims to involve people at all organisational levels. Leadership facilitators use a wide range of organisational development (OD) strategies or systematic approaches to improve organisational effectiveness by aligning strategy, people and processes. They help organisations achieve their goals by driving significant change, improving performance and achieving a competitive advantage. Leadership facilitators also enable groups to learn from their own interactions. This learning includes inventing new ways of relating as the group/organisation faces new challenges. The best way to describe leadership facilitators is as 'change agents'.

Change agents help organisations transform by focusing on effectiveness, improvement and development. They focus on people and their interactions and draw on a wide range of disciplines, such as psychology, sociology, anthropology, systems dynamics, coaching and creativity.

There are many approaches that can be used to facilitate leadership, but effective facilitation depends on responding to the specific needs of the group at any given time. Change agents using the outline here need to know group dynamic techniques and adult learning principles, have high-level facilitation skills, know social systems theory, and have specific knowledge and experience (and sometimes accreditation) in using their method of choice.

In this chapter I explain ten approaches:

1. action learning
2. case-in-point method
3. Tavistock-style group relations learning
4. Open Space Technology
5. sociometry, sociodrama and other action methods
6. Social Network Analysis

7. Creative Problem Solving

8. team coaching

9. teaming

10. eclectic interventions.

Entire books about each of these methodologies are available. My aim here is to introduce you to the basics and share some of my personal experiences in using them.

1. Action learning

Reg Revans (1907–2003), professor, original management thinker, and 1928 Olympic silver medallist in long jump and triple jump, developed the action learning concept in the 1940s. The World Institute for Action Learning defines action learning as:

> a process that involves a small group working on real problems, taking action, and learning as individuals, as a team, and as an organization. It helps organizations develop creative, flexible and successful strategies to pressing problems.[4]

Action learning is a self-managed learning process based on asking open questions to explore a challenge using the critical thinking of peers. Learning is an ongoing process that entails attentive listening with an open and inquisitive mind, while asking probing questions with the intention to understand and explore new ideas.

The main focus of action learning is learning by doing while addressing real-time challenges and solving problems through reflection, supported by a group of colleagues with the intention of getting things done.[5] Embedded in action learning is a strong emphasis on asking penetrating questions that promote reflection. This, in turn, engages participants in emotionally intense and team-focused experiences that directly address the immediate needs that strategically impact the organisation.[6]

Revans's dictum was: 'There can be no learning without action, and no (sober and deliberate) action without learning.'[7] Learning is 'cradled in the task', and happens by reflecting upon the experience of taking action.

Revans maintained that people and organisations flourish when their learning is equal to, or greater than, the rate of environmental change. This is his learning equation:

$$L = P + Q$$

L (learning) is a combination of P (programmed knowledge, or traditional instruction) and Q (questioning, and insight from new questions and reflection).[8]

Because action learning is highly collaborative, in that it requires individuals and groups working together on addressing each other's and common problems, it 'provides the means of linking leadership development with the solution of business problems'.[9]

Dr Michael Marquardt is a professor of Human Resource Development and International Affairs at George Washington University. He is also on the board of the World Institute for Action Learning. He explains that people become smarter and more creative in the process of solving problems together, and that everyone needs to provide leadership. Marquardt emphasises that the power of learning by going through the action learning process occurs naturally. He also highlights its cost-effectiveness by saying that participants get more done more in two hours of action learning than they would in two months using typical problem solving.[10]

Organisations with best-practice global leadership development programs that incorporate action learning include Johnson & Johnson and Cisco;[11] Motorola;[12] Boeing;[13] Alcoa, DuPont and Nokia;[14] and Ameritech, Citibank, General Electric, Prudential Assurance, Shell, the University of Michigan and Harvard Business School.[15]

Dr Yury Boshyk is an adviser, educator, coach, facilitator, speaker and author with over 25 years of experience in executive and management education with global companies, Chairman of Global

Executive Learning Network and the founder of Business Driven Action Learning. He says that action learning has evolved to generate multiple approaches, including 'traditional' (or Classic or Gold Standard) Action Learning; Americanised (or modified) Action Learning; Action Reflection Learning (ARL); Business Driven Action Learning (BDAL); and Learning Coach-Led Action Learning (WIAL).[16]

2. Case-in-point method

Case-in-point was pioneered, and is taught, by the program faculty at Harvard Kennedy School. This approach is explained by Ron Heifetz, Alexander Grashow and Marty Linsky in their 2009 book *The Practice of Adaptive Leadership: Tools and tactics for changing your organization and the world*. Case-in-point is a practical way to help organisations create cultures of adaptive leadership.[17] In essence, it is an experiential and provocative learning method to assist groups to deal with real-time issues during discussions facilitated by a trained practitioner.

As with any facilitation approach, case-in-point aims to enhance learning through self-discovery, as opposed to teaching by prescription via lectures or a traditional training style. It uses questioning and reflecting techniques instead of providing answers or solutions. Case-in-point promotes risk-taking, provocation, challenges and tension, by encouraging participants to test assumptions and behaviour ('putting the cat on the table'). The aim is to empower and build capabilities by bringing out the group's unique untapped resources, as opposed to emphasising its deficiencies through real-time leadership.

It's important to remember that case-in-point is based on the principles of adaptive leadership. This aims to mobilise groups to make changes, which requires the case-in-point facilitator to 'turn up the heat'. Heifetz and his colleagues use the analogy of a pressure cooker, saying the facilitator needs to put enough pressure into the system to enable change but not blow up the cooker.

It is not without reason that Heifetz and Linsky warn that exercising adaptive leadership is dangerous, but they suggest that it is worth the risk:

> By making the lives of people around you better, leadership provides meaning in life. It creates purpose. We believe that every human being has something unique to offer, and that a larger sense of purpose comes from using that gift to help your organisations, families, or communities thrive.[18]

This work entails igniting and sustaining the unusual levels of energy people need to be 'pumped up' enough to change the status quo.

The case-in-point facilitator needs to help people become aware of the group dynamics, patterns, connections, and factions or coalitions that emerge, develop, strengthen, diminish or die, as well as how individual members and the group react. The facilitator may choose 'critical incidents' (interactions that capture critical group dynamics or behavioural patterns) to challenge individuals or the group. For example, the facilitator could focus at the individual level and say something like, 'I noticed that when Mary speaks, some of you keep cutting her off, or don't pay attention to her'; or, 'I've noticed several times that when Tom says something, almost immediately Andrew has also something to say.'

Alternatively, the facilitator could focus at the group level and ask questions such as, 'What is the group doing right now?'; 'How is what's happening now serving the group?'; 'What's the group try to tell us right now?'; 'What's the group trying to achieve right now?'; 'What is this heated argument telling us about the group?'; or, 'If you could change something within the group right now, what would it be?'

Notice that in both instances, immediacy, or the ability to use the present moment or situation to help the group see what is happening, is important. Immediacy is arguably the most powerful technique a facilitator can use, as it invites the group to examine itself from a new perspective by considering what is going on in their relationships, as opposed to focusing on the content of the conversation. This often unveils a new reality, or dimension of it. In other words, a 'blind spot' for the group.

With a more strategic intent, and at the broader organisational level, the facilitator might ask the group, 'How does this pattern of interaction

over the past 20 minutes relate to the other patterns in the organisation?';
or, 'What patterns have emerged that resemble those of your teams?' This
time the questions are designed to help participants connect with other
parts of the organisation. This can also uncover blind spots.

Uncovering multiple small blind spots at different levels can result in
the discovery of a whole new reality. This is true leadership development
at its best! Why? Because participants can see the system in a new light.
A new reality has manifested right before them and, because people can
only act in a world they can see, new possibilities appear.

> *Uncovering multiple small blind spots at different levels can result in the discovery of a whole new reality.*

Michael Johnstone and Maxime Fern,
executive directors at Vantage Point
Consulting and adjunct faculty members
at Harvard Kennedy School, offer the
following ground rules, or rules of
engagement, for facilitators to establish
a climate of psychological safety to ensure challenges are constructive,
effective, and productive:

- Explain to participants that the learning will be experiential and
  that tensions and 'heat' are likely to emerge.

- Encourage participants to listen and respect each other.
  Emphasise, however, that being overly 'polite' by pretending
  or keeping social masks is undesirable. To this end, effective
  listening and statements of facts over opinions is important.

- Clearly distinguish between case-in-point (plenary sessions in
  which the entire group participates) and debriefing events (small
  group sessions that take place in separate rooms, often referred
  to as 'syndicate' rooms).

- Never take participants' negative reactions towards you
  personally. Instead, remain detached, focus on the group, use
  deflecting techniques and encourage participation. Remember,
  you are there for the group — not the other way around.

- Keep in mind that no-one, including you, is flawless.
  Acknowledge your own shortcomings by recognising and
  apologising, if necessary, for any mistakes.

- Treat all your interpretations as hypotheses — not as fact or truths. Invite people to consider their own reactions, thoughts and emotions, as data can help clarify what is happening in the group.

- Respect individuals' confidentiality.

- Take responsibility for your own actions and reject the blame game.

- Invite people to do the same by owning their piece of any 'mess' by asking them to reflect on how they might have contributed to it and how they can find a solution.[19]

Leaders, educators, trainers, facilitators, and consultants from corporate, public, and not-for-profit organisations around the world undertake case-in-point training each year.

3. Tavistock-style group relations learning

The Tavistock method, commonly known as group relations, originated from the work of Wilfred Bion (1897–1979), an influential British psychoanalyst who was president of the British Psychoanalytical Society from 1962 to 1965. He held a series of small study groups at the Centre for Applied Social Research in London's Tavistock Institute of Human Relations.[20]

Based on the work of prominent psychoanalyst Melanie Klein (1882–1960), central to this method is to consider both the individual and the group the individual belongs to. It is a way to conceptualise a group as a collective entity, as opposed to clusters of individuals. The group relations model views the group as a holistic system, and so questions such as why individual group members act differently are of little interest. From this perspective, the organisation is a system with conscious and unconscious subsystems that relate to and mirror one another. The overall assumption is that unconscious behaviour and its dynamics leads to a much deeper understanding of organisational behaviour.

There are three basic assumptions about group relations:

1. *Dependency*—the assumption that individuals depend on imagined or internalised parental figures or systems. People (employees) experience helplessness, powerlessness, frustration and disempowerment if this dependency is not realised. For example, employees question why their boss is not giving them more attention. Such projections indicate anxiety, insecurity and emotional immaturity, and manifest in people asking for structure by saying things like, 'We need a committee to deal with or investigate what happened.'

2. *Fight/flight*—ways of coping with the anxiety associated with organisational life. Fight reactions manifest in aggression towards the self or others, and can appear as competition, jealousy, envy, boycotting, back-stabbing, fighting for a team position, rivalry, and battling for honoured relationships with authority figures. Flight reactions can be avoidance of others, being sick, or resigning. Flight reactions also include avoiding threatening situations or emotions, rationalisation or intellectualisation (for example, talking about others to avoid self-examination).

3. *Pairing*—individuals or groups pairing up with individuals and/or subgroups that are perceived to be powerful, as a way to cope with anxiety, loneliness and alienation. From this perspective, the unconscious need to feel secure and create a fantasy takes place in pairs. Pairing also means splitting up when diversity creates anxiety. In such cases, the individuals or groups attempt to split the whole into smaller, more comfortable units. It also manifests in ganging up against perceived aggressors or authority figures. Intra- and intergroup conflict can result from pairings.

The Tavistock approach also considers other issues, such as anxiety, boundaries, roles, representation, authority, leadership (and followership), relationships and relatedness. Larry Hirschhorn, member, founder and past president of the International Society for the Psychoanalytic Study of Organizations, who also teaches Psychodynamics of Organizations at the University of Pennsylvania, is the author of several books, including

The Workplace Within and *The Psychodynamics of Organizations,* in which he explains these concepts in detail.

The Tavistock method attempts to see organisational life more fully and promotes the integration of intellectual capacity and emotional intelligence to produce creative and visionary leadership. It is an accelerated immersive learning experience that enables participants to understand effective leadership and better understand their own and others' resistance to change. Like in the case-in-point method, the group relations model is a 'real-time learning laboratory'. This uses plenary and small group sessions, referred to as 'search groups', in which 12 participants work with a consultant to analyse their leadership and experiment creatively to test and expand their repertoire of behaviour.

Group relations learning is done on three levels. The first is how individuals behave irrationally in the face of authority. The second is recognising that group functioning and collaborative working can be obstructed by irrational thinking by group members. The third level is the shifting to new ways of thinking. This happens only when participants discover their capacity to doubt the validity of previously unquestionable truths or realities. So, they need to learn how to be both involved and detached at the same time. This ability to reflect on one's own thinking and involvement (self-observation) is crucial to learning experientially.

As with case-in-point, leaders, educators, trainers, facilitators and consultants from corporate, public and not-for-profit organisations around the world undertake Tavistock training each year.

4. Open Space Technology

Harrison Owen, president of H.H. Owen and Company, author and consultant, created Open Space Technology (OST)—a purpose-driven leadership methodology—in the early 1980s.

OST facilitates meetings and groups of five to 1000 individuals to organise themselves to solve complex conflicts and urgent issues, including running conferences, symposiums or community events. The process begins without a formal agenda, just a theme or purpose;

and participants create the agenda during first 30 to 90 minutes of the process. Despite this apparent lack of structure, OST has four elements: four guiding principles, a law, certain allocated roles and operating mechanisms, and expected outcomes.[21]

Michael Lindfield, an organisational development consultant at Boeing in Seattle, refers to OST as a '... way of creating an environment where things are possible'. He adds:

> ... much of our business culture is driven by a need to control outcomes. While this may be good when attempting to control and reduce variations in our manufacturing processes, it is counter-productive when applied to the creative thinking process ... [22]

This is a good example of how bureaucracies, while maintaining businesses through systems of control, fail to support regeneration through impassioned vision and new possibilities.

OST uses an emergent agenda, which means it develops as participants engage in the process. Therefore, while it's impossible to know exactly what will happen during the meeting, the following outcomes or promises are built into the process:

- Participant's most important issues are raised, tabled, and discussed.

- Participants will take on all issues that they can do something about.

- The most important meeting items, such as discussions, ideas and recommendations, will be tabled in a report and disseminated to everyone.

- The group will prioritise the issues and actions documented, should they be required to.

- The group will draft an action plan for issues with a high priority, should time allow.

- Participants will feel engaged and energised by the process.

In preparation for running OST it is important to design good documentation of ideas, recommendations, discussions and action steps. OST uses the following four elements:

1. *The circle*—the initial group shape or social architecture that promotes a sense of community. Concentric circles can be used for very large groups. It also symbolises the non-hierarchical nature of collective leadership, in which everyone has an equal voice and is connected to everyone else.

2. *The breath*—symbolises vitality, as it establishes a rhythm in any project, person, organisation or community.

3. *The bulletin board*—provides a central place for people to post messages about what they wish to explore and what they offer. It allows people to make informed choices on what they do during the sessions.

4. *The marketplace*—the space in which people interact and share their concerns and business. This is where it all happens.

OST also has four guiding principles:

1. Whoever comes to the sessions is the right person.

2. Whatever happens is the only thing that could have happened.

3. Whenever it starts is the right time.

4. Whenever it's over, it's over.

OST, therefore, is centred on the present. It is governed by what is called 'the law of mobility' or 'law of two feet', which states that participants are responsible for their own learning. They are encouraged to move to, or visit, the various concurrent small groups formed to meet their needs or concerns, where they can either learn by listening and/or contribute.

Further, OST has four mechanisms:

1. The 'open space' meeting will begin with a brief introduction by the sponsor and a nominated lead facilitator.

2. The sponsor introduces the purpose and the facilitator explains the 'self-organising' process called 'open space'.

3. The group creates the working agenda as individuals post their issues in bulletin-board style.

4. Each 'convener' of a breakout session takes responsibility for naming the issue (or invitation), posting it on the bulletin board, assigning a space and time to meet, and later initiating the conversation and taking notes.

Michael Herman is an internationally recognised leader in the practice of OST who offers OST coaching and facilitation. He explains:

…leaders do inviting as an active business practice…and mostly what these leaders invite is leadership. They invite people to take responsibility, to take the lead, on the issues and opportunities they care about personally.[23]

OST is at its best when the issues the issues are complex, the passion is high, the team make up is diverse, and the time available is limited. Participants pledge to tell the truth and have no preconceived notions, say what it is, when it is, without blame or judgement, pay attention to what has heart and meaning, and be open to outcomes without attachment.

In a nutshell, Open Space supports integrative thinking, creativity, and behaviour based on interdependency. The connection between OST and collective leadership is that the group as a collective entity will, and must, generate its own leadership.

Both OST and leadership are characterised by the absence of control. OST is a space for empowerment. The underlying assumption is that leadership that is defined as control can only fail.

5. Sociometry, sociodrama and other action methods

Jacob Moreno, M.D. (1890–1974) was a psychiatrist, psychosociologist, educator, and a leading social scientist. He invented sociometry, sociodrama and psychodrama by pioneer role theory, group psychotherapy, creativity and spontaneity.

The three approaches are also referred to as 'action methods', which involve visual and role-based approaches to group work, and have been applied to multiple contexts such as organisations, schools and communities.

Psychodrama deals with the individual (the protagonist) and the issues they face, and has been used in leadership training.[24] Sociometry is a flexible, creative and spontaneous method for measuring social relationships and working with groups. The term 'sociometry' comes from the Latin terms *socius*, which means 'social', and *metrum*, which means 'measure'. Sociometry, then, measures how individuals associate with each other in trying to achieve something together.

Sociometry explores the formation, evolution and functioning of groups, and heightens awareness while identifying, correcting and sharpening perceptions by revealing covert group dynamics. Sociometry assesses interpersonal and intergroup relationships by asking about and making explicit the invisible patterns of preferences in a group, using either graphs or human sculptures. Group members make informed choices while being aware of the effect their choices have on the group. It can be used for personal and professional development, including making job and relationship choices, team building, conflict management, review meetings, strategic planning, training and development events and community consultation.[25]

Sociodrama is a learning process that uses group dynamics and enactment as a way to address human relationship issues. As a deep action method that deals with intergroup relations and collective ideologies, its focus is on the group as an entity, and it's rooted in role theory. Sociodrama assumes that individuals are role players with a repertoire available to them, and some of the roles dominate their behaviour. Every culture has a certain set of roles that, to varying degrees, it imposes upon its members.

Sociodrama helps groups clarify their values and review their behaviour through sessions that foster creativity and drive change. It can also promote critical thinking and group bonding and collaboration, foster motivation, and help groups clarify their purpose, values and priorities. During this process, a group selects and performs a chosen social situation that is common to them. Unlike role playing, sociodrama deepens and broadens the enactment, making it a kinesthetic, emotional and educational method. A trained facilitator directs and supervises the process.

The sculpture of an executive team

Some years ago, a client asked me to work with his senior management team. 'We are experiencing some differences of opinion', he said. He explained that they had tried 'everything', but nothing had worked.

The seven executives and I met away from their offices one early morning. I invited them into a spacious room that contained only chairs. Clearly this attracted their attention as they were used to sitting around a boardroom table. Following a brief exchange of pleasantries, I asked them to imagine that the room was the 'business world' in which they worked. I also explained that everything I asked them to do had to be done in absolute silence. We then put all of the chairs against one wall and I asked them to position themselves anywhere in the room that represented where saw themselves within the team. The CEO placed himself in the centre of the room and the others chose spots scattered around. Noticeably, one based himself by the door.

I asked them to reflect on the configuration, then reposition themselves by considering whether the distances apart represented the way they felt about how they were working as a team. The CEO didn't move. Three of them got closer to each other, and slightly away from the CEO. Two, although somewhat away from each other, were between the faction of three and the person who remained by the door. I then asked them to tell the rest of the team, starting with the CEO, how they felt in that position at that time, and why they chose that particular position in relation to the other team members, and in relation to the team. Briefly, this is what they said.

First, the CEO explained that he felt alone in middle of the room, which, he added, was a surprise. 'I placed myself in the centre of the room because I'm the CEO and this represents my role as the one who represents the organisation and everyone looks to for answers and direction.' The cluster of three said they felt completely exhausted and frustrated by a lack of trust and cooperation. They explained that they felt they were carrying the rest of the team—hence their exhaustion. The next two said they felt unappreciated and frustrated, as they believed their points of view and decisions were constantly scrutinised by the rest of the team, especially the CEO. Finally, the person by the door said he was feeling very isolated and unhappy. He explained that he was still feeling an outsider after six months on the team. The rest of the session was devoted to examining in detail their perspective, relationship and dynamics.

The interesting thing about this sociometric sculpture was that the seven members of this executive team—as they openly acknowledged later—had never said to each other what they said at that session, despite the fact they had had endless discussions. It became possible because each person had to physically express themselves in silence. This kind of expression was not filtered.

As you probably have already heard, body language speaks louder than words. Once 'the cat was out of the bag' (their secret had been made public), the individuals' verbal statements had to be congruent with the strength of their bodily statements. There was no hiding their true feelings, which was a relief for the whole team. From then on, their conversations were much more authentic and transparent, with the clear intention of working more effectively and productively as an executive team.

Incidentally, once the real conversations were unpacked, it was equally important to help the team notice what remained unsaid. For example, at the beginning no-one referred to the 'team'. It was all about them as individuals. But as they learned to attend to each other's needs, things changed and progressively, 'we' became a natural part of their vocabulary.

(continued)

During the following sessions, the conversations also became more lively and open. Each member learned to express what they needed in relation to responsibilities and communication, and they addressed the barriers in working together. They even started referring to their own teams with a sense of excitement and progress. During our sixth and last session, at the end of three months, I invited them to do another team sculpture. This time they could reach each other by just extending their arms. They had visibly shifted towards establishing more effective relationships.

6. Social Network Analysis

Social Network Analysis (SNA) refers to the set of processes, theories and tools for understanding the network's structures and relationships. In SNA, the 'nodes' represent the people and the 'links' show their relationships, as depicted in the following image.

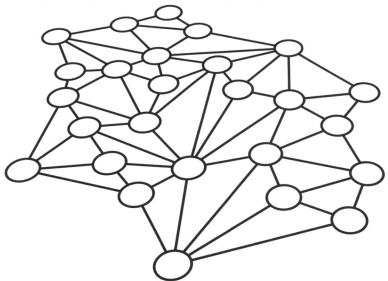

Source: © jmcreation/Getty Images

Practitioners of SNA collect data, which they analyse using special software, and produce network maps or graphic representations of the connections between the nodes. As you can probably tell, SNA extends the sociometric approach.

Linton Freeman is a research professor at the Department of Sociology and Institute for Mathematical Behavioral Sciences at the University of California. In his book *The Development of Social Network Analysis*, he refers to sociometry as the birth of SNA. It represents organisations as social groupings that show certain patterns of interaction evolving over time. SNA aims to identify these structures and patterns, as well as their evolving nature, causes and consequences.[26]

SNA is a relational approach that enables a multiplicity of leadership roles in groups and is well suited to understanding the mechanics of collective or distributed leadership. The analysis of network structures pays attention to the quality of ties between the actors as well as the frequency and intensity of such ties and their configuration. SNA uses visualisation and mathematics to map the structure of relationships between individuals within organisations and other entities within a larger system. This helps explain how social capital is created through an often-complex web of collaborative relationships, which in turn facilitates collective problem-solving and coordinated action to achieve common goals. Understanding how these networks evolve is important in developing leadership capacity.

In 2015 the Center for Creative Leadership conducted a survey to study how organisations develop relationships among individuals, teams and business units to build leadership capacity. The aim was to identify leadership development practitioners' areas of focus by comparing individual (human capital) versus collective (social capital) efforts. The sample included internal and external practitioners from 34 countries across the corporate, government, education and not-for-profit sectors. The results indicated there was a focus on developing human capital and individual leaders rather than on the leadership capacity of collectives. In fact, almost all leadership development practitioners (93 per cent) reported that they focused on improving individuals (usually formal leaders) and their effectiveness for their roles. Significantly fewer practitioners (69 per cent) focused on helping individuals improve the effectiveness of their

> *Well-networked leaders have access to people, information, and resources to help solve problems and create opportunities.*

teams, and fewer still (55 per cent) on helping teams improve their collective leadership capacity. Further, only 64 per cent of respondents believed organisations were effective at developing human capital, and only 44 per cent said organisations were effective at developing social capital. Finally, despite SNA being rated the most effective strategy for helping a group understand its relationships, only 23 per cent used it—the rest just talked about it. [27]

These relational and multilevel views of leadership include the networked patterns of social relationships linking individuals and teams to larger collectives. This leads to new approaches for network-enhancing leadership development to improve the leadership capacity of organisations.

Network leadership

Doug Macnamara is president and CEO of the Banff Centre for Arts and Creativity. He defines network leadership as a next-level systems-thinking form of leadership:

> It requires executives to engage, empower, facilitate, and bring 'connectedness' to an otherwise unwieldy mass of disparate elements. And, it is anchored by a study of the changing dynamics in the environment around us instead of the technical/analytical focus that has many an executive caught up in the tactical. [28]

Networking is a critical leadership component of modern organisations. To be effective, contemporary leaders have to be well-networked. This enables them to access the information, resources, and people required to solve problems effectively and generate opportunities. [29] The Center for Creative Leadership (CCL) advocates that 'networks are the fundamental way in which we can see and measure how collectives are engaging in leadership'. [30]

Charles Palus, senior faculty member in Research, Innovation and Product Development and director of Labs at the CCL, explains:

> People with network perspective understand the dynamic web of connections that have an impact on their work, their leadership, and the leadership culture of their organisation. They can identify patterns of relationships and people in their personal network and the broader

organisational network that will foster strategic success — and those that will inhibit or undermine it.[31]

Networking capabilities are critical to building relational capital. As you may recall, some of the unexpected benefits we found during the case study evaluation of the leadership development program presented in chapter 11 happened through networking. Today digital technology and social media offer great opportunities to reach a global ecosystem of relational capital which can open up endless possibilities.

Herminia Ibarra is a professor of Leadership and Learning, and a professor of Organisational Behaviour at INSEAD and Harvard Business School. In her *Harvard Business Review* article 'How leaders create and use networks', she insists that it is essential for leaders in today's competitive climate to network — that 'what you know is who you know'. Other things (such as experience and qualifications) being equal, it's what gives you an edge. 'It's the relationships that you have that allow you to augment what you know and allow you to take the 'what you know' and actually to translate it into practice, into something the organisation can use. It makes all the difference.'

Ibarra identified three types of networking: operational, personal and strategic. Each has a purpose. Operational networking helps leaders get their work done efficiently by ensuring coordination and cooperation. Personal networking generally is external to the organisation (for example, professional associations or alumni), and becomes a safe forum for development and a foundation for strategic networking. With strategic networking, both vertical and lateral relationships are included. It is key to leverage.

> What differentiates a leader from a manager ... is the ability to figure out where to go and to enlist the people and groups necessary to get there ... some managers ... dismiss such work as too 'political' ... [32]

7. Creative Problem Solving

Creative Problem Solving (CPS) was developed in partnership by two pioneers in the field of creativity and aims at producing new and innovative solutions to problems using a highly structured approach.

Alex Osborn (1888–1966) was an advertising executive who created 'brainstorming' — a creative group technique to solve specific problems by generating a list of ideas from members. Sidney Parnes (1922–2013) was a professor at Buffalo State College in Buffalo, New York, and the co-founder of the International Center for Studies in Creativity.

Overall, the original CPS format is a facilitated process that enables participants to progressively engage their natural creative thinking at various stages of the process. During stage one, the group explores the actual challenge by identifying the actual goal; collecting relevant data; and clarifying the nature of the problem. In stage two, the group generates multiple possible ideas to address those problems. Stage three entails moving from ideas to action planning and implementing solutions.

CPS is different from most creative problem solving or creativity approaches as it uses divergent and convergent thinking at each step of the process – not only when the group generates ideas aimed at solving the problem. Hence, divergent thinking is the beginning of each step, with sole purpose to elicit multiple alternatives (quantity and variety is the goal). Convergent thinking then follows. This is the process of narrowing down or selecting the most suitable solution by evaluating all options available (quality or suitability is now the goal).

Gerard Puccio is chair and professor at the International Center for Studies in Creativity at Buffalo State College, State University of New York. Puccio and his colleagues at Buffalo State, in their book *Creative Leadership: Skills that drive change,* refer to creativity as 'a core leadership competence' and the precursor, or catalyst, to innovation. They define leadership as 'the process of positively influencing people, contexts, and outcomes through a deliberate creative approach that is applied to open-ended, novel, and ambiguous problems — both opportunities and predicaments'.[33] Puccio is the creator of FourSight, a leading assessment tool that matches thinking styles to the CPS process.[34] This instrument enables groups and organisations to boost their critical and creative problem solving while achieving consistent breakthrough results.

Innovation takes bells and b#lls—not just good ideas!

The owner of a grocery shop was really worried about the growing number of mice that were spoiling the bread, biscuits and fruit in his shop. So he bought a big fat cat. The cat enjoyed hunting and killing the mice.

The mice had a brainstorming session to come up with ideas to get rid of the cat. A smart mouse said, 'The cat moves softly. That is the real problem. If we tie a bell around his neck, we'll be fine because we'll be able to hear when he is moving.'

'Yes, that's the answer', yelled the mice.

An older mouse simply asked, 'And who will tie the bell on the cat?'

There was a long silence and that was the end of the meeting.

Three weeks later, the shop was free of mice: the cat had killed them all.

Source: © makar / Shutterstock

There are two morals to this story:
1. There is no innovation without risk!
2. Innovate or die.

Innovation results from applying new and useful ideas (creativity). Many organisations want to achieve it, but—like the mice—they don't want to take risks, so they choose to conform to the status quo ('what is') as opposed to exploring possibilities ('what could be'). They play it safe.

Expecting to innovate by playing it safe is simply unrealistic, but that is what many organisations do. They wait for someone else to try it first.

The price of conformity

Conformity has two great advantages:

1. It enables us to collaborate with others to achieve common goals.

2. It allows us to learn from others by seeing how they test ideas. We observe them, take what's successful and apply it ourselves.

Conformity feels safe and comfortable for some. You don't have to think or do too much. You just have to 'copy' or 'follow'. But if conforming is all we do, we'll never grow. That's a very high price to pay, don't you think?

Growth requires trying new things and taking risks. In addition to creativity (coming up with new and useful ideas), innovation also requires courage and tolerance for failure. Whether in our personal lives or in business, this means investing without a guaranteed return. And, if it doesn't work, it's about being willing to try again and again.

Innovation leadership: nine critical functions

David Gliddon, professor of Business at Penn State University, uses the term 'innovation leadership' to refer to the leadership styles needed for employees to generate the creative ideas that produce innovative products, services and solutions.[35] David Horth is the director of Innovation, Venturing and Partnerships at the Center for Creative Leadership, and Dan Buchner is the founder and principal at Praktikel Innovation in British Columbia, Canada. In their white paper

'Innovation leadership: How to use innovation to lead effectively, work collaboratively, and drive results' they state:

> What leaders need now is innovation leadership. They need it for themselves as they learn to operate in challenging, unpredictable circumstances. They also need to create a climate for innovation within organisations. Innovative systems, tools, and thinking are essential for organisational health and future viability.[36]

Göran Ekvall is Professor Emeritus of Industrial and Organizational Psychology at the University of Lund in Sweden. He identifies nine critical dimensions that support a climate for change and creativity, as well as the leadership values and behaviour that work encourage creative productivity. The following are the dimensions, and questions that will help you ascertain how they relate to your team or organisation.[37]

1. *Challenge.* How challenged, emotionally involved, and committed to their work are your people? They may be engaged by demanding and meaningful work, but do they have, or are they taught, what is needed to meet the challenges ahead?

2. *Freedom.* How free are your team members to decide how to do their jobs? Do they have the resources and the autonomy to effectively make decisions?

3. *Trust/openness.* Do people in your team/organisation feel they can speak their minds and openly offer different views? Can they speak frankly to other employees and to their manager, and do they share mutual respect?

4. *Idea time.* Do your team members have time to think things through, develop new ideas, and produce quality products or services?

5. *Playfulness/humour.* How relaxed is the workplace — is it OK for employees to have and experience fun?

6. *Risk-taking.* Is it OK to fail — or make mistakes — when trying new things? Do your people feel they can take risks?

7. *Idea support.* Do employees have adequate resources to create and new try ideas? Do they feel creative ideas are encouraged? Do your managers listen when ideas are suggested? Do your people feel their ideas are properly considered by management?

8. *Debate.* To what extent do employees engage in lively, constructive debate about relevant issues? Are employees keen to offer ideas and perspectives and do they feel confident that these will be welcomed and can be discussed with their manager and others?

9. *Conflict.* To what degree do your people feel engaged in interpersonal conflict or 'warfare'? Is the emotional tension among employees and managers high, medium, or low? Are there power struggles?

The key question now is, how many boxes can you tick?

If you are serious about innovation, these questions can help you determine the scope and focus of your leadership development interventions.

8. Team coaching

Richard Hackman (1940–2013) was a professor of Social and Organizational Psychology at Harvard University, and a pioneer of the study of team dynamics and team psychology. He says that team coaching is 'an act of leadership, but it is not the only one or necessarily the most consequential one'.

Team leaders can engage in multiple ways to foster team effectiveness. For example, by re-establishing the team's purposes, arranging and coordinating resources, removing organizational barriers, and promoting positive social interactions.[38]

Peter Hawkins is a professor of Leadership at Henley Business School, and the founder and Emeritus Chairman of Bath Consultancy Group. He refers to systemic team coaching as:

…a process by which a team coach works with a whole team, both when they are together and when they are apart, in order to help them

both improve their collective performance and how they work together, and also how they develop their collective leadership to more effectively engage with all their key stakeholder groups to jointly transform the wider business.[39]

Broadly speaking, team coaching is an eclectic approach to assist groups to become teams by discovering their identity, purpose, goals and processes. It also can be used to assist teams improve their functioning and performance.

9. Teaming

Amy Edmondson is Novartis Professor of Leadership and Management at Harvard Business School. She proposes that teaming is an approach for leaders to create psychological safety, encourage reflection, and deal with defensive interpersonal dynamics that may inhibit the sharing of ideas. Given that teams don't learn naturally, teaming enables organisations to have the collaboration required to learn.[40]

Edmondson refers to teaming on the fly as a learning process needed more than ever in the current environment of rapid change, requiring high levels of flexibility, and where most of the work is open-ended, and people are no longer members of a stable team. Edmondson recommends the following five tips for effective teaming:

1. speak up

2. listen intensely

3. integrate different facts and points of views

4. experiment iteratively

5. reflect on your ideas and actions.[41]

10. Eclectic interventions

Eclectic interventions include team coaching or facilitation interventions, and other processes or activities (such as training) that have no particular theoretical background or perspective but are considered robust enough to achieve the goals they intend to achieve. Eclectic interventions may also include elements or processes from some of the methodologies presented in this chapter.

Conclusion

Leadership development doesn't happen by accident. It's a deliberate approach to building the leadership capacity of organisations. The ten methodologies presented in this chapter have a rich theoretical tradition and practical legacy of success. While these approaches have been available for a long time, most leadership development efforts in organisations are still focused on developing human capital and individual leaders rather than building collective leadership capacity. This is one of the main reasons most LDPs fail to deliver the expected results.

To varying degrees, multiple aspects or processes of the methods presented in this chapter could be integrated into your existing leadership development practices by using eclectic interventions.

Insight questions

- What approaches does your organisation use to build leadership capacity?

- What new approach could you consider to develop the leadership capacity of your team or organisations to achieve better results?

- How supportive of innovation is the climate of your team/ organisation?

- What's your organisation's approach to innovation and risk taking?

CHAPTER 13
Spectacular performance and business results

The greater danger for most of us lies not in setting our aim too high and falling short but in setting our aim too low and achieving our mark.
—Michelangelo

The themes of spectacular or extraordinary performance and excellence, what is possible or impossible, and their challenge to common wisdom, have been debated by great minds throughout history and by contemporary business leaders.

As I mentioned at the beginning of this book, the ideas and concepts presented here, properly applied, can make a significant difference to the way you lead others. I have explored how to lead yourself effectively, which is a prerequisite to leading others. I have also emphasised that this is an ongoing process that requires continuous self-development.

This chapter demonstrates what can be achieved when you successfully integrate and apply many of these concepts (for example, the language of possibility, keeping promises and commitments, self-fulfilling prophecies, locus of control and social loafing).

First, I invite you to do a little bit more of this self-development by examining the concept of spectacular performance. Specifically, becoming aware of the assumptions and conditioning that shapes how you see and interpret events (reality). This will uncover the 'lenses' through which you filter this topic (and other aspects of life, for that matter). These lenses are obstacles or barriers that limit what you can accomplish.

This 'thinking about thinking' is also known as 'metacognition'. It shapes, or has shaped, the way you think. So, before you read on, it is important that you complete the following short exercise. It will take just a few seconds, providing you are honest and do not judge yourself.

Write down the words that automatically come to mind when you hear terms such as 'spectacular performance', 'extraordinary', 'exceptional', 'breakthrough', 'ground-breaking', 'high performance' and 'stretch targets'.

Many of the executives I work with tell me that such expressions have been abused, and that they no longer mean anything. In fact, a common response, at least in Australia, is that such expressions are a bit 'wanky' (which, for those of you who don't know, is slang for masturbation, and means pretentious, stupid or pointless).

But many of these same executives work relentlessly, pushing themselves to the limit (working their butts off, to use a very popular expression), often at the expense of their health, family and social lives, to achieve the 'extraordinary'. I suspect that many of those individuals also consider that striving for 'work–life balance' is a bit wanky.

Myth or reality?

What is extraordinary or spectacular performance? Is it merely an ideal, or it is real? Can it really be achieved? How can it be achieved? Have we, as a society, been desensitised to striving for the extraordinary?

In this chapter I present the tools and mental software to explain how extraordinary performance (or what is sometimes perceived as impossible) can become possible.

One of the key roles of a leader is to get the best out of people. This involves influencing people's actions and outcomes or results (performance), whichever form they take. The best way to do this is by inviting your people to reflect upon, and question, what shapes their thinking—and ultimately their actions. But, to be effective, first you need to do that yourself.

It is important to distinguish between types, or levels, of performance so that you can be clear on what you're pursuing and determine what's possible for you, your team and organisation. This may challenge your current view.

Five stories, one theme

Here are five different real-life stories, with very different contexts, that share a common theme: people achieving the extraordinary—something spectacular—something that at some point seemed impossible.

The experts said it couldn't be done

Once upon a time, running a four-minute mile was thought to be impossible. Experts insisted that the human body was simply not capable of a four-minute mile. Doctors and scientists said it was impossible and that one would die trying. It wasn't just impossible — it was dangerous!

Even so, against all odds, on 6 May 1954 Roger Bannister ran the first ever sub-four-minute mile, at Oxford University's Iffley Road track in front of about 3000 spectators. In doing so, he demonstrated that the four-minute mile barrier was a myth.

Bannister accomplished what had been considered impossible. To do it, he had to develop a sense of extreme certainty, without having any proof that it could be done. It was only after he'd crashed through the four-minute barrier that the rest of the world saw it was possible; Australia's John Landy was the second man through. Now a mile is covered in less than 3.5 minutes.

The Collins Class submarine — No, it cannot be done!

The growth of the Australia economy came to a sudden halt in 1974, for the first time in almost 20 years. This coincided with the first oil shock, which produced a severe recession and rampant inflation. Between 1975 and 1983, high unemployment and inflation continued. After a century of centralised wage fixing and industry protectionism, the Australian manufacturing industry was inefficient, uncompetitive and focused on making products for the small domestic market. Australia's exports were overwhelmingly primary products, leaving the nation highly vulnerable to price fluctuations on world markets. This was an unusual situation for a developed country.

During this period, a team came up with the idea of building submarines in Australia. The key members were Hans Ohff, John

White and Graham White. Hans Ohff called the Minister for Defence Support to discuss the idea and was told, in essence, 'We can't build submarines—go away.' The attitude from industry was not much different. Graham White recalls a presentation at a Business Council lunch after which Brian Lotton, BHP's managing director, said to him, 'We can't do these things in Australia—give up the idea.'

The negativity was understandable given the industrial malaise that had gripped Australia since 1974, and the decades of protectionism that had produced a narrow, inward focus and pessimism about manufacturing.

In spite of the strong opposition, the team explored the capabilities of Australian industry, learned about innovations such as quality systems and modular construction, and investigated the likely macroeconomic impact. This culminated in the development of a central strategy with the following tenets: industrial regeneration, technology transfer, modular construction, quality assurance and industrial relations reform.

A central argument against building submarines in Australia was that it would be more expensive than elsewhere. So one of the first moves for the team was to ask the Australian Taxation Office (ATO) about the impact the workers' wages—and the extra money circulating—would have on the economy. The ATO responded that no-one had ever asked such a question before. However, it conducted a study and reported that the economic benefits would be dramatic. Those who had argued that building submarines in Australia would be too expensive had not taken this into account.

A critical event in the campaign was a seminar on 28 September 1984, hosted by the Institute of Engineers at the Academy of Science in Canberra. The project team put together an impressive panel of speakers, and attracted people from all the relevant areas—industry, politics, the unions and the navy. The attendance was huge and finally the pendulum swung: 'Yes, we can build submarines in Australia.'

(continued)

Kim Beazley became Australia's youngest ever Defence Minister (and in the view of most sailors, the best) when the Australian Labor Party took office following the December 1984 election. Beazley was well aware of the strategic value of submarines. More fundamentally, he supported the long-standing American alliance and appreciated that strategic intelligence exchanges could build trust and influence with the United States.

In 1992 Senator Robert Ray, then Labor Minister of Defence, argued quite independently of any military considerations that the decision to build submarines in Australia was 'to benefit Australia, not only through job creation but also through technology transfer, creation of modern management techniques and the introduction of new and more progressive industrial relations practices'.

The Collins Class submarine project overcame numerous challenges and political obstructions the project first tabled in the 1981–1982 budget and the last submarine delivered in 2003, at with a total cost of more than A$6 billion.

While the project was both expensive and controversial, this unique achievement is a testament to what many viewed as an impossible task.

A detailed account of this remarkable story is provided in the book *The Collins Class Submarine Story: Steel, spies and spin* by Peter Yule and Derek Woolner.[1]

The Rocky Flats story

Rocky Flats was an environmental disaster. It was the most contaminated nuclear plant in the United States, rampant with worker unrest. Operators of the former nuclear weapons plant pleaded guilty to environmental crimes and it was initially estimated that it would take 70 years and US$36 billion to clean up and close the facility. But something extraordinary happened.

Rocky Flats has been turned into a wildlife refuge and the project is running 60 years ahead of schedule and US$30 billion under budget. Kim Cameron and Marc Lavine, in a fascinating and thoroughly researched book *Making the Impossible Possible: Leading extraordinary performance: The Rocky Flats story*, reveal the ten leadership principles responsible for the turnaround. They explain how it was achieved and how it can be replicated in any business. Of particular relevance to the leadership contract is the fact the authors state that 'trust and credibility were crucial to the success of the project, and trust was almost entirely dependent on the demonstration of absolute integrity, consistency in keeping promises, and follow-through on commitments'.[2]

Janine Shepherd's story

Australian cross-country skier Janine Shepherd suffered life-threatening injuries when she was hit from behind by a truck during training. The accident broke her neck, her back in six places, her collarbone, five ribs, her arm and bones in her feet. It also caused head injuries, internal injuries and massive blood loss.

Prior to the accident, she was considered an excellent chance to win Australia's first ever Winter Olympic medal. Doctors told her parents that she was not expected to live, and if even if she did, she would never walk again.

Today, Janine Shepherd is a bestselling author and internationally renowned speaker who travels all over the world sharing her story and inspiring others. Imagine, however, Janine's internal journey before getting to this point. As she explains in her book *The Gift of Acceptance*, her journey included being ashamed of her body, feeling worthless, and riding an emotional roller-coaster between depression and anger.[3] You can see and hear her story in the TEDxKC talk 'You are not your body'.

Erik Weihenmayer's story

About 3000 people have successfully climbed Mount Everest, but Erik Weihenmayer's case is different. What makes his story unique is that although he reached the top of the highest peak in the world, he couldn't see the world's most beautiful view. He is blind.

Erik was a teacher in Phoenix, Arizona, and mountain climbing was one of his great passions, so he felt he had to climb the highest peak on Earth. He did that in May 2001. Seven years later, on 20 August 2008, he reached the top of the Carstensz Pyramid, Australasia's tallest peak, to complete his goal to climb the Seven Summits—the highest peaks on every continent. Today Erik inspires the world through his writings, public speaking, and film making.

It is fair to say that a blind man climbing the highest peaks on every continent puts most things into perspective. It makes you wonder how big your own challenges really are. Are they bigger than Mount Everest for a blind man?

Incidentally, until 1953, climbing Mount Everest was considered impossible.

At some point, the people in these stories saw the final goal as possible and worth pursuing. This shows the power of strong vision generating possibility. One of the main roles of a leader is to create that vision and highlight the possibilities that inspire others to make them reality. A good vision has the power to generate so much commitment that individuals will do whatever it takes to achieve the outcome, despite the inevitable barriers, obstacles and conflicts that will emerge along the way.

Perception is not reality

'Perception is reality' is an expression you have probably heard many times. As I recall, it was popularised by a management guru in the 1980s.

What he probably meant to say (and perhaps he did, and people misunderstood him) was that people act on their perception of reality as if it actually was reality.

Well, the fact is that perception is *not* reality. Perception relates to neurophysiological processes, including memory, by which we become aware of and interpret external stimuli or events. Psychologists have known for a long time that perception is the result of our 'interpretation' or 'translation' of events, which may or may not match actual events or reality.

Perception is a process of interpretation that is affected by many factors, such as our expectations, experiences, motivation, emotions and mental state. Common thought would have it that reality means 'perceptions, beliefs, and attitudes towards reality', as in, 'My reality is not your reality.' This is often used as a circuit-breaker in conversations to mean 'we have deeply different conceptions of what is real'. For example, in a business discussion between two executives, one might say (attempting humour): 'You might disagree, but in my reality, everyone in this team is doing the right thing.'

I read a funny story about this 'perception is reality' expression. A lecturer cracks a real egg and pours it into a glass to set up the class's perception, and then throws plastic eggs into the class. No surprisingly, the students' perception is that the eggs are real. This affects their behaviour, and they try to avoid eggs being smashed on them. The reality, regardless of perception and the behaviour perception causes, is that the 'eggs' were plastic.

This is the important distinction between perception and reality. We behave according to our perception of reality, not reality itself. Therefore, a leader must always question the current perception of reality.

In making his breakthrough in 1954, Roger Bannister demonstrated to the world that the perception (and belief) that a four-minute mile was impossible was actually wrong. Bannister changed everyone's perception. The same thing

> *Performance is directly correlated to people's perception of what's possible—the first principle of performance.*

occurred with the Collins Class submarine. Someone saw building submarines in Australia as possible, while others did not—completely different interpretations (perceptions) of the same situation, context, circumstance and landscape. Janine's and Erik's stories are two more examples. They both achieved what many perceived as impossible, because they saw it as possible.

The three laws of performance

Research shows that trying to achieve goals that are perceived as impossible produces poorer performances than pursuing goals that are perceived to be either easy or challenging.[4] As I will explain, trying to achieve 'pie in the sky' performance is futile. This is because people's performance is directly correlated to the way situations occur to them (their perception of what's possible). This is the first principle of performance.

While this first law of performance has been published somewhat recently,[5] psychologists have known it for a very long time. People perform not so much based on how situations 'are' (in themselves), but rather in relation to how they interpret or perceive situations. Take again the example of Roger Bannister. He had the conviction and commitment to do what he saw as possible, while others considered the same goal impossible. He created certainty and confidence in himself without seeing, or needing, the proof that it could be accomplished. He intrinsically believed it could be done. Not surprisingly, his performance matched the way the situation occurred to him — that is, as doable. And once he had done it, the rest of the world also saw it as possible.

What's possible for you and your team?

If your team, for example, perceives that what is expected of them is totally unrealistic (pie in the sky), they will respond accordingly. Possibly, they won't even try — 'Why bother?' The way the situation occurs to them shows up in their language. This is the second principle of performance. Some examples of this principle in action are when people say things like: 'It is impossible', 'It cannot be done', 'This target/time frame is unrealistic' or 'It's a waste of time and effort, we will never achieve this target.'

So, as a team leader, how do you respond? There are two possible ways. The most commonly used approach is to lower the target until it appears to be more realistic to the team. But there is an alternative approach. If people's actions are correlated to what they see as possible (or how things occur to them—the first principle of performance), then in changing the way people see things (their perception), their actions will change accordingly. The next question, of course, is how can you change what people see as possible (or how things occur to them)?

> Painting a strong vision... is a very effective way to generate possibility.

The answer is through language—the second principle of performance is 'how situations occur to people arises in language'.[5] However, it is future-based language that transforms how situations occur to people. This is the third principle of performance.

Yes, only through future-based language, which creates the possibility of a new future, can you alter how things occur to people. As discussed in chapter 3, this kind of language, also called the 'language of possibility', can include making 'declarations' about a future state of affairs. Painting a strong vision, for example, is a very effective way to generate possibility. Leaders 'implant' or 'seed', as it were, a picture of the future in followers' minds. Without wanting to undermine or diminish the preciousness and uniqueness of the human mind, I would like to use the analogy of a computer, in that creating this powerful vision is like placing software on your hard drive to execute a future task with certainty and precision. Ideally, this new future is one that has not been considered previously.

* * *

Let us explore further the realm of the extraordinary. Consider the Declaration of Independence—a statement adopted by the United States Continental Congress on 4 July 1776, that declared that the 13 American colonies then at war with Great Britain had become independent states, and were no longer part of the British Empire.

These events illustrate that achieving extraordinary performance also requires a shift from 'problem solving' to an 'abundance' mindset, which focuses on finding possibilities. Using this mindset, action precedes clarity, which contrasts with the business-as-usual (BAU) mindset, where clarity precedes action. (That is, when people need clarity about how things will happen.) People take action with the abundance mindset because they know clarity will come as they move towards their goal.

The journey to extraordinary performance then is a journey of self-discovery, and teams are able to live with a relatively high degree of uncertainty. This takes self-confidence, courage and commitment. However, above all it takes high levels of trust in their leader. It is not about understanding — it is about trusting. That is why in the Leadership Results (LR) model, the leader's credibility (of which trust is a main component) precedes followers' commitment. This is also the commitment that enables total alignment and engagement of your people.[6] Commitment and alignment are also achieved through language. Individuals or teams who cannot tolerate uncertainty seldom take risks. They never try anything new, as they are too afraid to fail or lose (or worse still, be seen as losers).

What results and level of performance do you want?

The LR model presented in this book begins with a clear end in mind, which is the outcome everyone (individuals, teams and organisations) wants — results! Given that 'results', of course, is a generic term, you may want to ask what kind of results I am talking about.

Well, what kind of results would you like?

Within the context of this book, I am talking about what has been described by Kim Cameron and Marc Lavine in their book *Making the Impossible Possible* as 'unusual, positively deviant, spectacular, or extraordinary levels of performance'. In the industries in which I have been working and researching, such high levels of performance are referred to as 'extraordinary outcomes'; 'breakthrough', or 'groundbreaking' results and 'superior', 'peak', or 'spectacular' performance. This is the kind of performance that is achieved when a team is so empowered it can move mountains, as it were. These are terms used to distinguish this kind of performance from BAU performance, which is underpinned by a 'mediocrity mindset'.

Let's explore the distinction between BAU and extraordinary or breakthrough performance in more detail. BAU refers to results based on what has been learned from experience, so it becomes an extension of the past. Hence, BAU is conservative and incremental by nature (a 10 to15 per cent improvement, or increase in performance indicators). With a BAU mindset, clarity is more important than action. This becomes obvious when people refuse to commit to any action unless they know exactly how the ultimate result will be achieved. They want clarity because that is how they are used to working. 'Show me how to do it', or 'prove to me how it can be done', and then I'll do it. This has been the prevailing model of performance for a long time. It shapes, constrains and limits our current practices—BAU itself. It also explains why after Roger Bannister broke the four-minute mile, others did likewise. Once it was proved that it could be done, they were happy to follow. Yet only Bannister initially saw it as possible.

From a BAU perspective, people are limited by their experience as opposed to being driven by their future learning (innovation). The underlying (unspoken) assumption is that more BAU levels of performance would have to be accomplished using their current way of thinking and working, as opposed to having to invent new ones. From this BAU perspective, extraordinary performance is seen as an unattainable goal in the light of prior performance.

> *The essence of extraordinary performance is achieving things that are a quantum leap, and independent, from the past.*

The essence of extraordinary performance is achieving things that are a quantum leap, and independent, from the past. Of course, this is without compromising the safety and wellbeing of those involved, the quality of outputs, ethics or issues related to social responsibility. Innovation becomes the key to this type of performance breakthrough. Take, for an example, the creative thinking of the Collins Class submarine team in looking where others were not looking. The team reframed what was seen as a 'no-go project' with only obstacles and challenges into a great social, economic, political and technological advancement and innovation. This is a good example of what happens when people get truly excited about a possibility and doing something worthwhile. By uncovering individuals' blind spots, and enabling them to see the previously unseen, a new real performance is revealed.

From this perspective, a team makes dramatic moves quickly, rather than incremental improvements. This also entails continually setting stretch targets that ultimately reach much higher levels of performance. There is more on stretch targets later in this chapter but first, let me introduce the performance ladder, and distinguish five distinct levels of performance.

The five-level performance ladder

Much of what appears in figure 13.1 is self-explanatory, but it is also necessary to explain the levels of performance in more detail.

Figure 13.1: the five levels of performance

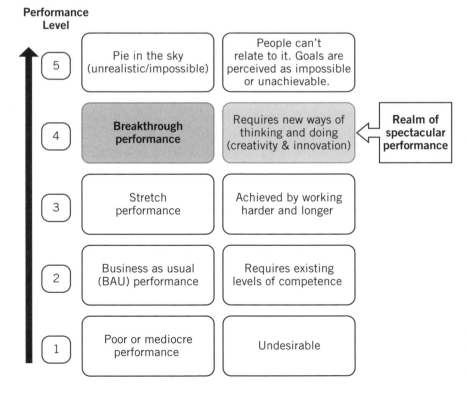

Level 1: Poor or mediocre performance

Level 1 relates to underperformance, reflecting the fact that the performance is far from optimal or what is desired. Most of us know too well what this looks like. This level of performance sends a business broke. While the causes are varied (a whole new book could be written about it), it should always be addressed urgently. Within the context of this book, however, I will say that this type of performance is often the result of a certain transactional style of leadership.[7] This is a poor and passive leadership style that relies heavily on passive management-by-exception. Leaders like this act only when things go wrong or targets are not met. The mindset is the old and too popular 'if it isn't broken, don't fix it' or, in the Australian vernacular, 'she'll be right, mate' leadership style.

I am always surprised, and concerned, to hear these words from leaders of a certain stature. While it is important to celebrate success, being absolutely comfortable with your current level of performance is resting on your laurels. It is a recipe for disaster: you are in danger of making no effort to improve or be open to innovation. This is why success can be very dangerous.

Level 2: Business as usual

Level 2 describes the kind of performance that fluctuates from average to good. BAU performance is somewhat predictable. Only the existing levels of knowledge, skill and ability are required to achieve or sustain this level of performance. It basically happens by default in going through the motions every day, even making minor improvements from time to time.

Level 3: Stretch performance

Level 3 involves using the same technologies and ways of working as at the BAU level. Stretch performance is achieved by doing more of the same, more often and with much more intensity—for example, by people working harder and longer hours (ten, 12 or up to 14 hours a day, six or seven days a week). This kind of effort, however, is not sustainable. People burn out and ultimately resent their work. Inevitably, there is also a negative spill-over, or ripple effect, that eventually affects family and social life.

Let's jump to Level 5: Pie in the sky performance

This level refers to the kind of performance (goals, targets or expectations) that are seen as impossible and unachievable. While the end result is appreciated, it is also perceived as unlikely to be achieved. People simply do not relate to it. Therefore, such goals or targets are unlikely to be realised. As mentioned earlier, goals that are perceived as impossible produce poorer performance than those that are perceived as easy or challenging. This is because people do not even bother trying to achieve unrealistic goals or targets. Hence, their actions are the same as those at the BAU level.

Level 4: Breakthrough performance

This is the realm of extraordinary performance, or ground-breaking results. It refers to results that are unprecedented. They require overcoming a fear of failure; resisting the need to look good or successful by setting targets that are predictable, based on what has worked in the past; and overcoming the language of 'it can't be done'.

Performance at this level as opposed to level 3 is achieved by using creative thinking and innovation. This may mean, for example, searching where others are not, doing the unthinkable, and connecting unconnected dots. A good example of this performance level is the team that challenged the belief that submarines could not be built in Australia.

Achieving an extraordinary or breakthrough performance requires setting stretch targets. These are discussed in the next section.

Stretch targets

Stretch targets represent commitments or 'contracts' made by individuals, teams and organisations to achieve specific performance outcomes. They are used to plan such performance outcomes and make expectations explicit. Stretch targets are goals that challenge and mobilise individuals and teams to action beyond the predictable, or

BAU, levels of performance. They take teams beyond their normal limits and comfort zones.

When a leader creates and commits to a stretch target, it is important to ensure it's not considered out of reach (level 5, pie in the sky). If it is, setting smaller, more achievable goals as milestones can help achieve the desired stretch target. The stretch target has to be seen as challenging, but also possible. From this perspective, target setting is the beginning of organisational transformation as it explicitly initiates a conversation about planning the performance to meet the challenge.

Mediocre or average teams typically avoid even talking about setting stretch targets. Team members will say that, based on their experience, stretch targets have failed in the past. Others will inadvertently assume that stretch targets will have to be achieved using the current ways of thinking and working, and cannot believe it is possible to achieve them. Not surprisingly, cynicism about doing more with less is likely to be heard. Is this a familiar scenario?

Stretch targets are performance objectives that force significant changes to thinking and working and elevate performances to superior and unprecedented levels. Teams need to use creative problem solving to achieve stretch targets, as they cannot be reached using old ways of working.

This level of performance means challenging, re-examining and transcending the language trap, which is anchored in the past. When work groups are first introduced to the concept of extraordinary performance they often make comments such as, 'We have always done it this way'; 'This is what has worked for us in the past'; 'These targets and time frames are unrealistic'; and 'If we don't achieve these results, we'll look like idiots.' These are based on the past and their fear of failure, or wanting—above all—to look good.

More often than not, such comments are not made explicitly, but they are real and pervasive. Principally, people are unaware of them. They are internal beliefs or assumptions and remain unquestioned, constituting a blind spot. As explained in chapter 12, such individuals treat their beliefs as the 'truth' or 'reality', creating a major barrier or limitation for themselves. In fact, they kill any possibility of extraordinary performance.

Why setting stretch targets pays off

I worked with project alliances, also referred to as 'relationship contracting' in industry, for a number of years. In essence, project alliances are alternative and collaborative approaches to delivering large, complex and high-value infrastructure projects. In such projects, the owners and service providers form new teams (alliances) to work together and share both project risks and opportunities. All members are appointed on a 'best-for-project' basis, without duplication of roles. Another key feature is the aim to deliver better value for money and improved project outcomes. From this perspective, an alliance is a particular form of high-performance team.

Successful project alliances need to be committed to achieving results beyond BAU. The terms 'extraordinary outcomes', 'ground-breaking' and 'breakthrough results' are frequently used. To outperform, the selected group must be transformed into a true alliance; that is, a true high-performance team. Needless to say, this does not happen naturally and it can be particularly challenging, as the team members come from different organisational cultures. The new entity needs to develop its own unique culture. Australia is recognised as a world leader in the application of project alliances, which is why I chose to undertake a PhD in this particular environment.

I would like to share the example of two project alliance teams I worked with. I will refer to them as the Black Swan and the Sunshine alliances to protect their identity. The Black Swan team was stuck in the 'this target is not realistic or possible' conversation. The Sunshine alliance team, however, for reasons I will explain, chose the 'Who says it is not possible? Let's go for it!' conversation.

Which team do you think performed best?

Yes, it was the Sunshine alliance, and while it did not actually reach the set target, it far outperformed the Black Swan alliance. Why? Because in its pursuit of much higher targets, the team members stretched themselves to a level of effort and innovation that delivered a performance much closer to what they believed was possible. When obstacles appeared, the Sunshine alliance kept trying new approaches, without giving up.

Members of the Black Swan alliance, on the other hand, did not even try. They actually led themselves to believe that the targets were impossible. In fact, when obstacles appeared they said to themselves, 'You see, we knew it all along. We told you. It's just not possible!' Not surprisingly, that conversation became a self-fulfilling prophecy.

Self-fulfilling prophecies are expectations, either positive or negative, that become true. In the case of the Black Swan alliance, the negative expected outcome evoked the necessary behaviours to make this actually become true. This explains how negative thoughts (perceptions) shape our reality. Self-fulfilling prophecies are cause-and-effect scenarios. They are stronger within teams than in individuals, because they have a synergistic and accumulative effect. The expectations of more than two people are more powerful than those of one person. Psychological research clearly tells us that the expectations of a team are the strongest predictors of performance.

The mechanism by which a self-fulfilling prophecy works is not magic. Individuals look for evidence to support their beliefs or expectations until they find it. So, eventually they can say, 'You see, I told you. I was right!' When individuals have this state of mind, even minor cues are interpreted as evidence that reinforces their thinking (hunch, hypothesis or prediction). Over time, the evidence gathered can become so weighty that it is extremely difficult to debunk. Self-fulfilling prophecy is a very insidious and powerful process—there's more about it in chapter 7.

Other very important factors contributed to the Sunshine alliance outperforming the Black Swan team. First, and partially as a result of having a clear vision, Sunshine team members had an internal LOC (locus of control; see chapter 7). It means the team members believed their thoughts, attitude and actions would determine their destiny, as opposed to relying on good luck or fate. Conversely, the Black Swan members falsely believed they could not, and were not going to, reach the proposed challenging targets. Consequently, their fear of failure caused them not to achieve them.

This highlights another factor in the underperformance of the Black Swan team—social loafing. This is the tendency of team members to exert less effort because they are part of a group. As members pool their efforts to achieve a common goal, each individual potentially contributes less than if they were individually responsible. (See chapter 10 for more on this.) Needless to say, this is exacerbated when the team is in a mood of doubt, as the Black Swan team was.

The Sunshine team members had much higher levels of self-confidence and self-efficacy, optimism and resilience, than the members of the Black Swan alliance. You might recognise these as attributes of PsyCap (see chapter 7).

Once I examined the data collected from both alliances, I noted something very interesting. There was striking contrast between the credibility scores of the two team leaders (alliance managers). Needless to say, the leader from the Sunshine alliance had much higher scores than Black Swan's leader.

> ... extraordinary leaders generate spectacular performance and results by first being at the service of their teams.

Another example is what I'll call the Grand Pipeline alliance. This team actually reached its targets, and earlier than expected, and so it set higher stretch targets. The team members kept stretching and challenging themselves because the expectations they created, even the obligations many members felt, were stronger and more emotionally binding than the targets set by someone else (such as the team leader, management team or project owner). This level of conviction and belief that they could go even higher is the key to extraordinary performance.

As stretch targets are difficult goals, they need to be accepted and embraced by all of the team members (and, for that matter, by all teams or business units in the organisation). This is vital to harness the collective force that makes breakthroughs possible.

In summary, extraordinary leaders generate spectacular performance and results by first being at the service of their teams. They use, generate and maintain high levels of credibility (that is, they fulfil team members' expectations, and generate the highest levels of trust and fairness), use the language of possibility (declarations) to help individuals see what's possible and create a new realm of performance, and set stretch targets.

In the next chapter, I discuss this language of possibility, and other linguistic distinctions, in detail.

Conclusion

Spectacular or extraordinary performance is achievable under certain conditions. People need to understand that perception is not reality, the three laws of performance, the five levels of the performance, how to use stretch targets, self-fulfilling prophecy, locus of control, and how to generate and maintain high levels of credibility among team members.

Insight questions

- What are your team's views on spectacular or extraordinary performance?

- Is your team aware of the various levels of performance?

- What does your team see as possible in relation to their performance achievements?

- What do your people perceive as possible in relation to their team performance?

- What language do they use?

- How do you use the language of possibility to affect your team's performance?

- Does your team understand how self-fulfilling prophecies work?

- Is your team's locus of control internal or external?

- How are the levels of credibility within your team?

CHAPTER 14

A call to decisive, bold action and results

Begin, be bold, and venture to be wise.
— **Horace**

The village chief and the tsunami

An old Japanese tale recounts how a highly respected village chief one day felt a tremor while looking down from his house on a hilltop. He saw the sea quickly pulling away from the land and puzzled villagers running onto the beach. Without hesitation, he instructed his grandson to set fire to the large freshly harvested rice stacks on the hill.

(continued)

The huge fire caught the villagers' attention: their most precious asset was being destroyed. Alarmed and enraged they quickly ran uphill from the shore to extinguish the flames. Then, in horror, they watched from safe ground as the tsunami wiped out the village. The chief was recognised as a hero as it became clear he had set the fire to save the villagers.

What's the moral of this story?

How does it apply to you?

How can you save your village?

Furthermore, how can you contribute to saving our global village?

Crises call for decisive and bold action. Inaction leads to missed opportunities, no change in the status quo, and no improvements in results. In the worst-case scenario, inaction causes human suffering or lost lives.

Let me make it perfectly clear that I'm not advocating setting fire to anything! The story actually suggests a much better course of action.

To my mind, the chief was able to read the signs in the suddenly changing context by sensing the tremor and looking at the bigger picture from above. This presence and alertness allowed him to quickly use his sense-making—his ability to make sense of the world around him and create a meaningful picture that enabled him to act. Had he got it wrong, he would have been the villain who burned the harvest, not the hero who saved his village from the deadly tsunami. Sense-making entails reading the context swiftly and doing what seems reasonable and valid at the time.

Do you believe you can detect any change in your context? Are you able to make sense of your organisation's current context and situation quickly? Do you have the contextual intelligence, situational awareness, data, agility and global mindset to identify threats?

Further, the story illustrates the chief's vision, clarity of purpose, self-confidence and self-assurance in taking a strong stand. Do you believe you have the self-leadership to make these kinds of calls?

The story also tells us that the chief had a good understanding of human nature, communication and how relationships work. He could mobilise his people in the most rapid and effective way for their own benefit. He acted in the villagers' best interests, not his own. Do you understand what's important to your village (organisation)? Do you know what drives your enterprise and the people working in it?

The chief understood his people so well that he could predict their actions. Are you able to do the same with your stakeholders? Are you seen as having the integrity it takes to command the highest levels of respect and credibility? Do your stakeholders trust you? Are you able to get the best out of them?

Relational leadership requires you to connect and engage with many stakeholders. And opportunities to do this are available to you every day. To do it effectively, however, requires intention and thoughtfulness. By being strategic and deliberate, you'll have the greatest impact on your people and your organisation. It requires careful planning, which is what I'm inviting you to do next.

It would be easy for what you have learned from this book to remain aspirational. But I encourage you to reflect on what's next by formulating an action plan so you can achieve lofty results together with the people you lead.

But first, let's briefly review the core ideas in this book.

* * *

Part I explores the new context for leadership and its implications for leading and developing current and future leaders.

The story of the psychology student who observed the long-handled spoons experiment in chapter 1 exemplifies how easy it can be to underestimate the amazing power of human relationships. It shows how being of service to others through collaboration can yield extraordinary win–win outcomes—as in the case of project alliances. The quality of our relationships is not only the very essence of our existence, it's also the means to our prosperity.

The tale of the organisation who believed in consultants, in chapter 2, illustrates that context and leadership are inseparable, and that the context for leadership has been turned upside down. The new context is complex, turbulent and unpredictable. It requires us to shift our attention away from individual-based models of leadership to more contextual, relational and collective models. As the organisation found out, this involves using collective wisdom and shifting towards the use of meta-competencies such as contextual intelligence and learning agility. It's also essential to keep up to date with the latest research findings, despite the terms they use initially sounding like buzzwords.

The example of the sales director of the global company who must launch a new sales management system, also presented in chapter 2, shows that the new challenges are not technical, but adaptive. This means solutions are not known, so they require very uncomfortable work involving the people directly connected to them. The case of the global insurer, also featured in this chapter, reinforces the business risks associated with culture, and the need for global mindsets, cultural intelligence and intercultural competence.

The account in chapter 3 of the group of managers who lost their way climbing Mount Everest highlights that the context for leadership is chaotic, confusing, and doesn't have maps. Leaders need to use sense-making to map the new context for themselves by answering the question, 'What's the story?' Next, by mastering storytelling, speakership and the unique power of language, we can reframe this new reality, and provide others with hope, confidence, and a springboard for action.

Ruben and his Italian team in chapter 4 illuminate the risks of cultural assumptions and blind spots. The story of Monica's upbringing and socialisation demonstrates how our conditioning shapes our mental models of leadership, and how easily they blind leaders and organisations. This also flows through to why organisations keep making the same fundamental mistakes and fail to develop leaders ready to deal effectively with current and future challenges—and why change is needed urgently.

The all-in-one solution of a relational and integrity model of leadership in chapter 5 offers the opportunity to correct those mistakes by developing individual leaders, boosting employee engagement and building collective leadership across your organisation. It offers a pathway (a sequence with integrity) to self-leadership, leadership credibility, leadership impact and collective results.

Part II of the book is concerned with self-leadership and leader development. The allegory in chapter 6, of the father who 'kills' his boy to turn him into a man, challenges the perennial closed-ended, and arguably misleading, question of whether leaders are born or made. It does this by illuminating the possibility that true leadership comes through initiation, which traditionally has involved rites or ceremonies that catapult the individual from one life stage into another.

Contemporary leadership development approaches emphasise the cognitive (*knowing*) and behavioural (*doing*) dimensions of leadership but tend to neglect the deeper attitudinal and emotional (*being*) dimension.

Matt's case in chapter 7 illustrates how self-leadership — achieving direction and motivation — is about more than just competencies. Self-leadership is achieved through consciously and purposefully building and maintaining high self-esteem, identifying and applying your strengths, experiencing 'flow' regularly, building character, acting ethically and with integrity, and building psychological capital.

Jean-Pierre's story in chapter 8 highlights the perils of judging books (situations and people) by their covers, and the fact that we can be oblivious to things within our reach. The story also highlights the roles virtues, emotions, and signature strengths play in boosting self-leadership. When developing effective and ethical leaders — as well as engaging employees — organisations should consider whether the time has come to replace values with virtues, principles, ethics and character strengths. They seem to connect more deeply both intellectually and emotionally, offering richer human and financial benefits for employees and organisations.

The fable in chapter 9, of the two frogs that fell into the vat, demonstrates that commitment — not motivation — leads to results. While motivation is necessary to start anything, it won't always get you there. Motivation is about desire, but it's often short-lived. Commitment, on the other hand, is about determination, dedication and perseverance. It's far more important. Commitment also relates to an employee's emotional attachment, loyalty, or allegiance to the organisation, which effective leaders are able to generate from their teams.

Part III examines collective leadership and leadership development.

Jasmine's story of victimisation at the orphanage in chapter 10 unpacks the essence of collective, collaborative, shared or distributed leadership. The story illustrates how collective leadership is about empowering people by providing them with a voice and enhancing their confidence in their abilities to cope, perform successfully and be more creative. By diminishing or eliminating dependency, diffusion of responsibility and social loafing among team members, collective leadership helps organisations become more relational, collaborative, innovative, and mobilise towards collective action and change.

The cases of Cisco, the King's Fund, the All Blacks, IDEO, and AA, also presented in chapter 10, demonstrate that collective leadership involves individuals assuming leadership roles in groups or organisations in response to specific situations, settings or contexts, by taking responsibility for the success of the entire organisation. This requires power to be distributed to wherever expertise, capability and motivation sit.

The story in chapter 11 of the Australian Football League players who had difficulty letting go of the ball sheds light on the differences between management education/development and leadership development; leader and leadership development; and human, social and relational capital. The global case study, also presented in this chapter, identifies and discusses 14 best-practice principles of leadership development, and the practical implications for OD practitioners. It also outlines the benefits of ensuring leadership pipelines are ready and able to execute the strategies critical for long-term success. Finally, it offers 12 recommendations for OD and L&D practitioners conducting leadership development program evaluations.

The expression 'putting the cat on the table', introduced in chapter 12, represents the all-too-familiar effort and courage required to have direct and honest conversations (often referred to as 'tough' or 'difficult' conversations). As an agent of change, the various approaches presented in this chapter can help you develop collective leadership capacity and boost employee engagement to make a real difference.

The five cases in chapter 13 provide evidence of the importance of mental control and the use of language. While people act according to their perceptions, perception is not reality. Performance is directly correlated to people's perception of what's possible. It's always important to question perceptions of reality in relation to performance. Future-based language (the language of possibility) transforms the way situations are perceived. Self-fulfilling prophecies are not magic, but are real and pervasive. Self-belief, internal locus of control, playing to your strengths, and setting stretch targets are critical to achieving specific performance outcomes, and imperative to achieving spectacular results. Generating and maintaining the highest possible levels of credibility by being true to your word is essential in leading teams to the extraordinary.

Planning for action

I mentioned in the introduction that this is a book of action that will lead you to a brighter and better future. This, of course, is your choice.

Ron Heifetz, Alexander Grashow and Marty Linsky, in their book *The Practice of Adaptive Leadership: Tools and tactics for changing your organization and the world*, say: 'Acts of leadership are sacred, and every moment counts. The world would be a better place if we all, including us, practiced leadership a bit more of our time.'

To this end, I invite you to review your leadership agenda and consider the following seven questions:

1. What offer(s), and to whom, can you make today that will make a significant impact to those you serve?

2. What personal stand can you take today that will make an important positive difference to the way you lead?

3. What declaration can you make today that will create a new realm of possibility for those you lead?

4. What request(s), and to whom, can you make today that will mobilise others to take bold action and thrive?

5. What new leadership development approaches can you adopt today to take the leadership capacity of your team, organisation or community to the next level so they can thrive while tackling intractable challenges and achieve better leadership results?

6. Which new networks do you need to plug into today to mobilise engagement, propel others to action, and enrich or replenish your organisation's social capital?

7. What are you grateful for today, and to whom do you need to express your gratitude?

In most chapters, I started with a short story. I would like to close this book by sharing one last story that I use often as a reminder.

The wise man and the two youngsters

Once upon a time, there were two smart youngsters who loved playing pranks on the people in their village.

On a nearby mountaintop lived a wise old man, a sage with white hair and a long beard, to whom the people of the village would go for advice whenever they were troubled.

One day, the two youngsters decided to test the old man's wisdom. They caught a chicken and planned to approach the old man with their hands behind their backs and ask him which of them was holding something.

'What if he guesses correctly?' one youngster asked the other.

'Then I will ask him what I am holding. It is unlikely he'll be able to answer that.'

'But... what if he does?'

The other youngster thought awhile in silence, then replied triumphantly, 'I've got it! I'll ask him whether the chicken is dead or alive. If he says it's alive, I'll break its neck and kill it, and if he says it's dead, I'll pull it out alive and kicking! We can't go wrong!'

And they went off chortling.

The next morning, they visited the old man, as planned.

'Good morning', said the old man. 'What can I do for you?'

'Tell me old man, you who are so wise, one of us is holding something behind our back—which of us is it?'

'It is you', said the wise man, with a smile.

'Aha! Then tell me, what is it that I'm holding, old man?' asked the youngster, grinning.

'You are holding a chicken', said the old man.

Slightly taken aback, the youngster played his ace: 'Tell me, smart old man, is the chicken dead or alive?'

'Well, that is in your hands', replied the wise man.

REFERENCES AND SUGGESTED READING

Introduction

References

1. Crabtree, S 2013, 'Worldwide, 13% of employees are engaged at work', Gallup, 8 October, www.gallup.com/poll/165269/worldwide-employees-engaged-work.aspx.

2. World Economic Forum 2014, *Outlook on the Global Agenda 2015*, www3.weforum.org/docs/GAC14/WEF_GAC14_OutlookGlobalAgenda_Report.pdf.

3. Boatman, J & Wellins, R 2011, *DDI Global Leadership Forecast 2011: Time for a leadership revolution!*, Development Dimensions International, www.ddiworld.com/glf201.

4. Kellerman, B 2004, *Bad leadership: What it is, how it happens, why it matters*, Harvard Business School Publishing, Boston.

5. Grant Thornton Australia 2015, *Fraud in focus: Fraud and corruption in banking and financial services*, www.grantthornton.com.au/en/client-alerts/2015/fraud-and-corruption-in-banking-financial-services/.

6. Gahan, P, Adamovic, M, Bevitt, A, Harley, B, Healy, J, Olsen, JE & Theilacker, M 2016, *Leadership at work: Do Australian leaders have what it takes?*, Centre for Workplace Leadership, University of Melbourne, http://workplaceleadership.com.au/sal.

7. Productivity Commission 2010, *Performance benchmarking of Australian business regulation: Occupational health & safety*, Canberra, www.pc.gov.au/inquiries/completed/regulation-benchmarking-ohs/report.

8. Australian Industry Group 2015, *Addressing enterprise leadership in Australia*, http://cdn.aigroup.com.au/Reports/2015/ai_group_leadership_policy_june_2015.pdf.

9. Martin, Y 2013, 'Helping Australia's stressed-out workers', *Gallup Business Journal*, 24 December, www.gallup.com/businessjournal/166355/helping-australia-stressed-workers.aspx.

10. Sarros, JC, Cooper, BK, Hartican, AM & Barker, C J 2006, *The character of leadership: What works for Australian leaders — making it work for you*, John Wiley & Sons, Milton, QLD.

11. Kouzes, JM, Posner, BZ & Bunting M 2015, *Extraordinary leadership in Australia and New Zealand: The five practices that create great workplaces*, John Wiley & Sons, Milton, QLD.

12. Plinio, AJ, Young, JM, & Lavery, LM 2010, 'The state of ethics in our society: A clear call for action', *International Journal of Disclosure and Governance*, 7(3), 172–97.

13. Kellerman, B 2012, *The end of leadership*, HarperCollins, New York.

14. World Economic Forum 2013, *Network of Global Agenda Councils Reports 2011–2012*, http://www3.weforum.org/docs/GAC/2013/WEF_GAC_MidtermReports_2012-14.pdf.

15. Kaiser, RB & Gurphy, G 2013, 'Leadership development: The failure of an industry and the opportunity for consulting psychologists', *Consulting Psychology Journal: Practice and Research*, 65(4), 294–302.

16. Deloitte University Press 2016, *Global human capital trends: The new organization: Different by design*, www2.deloitte.com/au/en/pages/human-capital/articles/introduction-human-capital-trends.html.

17. O'Leonard, K & Krider, J 2014, *Leadership development factbook 2014: Benchmarks and trends in U.S. leadership development*, Bersin by Deloitte, www.bersin.com/Practice/Detail.aspx?id=17478.

18. Pfeffer, J 2015, *Leadership BS: Fixing workplaces and careers one truth at a time*, HarperBusiness, New York.

19. Beer, M., Finnström, M. and Schrader, D., 2016. Why leadership training fails—and what to do about it. *Harvard Business Review*, 94(10), pp.50–57.

20. Heifetz, RA, Linsky, M & Grashow, A 2009, *The practice of adaptive leadership: Tools and tactics for changing your organization and the world*, Harvard Business Press, Boston.

Chapter 1

References

1. Slocombe, C 2014, 'Standard project alliance agreements', *Public Infrastructure Bulletin*, 1(9), Article 2, http://epublications.bond.edu.au/pib/vol1/iss9/2.

2. Ross, J 2008, 'Procurement models: Interactive forum', *Major Projects Conference*, Department of Infrastructure and Planning, Brisbane.

3. Lloyd-Walker, B & Walker, D 2011, 'Authentic leadership for 21st century project delivery', *International Journal of Project Management*, 29(4), 383–95.

Suggested reading

Argyris, C 1960, *Understanding organizational behaviour*, Dorsey, Oxford.

——1982, *Reasoning, learning and action*, Jossey-Bass, San Francisco.

——1991, 'Teaching smart people how to learn', *Harvard Business Review*, 69(3), 99–109.

Argyris, C & Schon, DA 1978, *Organizational learning: A theory of action perspective*, Addison-Wesley, Reading, MA.

Coyle-Shapiro, J & Kessler, I 2000, 'Consequences of the psychological contract for the employment relationship: A large scale survey', *Journal of Management Studies*, 37(7), 903–30.

Guest, DE 1998, 'Is the psychological contract worth taking seriously?', *Journal of Organizational Behavior*, 19, 649–64.

—— 1998, 'On meaning, metaphor and the psychological contract: A response to Rousseau', *Journal of Organizational Behavior*, 19, 673–7.

Morrison, EW & Robinson, SL 1997, 'When employees feel betrayed: A model of how psychological contract violation develops', *Academy of Management Review*, 22(1), 226–56.

Nicholson, N & Johns, G 1985, 'The absence culture and psychological contract—Who's in control of absence?', *Academy of Management Review*, 10(3), 397–407.

Robinson, SL 1996, 'Trust and breach of the psychological contract', *Administrative Science Quarterly*, 41(4), 574–99.

Robinson, SL, Kraatz, MS & Rousseau, DM 1994, 'Changing obligations and the psychological contract: A longitudinal study', *Academy of Management Journal*, 37(1), 137–52.

Rousseau, DM 1995, *Psychological contracts in organizations: Understanding written and unwritten agreements*, Sage Publications, Thousand Oaks, CA.

Salicru, S 2015, 'The global leadership psychological contract model—Actionable to shape the future to 2050', in M Sowcik, M (ed.) with International Leadership Association, *Leadership 2050: Critical challenges, key contexts and emerging trends*, Emerald Group Publishing, Bingley, UK.

—— 2016, 'Global leadership development', in P Grant (ed.) with Association for Business Psychology, *Business psychology in action: Creating flourishing organisations through evidence-based and emerging practices*, Matador, Troubador Publishing, Leicestershire, UK.

Salicru S & Chelliah, J 2014, 'Messing with corporate heads? Psychological contracts and leadership integrity', *Journal of Business Strategy*, 35(3), 38–46.

Thompson, M & Heron, P 2001, *Innovation and the psychological contract in the knowledge business*, Templeton College, Oxford.

Turnley, WH & Feldman, DC 1999, 'The impact of psychological contract violations on exit, voice, loyalty, and neglect', *Human Relations*, 52(7), 895–922.

Zhao, HAO, Wayne, SJ, Glibkowski, BC & Bravo, J 2007, 'The impact of psychological contract breach on work-related outcomes: A meta-analysis', *Personnel Psychology*, 60(3), 647–80.

Chapter 2

References

1. Bennett, N & Lemoine, GJ 2014, 'What a difference a word makes: Understanding threats to performance in a VUCA world', *Business Horizons*, 57(3), 311–17.

2. Sergi, V, Denis, JL & Langley, A 2012, 'Opening up perspectives on plural leadership', *Industrial and Organizational Psychology*, 5(4), 403–7.

3. Kutz, M 2017, *Contextual intelligence: How thinking in 3D can help resolve complexity, uncertainty and ambiguity*, Palgrave Macmillan, Basingstoke, UK.

4. De Meuse, KP, Dai, G & Hallenbeck, GS 2010, 'Learning agility: A construct whose time has come', *Consulting Psychology Journal: Practice and Research*, 62(2), 119.

5. Ancona, D, Malone, TW, Orlikowski, WJ & Senge, PM 2007, 'In praise of the incomplete leader', *Harvard Business Review,* 85(2), 92–100.

6. Heifetz, RA, Linsky, M & Grashow, A 2009, *The practice of adaptive leadership: Tools and tactics for changing your organization and the world,* Harvard Business Press, Boston.

7. Park, MJ 2014, 'Leadership 2030: The six megatrends you need to understand to lead your company into the future', *Journal of Applied Management and Entrepreneurship,* 19(2), 137–9.

8. Rousseau, DM 2004 'Psychological contracts in the workplace: Understanding the ties that motivate', *The Academy of Management Executive,* 18(1), 120–7.

9. Mendenhall, ME, Reiche, BS, Bird, A & Osland, JS 2012, 'Defining the "global" in global leadership', *Journal of World Business,* 47(4), 493–503.

10. Osland, J, Bird, A & Oddou, GR 2012, 'The context of expert global leadership', in WH Mobley, Y Wang & M Li (eds), *Advances in global leadership,* vol. 7, 107–24, Elsevier, Oxford, MA.

11. Ang, S & Van Dyne, L 2015, *Handbook of cultural intelligence,* Routledge, New York.

12. Zheng, M 2015, 'Intercultural competence in intercultural business communication', *Open Journal of Social Sciences,* 3(03), 197.

Suggested reading

Javidan, M & Teagarden, MB 2011, 'Conceptualizing and measuring global mindset', *Advances in global leadership* (pp. 13-39). Emerald Group Publishing Limited.

Kuada, JE, & Bujac, AI 2016, 'Two Decades of Global Mindset Research–Issues and Approaches', *Global Mindsets.* Routledge.

Chapter 3

References

1. Ancona, D 2012, 'Sensemaking: Framing and acting in the unknown', in SA Snook, N Nohria & R Khurana (eds), *The handbook for teaching leadership: Knowing, doing, and being*, Sage Publications, Thousand Oaks, CA.

2. Weick, KE 2010, 'Reflections on enacted sensemaking in the Bhopal disaster', *Journal of Management Studies*, 47(3), 537–50.

3. Schuyler, KG, Baugher, JE, Jironet, K & Lid-Falkman, L (eds) 2014, *Leading with spirit, presence, and authenticity: A volume in the international Leadership Association series, Building leadership bridges*, John Wiley & Sons, San Francisco.

4. McCarthy, J 2016, 'U.S. Economic Confidence Highest in Nine Years', 29 November, Gallup, http://www.gallup.com/poll/198200/economic-confidence-highest-nine-years.aspx.

5. Denning, S 2005, *The leader's guide to storytelling: Mastering the art and discipline of business narrative*, Jossey-Bass, San Francisco.

6. Boje, David M. 1991 'The Storytelling Organization: A Study Of Story Performance In An Office-Supply Firm', *Administrative Science Quarterly*, 36 (1): 106.

7. Heifetz, RA, Linsky, M & Grashow, A 2009, *The practice of adaptive leadership: Tools and tactics for changing your organization and the world*, Harvard Business Press, Boston.

8. Church, M, Coburn, S & Fink, C 2015, *Speakership: The art of oration, the science of influence'*, Thought Leaders, Balgowlah, NSW.

9. Baldwin, C 2005, *Storycatcher: Making sense of our lives through the power and practice of story*, New World Library, Novato, CA.

10. Sull, DN & Spinosa, C 2007, 'Promise-based management', *Harvard Business Review*, 85(4), 79–86.

Suggested reading

Austin, JL 1962, *How to do things with words*, Harvard University Press, Cambridge, MA.

Searle, JR 1970, *Speech acts*, Cambridge University Press, Cambridge, UK.

Chapter 4

References

1. Ghaemi, N 2011, *A first-rate madness: Uncovering the links between leadership and mental illness*, The Penguin Press, New York.

2. Carson, SH & Langer, EJ 2006, 'Mindfulness and self-acceptance', *Journal of Rational-emotive and Cognitive-behavior Therapy*, 24(1), 29–43.

3. Day, DV 2001, 'Leadership development: A review in context', *The Leadership Quarterly*, 11(4), 581–613.

4. Raelin, JA 2010, *The leaderful fieldbook: Strategies and activities for developing leadership in everyone*, Davies-Black, Boston.

5. Day, DV & Dragoni, L 2015, 'Leadership development: An outcome-oriented review based on time and levels of analyses', *Annual Review of Organizational Psychology and Organizational Behavior*, 2(1), 133–56.

6. McCallum, S & O'Connell, D 2009, 'Social capital and leadership development: Building stronger leadership through enhanced relational skills', *Leadership & Organization Development Journal*, 30(2), 152–66.

7. Blanchard, KH & Johnson, S 1982, *The one minute manager*, William Morrow & Co.

8. Heifetz, RA & Linsky M 2002, *Leadership on the line: Staying alive through the dangers of leading*, Harvard Business Review Press, Boston.

9. Bolden, R & Gosling, J 2006, 'Leadership competencies: Time to change the tune?', *Leadership*, 2(2), 147–63.

10. Grint, K. (2013). Leadership: The Enemy of the People? Management and Leadership Conference, Titanic Belfast. https://www.youtube.com/watch?v=FFpO9l4RYTE

11. Carroll, B, Levy, L & Richmond, D 2008, 'Leadership as practice: Challenging the competency paradigm', *Leadership*, 4(4), 363–79.

12. Zenger, JH & Folkman, J 2009, *The extraordinary leader: Turning good managers into great leaders*, McGraw-Hill, New York.

13. Ruderman, MN, Clerkin, C & Connolly, C 2014, *Leadership development beyond competencies: Moving to a holistic approach*, Center for Creative Leadership, Greensboro, NC.

14. Freedman, DH 2010, *Wrong: Why experts keep failing us – and how to know when not to trust them*, Little, Brown and Co., New York.

15. DeRue, DS, Ashford, SJ & Myers, CG 2012, 'Learning agility: In search of conceptual clarity and theoretical grounding', *Industrial and Organizational Psychology*, 5(3), 258–79.

16. Kouzes, JM & Posner, BZ 2011, *Credibility: How leaders gain and lose it, why people demand it*, John Wiley & Sons, San Francisco.

17. Kellerman, B 2008, *Followership: How followers are creating change and changing leaders*, Harvard Business Press, Boston.

18. Bird, A 2013, 'Mapping the content domain of global leadership competencies', *Global leadership: Research, practice, and development*, 2, 80–96.

19. World Economic Forum 2016, *The Future of Jobs report: Employment, skills and workforce strategy for the fourth industrial revolution*, World Economic Forum, Geneva.

20. Martineau, J 2004, 'Laying the groundwork: First steps in evaluating leadership development', *Leadership in Action*, 23(6), 3–8,

21. Kirkpatrick, JD & Kirkpatrick, WK 2014, *The Kirkpatrick Four Levels: A fresh look after 55 years (1959–2014)*, Kirkpatrick Partners, www.kirkpatrickpartners.com/Portals/0/Resources/White%20Papers/Kirkpatrick%20White%20Paper%20-%20May%202014.pdf.

22. Salicru, S, Wassenaar, E, Suerz, E & Spittle, J 2016, 'A case study of global leadership development best practice', *OD Practitioner*, 48(2), 12–20.

23. Harvard Business School Publishing 2016, *State of leadership development survey*, Harvard Business Publishing Corporate Learning, www.harvardbusiness.org/state-leadership-development.

Suggested reading

Carson, S 2010, *Your creative brain: Seven steps to maximize imagination, productivity, and innovation in your life*, Jossey-Bass, San Francisco.

Elenkov, DS & Pimentel, JR 2015, 'Social intelligence, emotional intelligence, and cultural intelligence', in S Ang & L Van Dyne (eds), *Handbook of cultural intelligence*, 289–305, Routledge, London.

Junker, NM & van Dick, R 2014, 'Implicit theories in organizational settings: A systematic review and research agenda of implicit leadership and followership theories', *The Leadership Quarterly*, 25(6), 1154–73.

Kaplan, A 1964, *The conduct of inquiry*, Transaction Publishers, New Brunswick, NJ.

Langer, EJ 2016, *The power of mindful learning*, Da Capo Lifelong Books, Boston.

Lauring, J, Paunova, M & Butler, CL 2015, 'Openness to language and value diversity fosters multicultural team creativity and performance', in *Academy of Management Proceedings 2015*(1) 13090, Academy of Management.

Lee, YT 2012, 'Global leadership in multicultural teams', in J Canals (ed.), *Leadership development in a global world*, 188–213, Palgrave Macmillan, London.

Meindl, JR, Ehrlich, SB & Dukerich, JM 1985, 'The romance of leadership', *Administrative Science Quarterly*, 30(1) 78–102.

Schyns, B & Riggio, RE 2016, 'Implicit leadership theories', *Global Encyclopaedia of Public Administration, Public Policy, and Governance*, 1–7.

Zander, L, Butler, CL, Mockaitis, AI, Herbert, K, Lauring, J, Mäkelä, K & Zettinig, P 2015, 'Team-based global organizations: The future of global organizing', in *The future of global organizing*, 227–43, Emerald Group Publishing Limited.

Chapter 5

References

1. *Steve Jobs introducing the iPhone at MacWorld 2007*, video, 9 January, www.youtube.com/watch?v=x7qPAY9JqE4.

2. Boatman, J & Wellins, R 2011, *DDI Global Leadership Forecast 2011: Time for a leadership revolution!*, Development Dimensions International, www.ddiworld.com/glf201.

3. Narain, J 2016, 'Selfish baby boomers: Generation wants to spend, spend, spend, rather than leave cash to their children', *Daily Mail*, 17 August, www.dailymail.co.uk/news/article-3744303/Selfish-baby-boomers-generation-wants-spend-spend-spend-leave-cash-children.html#ixzz4Wk3mU4W3.

4. The Week staff 2013, 'Millennials: The most selfish generation yet?', *The Week*, 15 May, http://theweek.com/articles/464375/millennials-most-selfish-generation.

5. Tate, R & White, J 2005, *People leave managers ... Not organizations!: Action based leadership*, iUniverse, Lincoln, NE.

6. Salicru S & Chelliah, J 2014, 'Messing with corporate heads? Psychological contracts and leadership integrity', *Journal of Business Strategy*, 35(3), 38–46.

7. Erhard, W, Jensen, MC & Zaffron, S 2016, *Integrity: A positive model that incorporates the normative phenomena of morality,*

ethics, and legality—Abridged (English language version), Harvard Business School NOM Unit Working Paper No. 10-061; Barbados Group Working Paper No. 10-01; Simon School Working Paper No. 10-07; http://dx.doi.org/10.2139/ssrn.1542759.

8. Kouzes, J & Posner, B 2012, *The leadership challenge,* John Wiley & Sons, San Francisco.

Suggested reading

Argyris, C 1960, *Understanding organisational behaviour,* Dorsey Press, Homewood, IL.

Guest, DE 1998, 'Is the psychological contract worth taking seriously?', *Journal of Organizational Behavior,* 19(1), 649–64.

Rousseau, DM 1995, *Psychological contracts in organisations: Understanding written and unwritten agreements,* Sage Publications, Thousand Oaks, CA.

Part II

Suggested reading

Neck, CP, Manz, CC & Houghton, JD 2017, *Self-leadership: The definitive guide to personal excellence,* Sage Publications, Thousand Oaks, CA.

Chapter 6

References

1. Bennis, WG & Thomas RJ 2002, 'Crucibles of leadership', *Harvard Business Review,* 80(9), 61–8.

2. Moore, RL 2001, *The archetype of initiation: Sacred space, ritual process, and personal transformation,* ed. MJ Havlick, Xlibris Corporation.

3. Productivity Commission 2010, *Performance benchmarking of Australian business regulation: Occupational health & safety*, Canberra, www.pc.gov.au/inquiries/completed/regulationbenchmarking-ohs/report.

4. Eliade, M 1958, *Rites and symbols of initiation (birth and rebirth)*, trans. W Trask, Harvill Press, London.

5. Eisler, RT 1998, *The equal rights handbook*, iUniverse, Lincoln, NE.

6. Turner, V 1974, *Dramas, fields, and metaphors: Symbolic action in human society*, Cornell University Press, Ithaca, NY.

7. Jung, CG 1968, *Man and his symbols*, Dell Publishing.

8. Rohr, R., Durepos, J., & McGrath, T. 2010. *On the threshold of transformation*. Loyola Press, Chicago.

9. Campbell, J 2003, *The hero's journey: Joseph Campbell on his life and work*, 3rd edn, ed. P Cousineau, 186–7, New World Library, Novato, California.

10. —— 1949, *The hero with a thousand faces*, Princeton University Press, Princeton.

11. Coelho, P 2006, *The alchemist: A fable about following your dream*, HarperCollins, San Francisco.

12. French, SE 2003, *The code of the warrior: Exploring the values of warrior cultures, past and present*, Rowman and Littlefield Publishers, New York.

13. Gilligan, C 1982, *In a different voice*, Harvard University Press, Cambridge, MA.

14. Kasser, TE & Kanner, AD 2004, *Psychology and consumer culture: The struggle for a good life in a materialistic world*, American Psychological Association, Washington, DC.

15. David, S 2016, *Emotional agility: Get unstuck, embrace change, and thrive in work and life*, Penguin, New York.

16. Keen, S 2010, *Fire in the belly: On being a man*, Bantam, New York.

Suggested reading

Boyatzis, RE, Goleman, D & Rhee, K 2000, 'Clustering competence in emotional intelligence: Insights from the Emotional Competence Inventory (ECI)', *Handbook of emotional intelligence*, 99(6), 343–62.

Finley, J 1980, *Merton's palace of nowhere: A search for god through awareness of the true self*, Ave Maria Press, Notre Dame, IN.

Merton, T., 1970. *The wisdom of the desert*. New Directions Publishing.

Moore, R.L. & Gillette, D. (1990). *King, Warrior, Magician, Lover: Rediscovering The Archetypes of the Mature Masculine*. San Francisco: Harper Collins.

Van Knippenberg, D, Van Knippenberg, B, De Cremer, D & Hogg, MA 2004, 'Leadership, self, and identity: A review and research agenda', *The Leadership Quarterly*, 15(6), 825–56.

Wren, JT 2013, *The leader's companion: Insights on leadership through the ages*, Simon & Schuster, New York.

Chapter 7

References

1. George, B 2015, *Discover your true north*, John Wiley & Sons, New York.

2. Senge, PM 2006, *The fifth discipline: The art and practice of the learning organization*, Doubleday, New York.

3. Cashman, K 2014, *Competencies and character in leadership*, video, 29 September, www.youtube.com/watch?list=UUsJ8bEQ-O4dFCjePSeOr68Q&v=NC8j8nkZUEo.

4. Clance, PR & Imes, SA 1978, 'The imposter phenomenon in high achieving women: dynamics and therapeutic intervention', *Psychotherapy: Theory, Research and Practice*, 15(3): 241–7.

5. Sakulku, J & Alexander, J 2011, 'The impostor phenomenon', *International Journal of Behavioral Science*, 6(1).

6. Cuddy, A 2015, *Presence: Bringing your boldest self to your biggest challenges*, Little, Brown and Company, New York.

7. Rotter, JB 1966, 'Generalized expectancies for internal versus external control of reinforcement', *Psychological Monographs: General & Applied*, 80(1), 1–28.

8. Seligman, M 1992, *Learned optimism*, Pocket Books, New York.

9. Merton, RK 1948, 'The self-fulfilling prophecy', *The Antioch Review*, 8(2), 193–210.

10. McCauley, CD, Van Veslor, E & Ruderman, MN 2010, 'Introduction: Our viewpoint of leadership development', in E Van Veslor, CD McCauley & MN Ruderman (eds), *The Center for Creative Leadership handbook of leadership development*, 1–26, John Wiley & Sons, San Francisco.

11. Day, DV 2001, 'Leadership development: A review in context', *The Leadership Quarterly*, 11(4), 581–613.

12. Branden, N 1995, *The six pillars of self-esteem*, Bantam Publishing, New York.

13. Seligman, ME & Csikszentmihalyi, M 2014, *Positive psychology: An introduction*, 279–98, Springer, Netherlands.

14. Drucker, PF 2006, *Classic Drucker: Essential wisdom of Peter Drucker from the pages of Harvard Business Review*, Harvard Business Press, Boston.

15. Rath, T & Conchie, B 2008, *Strengths based leadership: Great leaders, teams, and why people follow*, Gallup Press, New York.

16. Clifton, DO 2003, in Rath, T & Conchie, B 2008, 'Finding your leadership strengths', *Gallup Business Journal*, 11 December, www.gallup.com/businessjournal/112729/finding-your-leadership-strengths.aspx.

17. Jaussi, KS & Dionne, SD 2003, 'Leading for creativity: The role of unconventional leader behavior', *The Leadership Quarterly*, 14(4), 475–98.

18. Sarros, JC, Cooper BK, Hartican, AM & Barker CJ 2006, *The character of leadership: What works for Australian leaders — Making it work for you*, John Wiley & Sons, Milton, QLD.

19. Kiel, F 2015, 'Return on character: The real reason leaders and their companies win', Harvard Business Review Press.

20. Toner, JH 1998, 'Mistakes in teaching ethics', *Air Univ Maxwell AFB A1 Airpower Journal*.

21. Giles, Sunnie 2016, 'The most important leadership competencies, according to leaders around the world', *Harvard Business Review*, 15 March, https://hbr.org/2016/03/the-most-important-leadership-competencies-according-to-leaders-around-the-world.

22. Colquitt, JA, Scott, BA, Rodell, JB, Long, DM, Zapata, CP, Conlon, DE & Wesson, MJ 2013, 'Justice at the millennium, a decade later: A meta-analytic test of social exchange and affect-based perspectives', *Journal of Applied Psychology*, 98(2), 199–236.

23. Dyer, W 2001, *Your erroneous zones: Step-by-step advice for escaping the trap of negative thinking and taking control of your life*, HarperCollins, New York.

24. Hannah, ST & Avolio, BJ 2010, 'Moral potency: Building the capacity for character-based leadership', *Consulting Psychology Journal: Practice and Research*, 62(4), 291–310.

25. Luthans, F, Avey, JB, Avolio, BJ & Peterson, SJ 2010, 'The development and resulting performance impact of positive psychological capital', *Human Resource Development Quarterly*, 21(1), 41–67.

26. Luthans, F 2002, 'Positive organizational behavior: Developing and managing psychological strengths', *The Academy of Management Executive*, 16(1), 57–72.

27. Cascio, WF & Luthans, F 2014, 'Reflections on the metamorphosis at Robben Island: The role of institutional work and positive psychological capital', *Journal of Management Inquiry*, 23(1), 51–67.

28. Luthans, F, Avey, JB, Avolio, BJ, Norman, SM & Combs, GM 2006, 'Psychological capital development: Toward a micro-intervention', *Journal of Organizational Behavior*, 27(3), 387–93.

Suggested reading

Csikszentmihalyi, M 1990, *Flow: The psychology of optimal experience*, Harper Perennial, New York.

De Vries, MFRK 2005, 'The dangers of feeling like a fake', *Harvard Business Review*, 83(9), 108.

Dudău, DP 2014, 'The relation between perfectionism and impostor phenomenon', *Procedia-Social and Behavioral Sciences*, 127, 129–33.

Eden, D 1993, 'Leadership and expectations: Pygmalion effects and other self-fulfilling prophecies in organizations', *The Leadership Quarterly*, 3(4), 271–305.

Flett, GL & Hewitt, PL 2002, *Perfectionism*, 5–31, American Psychological Association, Washington, DC.

Gardner, W L, Cogliser, CC, Davis, KM & Dickens, MP 2011, 'Authentic leadership: A review of the literature and research agenda', *The Leadership Quarterly*, 22(6), 1120–45.

Gillham, JE, Shatte, AJ, Reivich, KJ & Seligman, ME 2001, 'Optimism, pessimism, and explanatory style', in EC Chang (ed.), *Optimism and pessimism: Implications for theory, research, and practice*, 53–75, American Psychological Association, Washington, DC.

Hannah, ST, Avolio, BJ & May, DR 2011, 'Moral maturation and moral conation: A capacity approach to explaining moral thought and action', *Academy of Management Review*, 36(4), 663–85.

Lickona, T 1991, *Educating for character*, Bantam, New York.

Lorenz, T, Beer, C, Pütz, J & Heinitz, K 2016, 'Measuring psychological capital: Construction and validation of the compound PsyCap scale (CPC-12)', *PloS one*, 11(4), e0152892.

Luthans, F 2002, 'Positive organizational behavior: Developing and managing psychological strengths', *Academy of Management Executive,* 16(1), 57–72.

Luthans F & Youssef, CM 2004, 'Human, social, and now positive psychological capital management: Investing in people for competitive advantage', *Organizational Dynamics,* 33(2), 143–60.

Luthans, F, Youssef-Morgan, CM & Avolio, B 2015, *Psychological capital and beyond,* Oxford University Press, New York.

Manz, CC 2015, 'Taking the self-leadership high road: Smooth surface or potholes ahead?', *The Academy of Management Perspectives,* 29(1), 132–51.

Parris, DL & Peachey, JW 2013, 'A systematic literature review of servant leadership theory in organizational contexts', *Journal of Business Ethics,* 113(3), 377–93.

Pearce, CL, Conger, JA & Locke, EA 2008, 'Shared leadership theory', *The Leadership Quarterly,* 19(5), 622–8.

Rath, T 2007, *StrengthsFinder 2.0,* Gallup Press, New York.

Rath, T & Conchie, B 2008, *Strengths based leadership: Great leaders, teams, and why people follow,* Gallup Press, New York.

Ruderman, MN, Clerkin, C & Connolly, C 2014, *Leadership development beyond competencies: Moving to a holistic approach,* Center for Creative Leadership, Greensboro, NC.

Schaubroeck, JM, Hannah, ST, Avolio, BJ, Kozlowski, SW, Lord, RG, Treviño, LK, Dimotakis, N & Peng, AC 2012, 'Embedding ethical leadership within and across organization levels', *Academy of Management Journal,* 55(5), 1053–78.

Van Wyk, R 2014, 'Nelson Mandela's defence: A psychological capital documentary analysis', *South African Journal of Science,* 110(11–12), 01–07.

Worden, S 2003, 'The role of integrity as a mediator in strategic leadership: A recipe for reputational capital', *Journal of Business Ethics,* 46(1), 31–44.

Young, V 2011, *The secret thoughts of successful women: Why capable people suffer from the impostor syndrome and how to thrive in spite of it,* Crown Publishing, New York.

Chapter 8

References

1. Fredrickson BL 2010, 'The role of positive emotions in positive psychology: The broaden-and-build theory of positive emotions', *American Psychologist*, (56), 218–26.

2. Lyubomirsky, S 2007, *The how of happiness: A new approach to getting the life you want*, Penguin, New York, NY.

3. Emmons, RA 2008, *Thanks!: How practicing gratitude can make you happier*, Houghton Mifflin Harcourt, Boston.

4. Costas, J & Kärreman, D 2016, 'The bored self in knowledge work', *Human Relations*, 69(1), 61–83.

5. Turriago-Hoyos, A, Thoene, U & Arjoon, S 2016, 'Knowledge workers and virtues in Peter Drucker's management theory', *SAGE Open*, 6(1), 2158244016639631.

6. Peterson, C & Seligman, MEP 2004, *Character strengths and virtues: A classification and handbook*, Oxford University Press, New York/American Psychological Association, Washington, DC.

7. Galunick, C 2017, 'Does articulating your corporate values matter?', Insead Knowledge, http://knowledge.insead.edu/node/4126/pdf.

8. Lencioni, PM 2002, 'Make your values mean something', *Harvard Business Review*, 80(7), 113–17.

9. Wood, R 2009, *Ethical leadership framework*, Centre for Ethical Leadership, Ormond College, University of Melbourne, https://cel.edu.au/our-research/ethical-leadership-framework.

Suggested reading

Arjoon S, Turriago-Hoyos A, Thoene U 2015, 'Virtuousness and the common good as a conceptual framework for harmonizing the goals of the individual, organizations, and the economy', *Journal of Business Ethics*, advance online publication, doi:10.1007/s10551-015-2969-6.

Frankl, VE 1985, *Man's search for meaning*, Simon & Schuster, New York.

Fredrickson BL 2010, 'The role of positive emotions in positive psychology: The broaden-and-build theory of positive emotions', *American Psychologist*, 56:218–26.

—— 2013, 'Updated thinking on the positivity ratio', *American Psychologist*, 68, 814–22.

Fredrickson, BL & Branigan, C 2005, 'Positive emotions broaden the scope of attention and thought-action repertoires', *Cognition & Emotion*, 19(3), 313–32.

Grant, AM & Gino, F 2010, 'A little thanks goes a long way: Explaining why gratitude expressions motivate prosocial behavior', *Journal of Personality and Social Psychology*, 98(6), 946–55.

Jonsen, K, Galunic, C, Weeks, J & Braga, T 2015, 'Evaluating espoused values: does articulating values pay off?', *European Management Journal*, 33(5), 332–40.

Lewis, M, Haviland-Jones, JM & Barrett, LF (eds) 2010, *Handbook of emotions*, Guilford Press, New York.

Lyubomirsky, S, Sheldon, KM & Schkade, D 2005, 'Pursuing happiness: The architecture of sustainable change' *Review of General Psychology*, 9(2), 111.

Muzur, A 2009, *The moral brain: Essays on the evolutionary and neuroscientific aspects of morality*, J Verplaetse, J De Schrijver, S Vanneste, J Braeckman (eds), Business Media BV, Springer Science, Dordrecht.

Niemiec, RM 2013, *Mindfulness and character strengths: A practical guide to flourishing*, Hogrefe, Cambridge.

Park, N, Peterson, C & Seligman, MEP 2006, 'Character strengths in fifty-four nations and the fifty US states', *The Journal of Positive Psychology*, 1(3), 118–29.

Peterson, C & Park, N 2004, 'Classification and measurement of character strengths: Implications for practice', *Positive Psychology in Practice*, 433–46.

Rash, JA, Matsuba, MK & Prkachin, KM 2011, 'Gratitude and well-being: Who benefits the most from a gratitude intervention?', *Applied Psychology: Health and Well-Being*, 3(3), 350–69.

VIA Survey, www.viacharacter.org/www/Character-Strengths-Survey.

Chapter 9

References

1. Herzberg, F, Mausner, B & Snyderman, BB 1959, *The motivation to work*, 2nd edn, John Wiley & Sons, New York.

2. Buckingham, M & Coffman, C 2014, *First, break all the rules: What the world's greatest managers do differently*, Gallup Press, New York.

3. Latham, GP 2012, *Work motivation: History, theory, research, and practice*, Sage Publications, Los Angeles.

4. Coelho, P 1993, *The alchemist*, HarperCollins, San Francisco.

5. Latham, GP 2004, 'The motivational benefits of goal-setting', *The Academy of Management Executive*, 18(4), 126–9.

6. Grant, AM 2012, 'An integrated model of goal-focused coaching: An evidence-based framework for teaching and practice', *International Coaching Psychology Review*, 7(2), 146–65.

7. Goldsmith, M 2007, *What got you here won't get you there: How successful people become even more successful*, Profile books, London.

8. Mann, A & Harter J 2106, 'The worldwide employee engagement crisis', *Gallup Business Journal*, 7 January,

www.gallup.com/businessjournal/188033/worldwide-employee-engagement-crisis.aspx.

9. Bersin by Deloitte 2016, 'Predictions for 2016: A bold new world of talent, learning, leadership, and HR technology ahead', webinar, http://marketing.bersin.com/Predictions-for-2016-A-Bold-New-World-of-Talent-Learning-Leadership-and-HR-Technology-ahead_012616.html?mkt_tok=3rkmmjwwff9wsron s6nac%2b%2fhmjteu5z16oktwqowhikz2efye%2blihetpodcmtcp hnr%2fydbceejhqyqjxpr3mk9yn1thtrhfraq%3d%3d.

10. Welch, J in Saunders, L & Tiwari, D 2014, 'Employee Engagement and disengagement: Causes and benefits', *The International Journal of Business & Management*, 2(5), 44, http://theijbm.com/may2014/5.BM1405-009.pdf.

11. Saks, AM 2006, 'Antecedents and consequences of employee engagement', *Journal of Managerial Psychology*, 21(7), 600–19.

12. Robinson, D, Perryman, S & Hayday, S 2004, *The drivers of employee engagement*, Institute for Employment Studies, Brighton, UK.

13. Kahn, WA 1990, 'Psychological conditions of personal engagement and disengagement at work', *Academy of Management Journal*, 33(4), 692–724.

14. Reilly, R 2014, 'Five ways to improve employee engagement now', *Gallup Business Journal*, 7 January, www.gallup.com/businessjournal/166667/five-ways-improve-employee-engagement.aspx.

15. Harter, JK, Schmidt, FL & Hayes, TL 2002, 'Business-unit-level relationship between employee satisfaction, employee engagement, and business outcomes: A meta-analysis', *Journal of Applied Psychology* 87(2), 268–79.

16. Aon Hewitt 2016, *2016 Trends in global employee engagement: Employee engagement is on the rise, but volatility abounds*, Aon Hewitt Corporation.

17. Schaufeli, WB, Salanova, M, González-Romá, V & Bakker, AB 2002, 'The measurement of engagement and burnout: A

two sample confirmatory factor analytic approach', *Journal of Happiness Studies*, 3(1), 71–92.

18. Vance, RJ 2006, *Employee engagement and commitment: A guide to understanding, measuring and increasing engagement in your organization*, Society for Human Resource Management, Alexandria, VA.

19. Human Capital Institute in Jones, D 2012, 'The dollars and sense of employee engagement', blog post, 6 March, Halogen Software, www.halogensoftware.com/blog/the-dollars-and-sense-of-employee-engagement.

Suggested reading

Bergami, M & Bagozzi, RP 2000, 'Self-categorization, affective commitment and group self-esteem as distinct aspects of social identity in the organization', *British Journal of Social Psychology*, 39(4), 555–77.

Britt, TW, McKibben, ES, Greene-Shortridge, TM, Beeco, A, Bodine, A, Calcaterra, J & West, A 2010, 'Self-engagement as a predictor of performance and emotional reactions to performance outcomes', *British Journal of Social Psychology*, 49(2), 237–57.

Britt, TW, McKibben, ES, Greene-Shortridge, TM, Odle-Dusseau, HN & Herleman, HA 2012, 'Self-engagement moderates the mediated relationship between organizational constraints and organizational citizenship behaviors via rated leadership', *Journal of Applied Social Psychology*, 42(8), 1830–46.

Gagné, M & Deci, EL 2005, 'Self-determination theory and work motivation', *Journal of Organizational Behavior*, 26(4), 331–62.

Goldsmith, M & Reiter, M 2015, *Triggers: Creating behavior that lasts—becoming the person you want to be*, Crown Business, New York.

Herzberg, F 1968, *One more time: How do you motivate employees*, Harvard Business Review, Boston.

Jeung, CW 2011, 'The concept of employee engagement: A comprehensive review from a positive organizational behavior perspective', *Performance Improvement Quarterly*, 24(2), 49–69.

Latham, GP 2012, *Work motivation: History, theory, research, and practice*, Sage Publications, Los Angeles.

Latham, GP, Budworth, MH 2007, 'The study of work motivation in the 20th century', in LL Koppes, PW Thayer, AJ Vinchur & E Salas (eds), *Historical perspectives in industrial and organizational psychology*, series in applied psychology, 353–82, Lawrence Erlbaum Associates, Mahwah, NJ.

Locke, EA & Latham, GP 2002, 'Building a practically useful theory of goal setting and task motivation', *American Psychologist*, 57(9), 705–17.

Macey, WH & Schneider, B 2008, 'The meaning of employee engagement', *Industrial and organizational Psychology*, 1(1), 3–30.

Meyer, JP & Allen, NJ 1991, 'A three-component conceptualization of organizational commitment', *Human Resource Management Review*, 1(1), 61–89.

Rhoades, L, Eisenberger, R & Armeli, S 2001, 'Affective commitment to the organization: The contribution of perceived organizational support', *Journal of Applied Psychology*, 86(5), 825.

Ryan, RM & Deci, EL 2000, 'Intrinsic and extrinsic motivations: Classic definitions and new directions', *Contemporary Educational Psychology*, 25(1), 54–67.

Shamir, B 1991, 'Meaning, self and motivation in organizations', *Organization Studies*, 12(3), 405–24.

Wellins, R & Concelman, J 2005, 'Personal engagement: Driving growth at the see-level', www.ddiworld.com/pdf/ddi_personalengagement_ar.pdf.

Xanthopoulou, D, Bakker, AB, Demerouti, E & Schaufeli, WB 2009, 'Work engagement and financial returns: A diary study on the role of job and personal resources', *Journal of Occupational and Organizational Psychology*, 82(1), 183–200.

Zhang, X & Bartol, KM 2010, 'Linking empowering leadership and employee creativity: The influence of psychological empowerment, intrinsic motivation, and creative process engagement', *Academy of Management Journal*, 53(1), 107–28.

Chapter 10

References

1. Denis, JL, Langley, A & Sergi, V 2012, 'Leadership in the plural', *Academy of Management Annals,* 6(1), 211–83.

2. James, W, www.quotes.net/quote/1912.

3. Darley, JM & Latané, B 1968, 'Bystander intervention in emergencies: Diffusion of responsibility', *Journal of Personality and Social Psychology,* 8(4), 377–83.

4. Zaccaro, S-J 1984, 'Social loafing: The role of task attractiveness', *Personality and Social Psychology Bulletin,* 10(1), 99–106.

5. Edmondson, A 1999, 'Psychological safety and learning behavior in work teams', *Administrative Science Quarterly,* 44(2), 350–83.

6. —— 2014, *Building a psychologically safe workplace,* video, TEDxHGSE, https://www.youtube.com/watch?v=LhoLuui9gX8.

7. Foushee, HC 1984, 'Dyads and triads at 35,000 feet: Factors affecting group process and aircrew performance', *American Psychologist,* 39(8), 885–93.

8. Wiener, EL & Nagel, DC (eds) 2014, *Human factors in aviation,* Academic Press, San Diego.

9. Grote, G 2016, 'Leading high-risk teams in aviation', in *Leadership lessons from compelling contexts,* 189–208, Emerald Group Publishing Limited.

10. Hirak, R, Peng, AC, Carmeli, A & Schaubroeck, JM 2012, 'Linking leader inclusiveness to work unit performance: The importance of psychological safety and learning from failures', *The Leadership Quarterly,* 23(1), 107–17.

11. Carmeli, A, Reiter-Palmon, R & Ziv, E 2010, 'Inclusive leadership and employee involvement in creative tasks in the

workplace: The mediating role of psychological safety', *Creativity Research Journal*, 22(3), 250–60.

12. Baer, M, & Frese, M 2003, 'Innovation is not enough: Climates for initiative and psychological safety, process innovations, and firm performance', *Journal of Organizational Behavior*, 24(1), 45–68.

13. Wilson, P 2016, 'Lessons from Google: 5 Ways to Create Psychological Safety', *Approachable Leadership*, 18 March, 1–10, http://approachableleadership.com/google-psychological-safety/.

14. Giber, D, Lam, SM, Goldsmith, M & Bourke, J (eds) 2009, *Linkage Inc's Best practices in leadership development handbook: Case studies, instruments, training*, 2nd edn, Pfeiffer, San Francisco.

15. Rifkin, G 2011, 'Brains on fire', Koen Ferry Institute, www.kornferry.com/institute/27-brains-on-fire.

16. Collins, B 2016, 'New care models: emerging innovations in governance and organisational form', The Kings Fund, London.

17. Dunn, P, McKenna, H & Murray, R 2016, 'Deficits in the NHS', The Kings Fund, London.

18. Johnson, T, Martin, AJ, Palmer, FR, Watson, G & Ramsey, P 2012, 'Collective leadership: A case study of the All Blacks', *Asia-Pacific Management and Business Application*, 1(1), 53–67.

19. Raelin, JA 2010, *The leaderful fieldbook: Strategies and activities for developing leadership in everyone*, Davies-Black, Boston.

20. Kelley D, Center for Building a Culture of Empathy, http://cultureofempathy.com/References/Experts/David-Kelley.htm.

21. Alcoholics Anonymous 2001, *Alcoholics Anonymous*, 4th edn, A.A. World Services, New York.

22. Borkman, T 2006, 'Sharing experience, conveying hope: Egalitarian relations as the essential method of Alcoholics Anonymous', *Nonprofit Management and Leadership*, 17(2), 145–61.

23. 'Famous alcohol abusers', DrugAbuse.com, drugabuse.com/
library/famous-alcohol-abusers/.

Suggested reading

Alderwick, H, Dunn, P, McKenna, H, Walsh, N & Ham, C 2016, *Sustainability and transformation plans in the NHS: How are they being developed in practice?*, The King's Fund, www.kingsfund.org.uk/sites/files/kf/field/field_publication_file/STPs_in_NHS_Kings_Fund_Nov_2016.pdf.

Amabile, T 2012, *Componential theory of creativity*, Harvard Business School, Boston.

Amabile, TM & Pillemer, J 2012, 'Perspectives on the social psychology of creativity', *The Journal of Creative Behavior*, 46(1), 3-15.

Denis, JL, Lamothe, L & Langley, A 2001, 'The dynamics of collective leadership and strategic change in pluralistic organizations', *Academy of Management Journal*, 44(4), 809–37.

Edmondson, A 2003, 'Managing the risk of learning: Psychological safety in work teams', in M West (ed.), *International handbook of organizational teamwork and cooperative working*, 255–76, Blackwell, London.

Edmondson, A & Lei, Z 2014, 'Psychological safety: The history, renaissance, and future of an interpersonal construct', *The Annual Review of Organizational Psychology and Organizational Behavior*, 1: 23–43.

Gupta, VK, Huang, R & Yayla, AA 2011, 'Social capital, collective transformational leadership, and performance: A resource-based view of self-managed teams', *Journal of Managerial Issues*, 23(1), 31–45.

Kark, R, Shamir, B & Chen, G 2003, 'The two faces of transformational leadership: empowerment and dependency', *Journal of Applied Psychology*, 88(2), 246.

Kets de Vries, MF 1988, 'Origins of charisma: Ties that bind the leader and the led', in JA Conger & RN Kanungo (eds), *Charismatic leadership*, 237–52, Jossey-Bass, San Francisco.

Lemay L 2009, 'The practice of collective leadership in the public sector', *The Public Sector Innovation Journal*, 14(1), Article 2.

Levine, M & Crowther, S 2008, 'The responsive bystander: How social group membership and group size can encourage as well as inhibit bystander intervention', *Journal of Personality and Social Psychology*, 95(6), 1429.

Marinnez-Moyano, IJ 2006, 'Exploring the dynamics of collaboration in interorganizational settings', in S Schuman (ed.), *Creating a culture of collaboration*, 69–86, Jossey-Bass, San Francisco.

Militello, M & Benham, MK 2010, '"Sorting Out" collective leadership: How Q-methodology can be used to evaluate leadership development', *The Leadership Quarterly*, 21(4), 620–32.

Mudrack, PE 1989, 'Defining group cohesiveness: A legacy of confusion?', *Small Group Behavior*, 20(1), 37–49.

Pearce, CL, Conger, JA & Locke, EA 2008, 'Shared leadership theory', *The Leadership Quarterly*, 19(5), 622–8.

Peck, MS 1978, *The road less travelled: A new psychology of love*, Rider, London.

—— 2010, *The different drum: Community making and peace*, Simon & Schuster, New York.

Rutkowski, GK, Gruder, CL & Romer, D 1983, 'Group cohesiveness, social norms, and bystander intervention', *Journal of Personality and Social Psychology*, 44(3), 545.

West, M, Eckert, R, Steward, K & Pasmore, B 2014, *Developing collective leadership for health care*, The King's Fund, London.

Chapter 11

References

1. McCauley, CD, Van Velsor, E & Ruderman, MN 2010, 'Interdiction: Our view of leadership development', in E Van Velsor, CD McCauley & MN Ruderman (eds), *The Center for*

Creative Leadership handbook of leadership development, 1–26, Jossey-Bass, San Francisco.

2. Denis, JL, Langley, A & Sergi, V 2012, 'Leadership in the plural', *Academy of Management Annals*, 6(1), 211–83.

3. Raelin, JA 2016, 'Imagine there are no leaders: Reframing leadership as collaborative agency', *Leadership*, 12(2), 131–58.

4. —— 2011, 'From leadership-as-practice to leaderful practice', *Leadership*, 7(2), 195–211.

5. Mintzberg, H 2004, *Managers, not MBAs: A hard look at the soft practice of managing and management development*, Berrett-Koehler Publishing, San Francisco.

6. Day, DV & Dragoni, L 2015, 'Leadership development: An outcome-oriented review based on time and levels of analyses', *Annual Review of Organizational Psychology and Organizational Behavior*, 2(1), 133–56.

7. Bennis, WG 1989, 'Managing the dream: leadership in the 21st century', *Journal of Organizational Change Management*, 2(1), 6–10.

8. Hitt, MA & Duane, R 2002, 'The essence of strategic leadership: Managing human and social capital', *Journal of Leadership & Organizational Studies*, 9(1), 3–14.

9. Dalziel, T, Gentry, RJ & Bowerman, M 2011, 'An integrated agency–resource dependence view of the influence of directors' human and relational capital on firms' R&D spending', *Journal of Management Studies*, 48(6), 1217–42.

10. Uhl-Bien, M 2006, 'Relational leadership theory: Exploring the social processes of leadership and organizing', *The Leadership Quarterly*, 17(6), 654–76.

11. Salicru, S, Wassenaar, E, Suerz, E & Spittle, J 2016, 'A case study of global leadership development best practice', *OD Practitioner*, 48(2), 12–20.

12. Kolb, AY & Kolb, DA 2009, 'Experiential learning theory: A dynamic, holistic approach to management learning, education

and development', in SJ Armstrong & CV Fukami (eds), *The Sage handbook of management learning, education and development*, 42–68, Sage Publications, Los Angeles.

13. Charlton, K & Osterweil, C 2005, 'Measuring return on investment in executive education: A quest to meet client needs or pursuit of the Holy Grail', *Ashridge Journal*, 6–13.

14. PricewaterhouseCoopers 2015, *18th annual global CEO survey*, www.pwc.com/gx/en/ceo-survey/2015/assets/pwc-18th-annual-global-ceo-survey-jan-2015.pdf.

15. Korn Ferry Institute 2015, *Real world leadership: Part One*, www.kornferry.com/institute/real-world-leadership-part-two-build-a-pipeline-of-ready-now-leaders?reports-and-insights.

16. Deloitte University Press 2015, *Global human capital trends report: Leading in the new world of work*, www2.deloitte.com/content/dam/Deloitte/at/Documents/human-capital/hc-trends-2015.pdf.

17. Harvard Business School Publishing 2016, *State of leadership development survey*, Harvard Business Publishing Corporate Learning, www.harvardbusiness.org/sites/default/files/19770_CL_StateOfLeadership_Report_July2016.pdf.

18. Kirkpatrick, JD & Kirkpatrick, WK 2014, *The Kirkpatrick Four Levels: A fresh look after 55 years (1959–2014)*, Kirkpatrick Partners.

19. —— 2010, 'ROE's Rising Star', *T+D Magazine*, www.kirkpatrickpartners.com/Resources/tabid/56/Default.aspx.

20. Phillips, PP, Phillips, JJ & Ray, R 2015, *Measuring the success of leadership development: A step-by-step guide for measuring impact and calculating ROI*, Association for Talent Development (ATD) Press, Alexandria, VA.

21. Rothbauer, P 2008, 'Triangulation', in L Given (ed.), *The Sage encyclopedia of qualitative research methods*, 892–4, Sage Publications, Thousand Oaks, CA.

Suggested reading

Adler, PS & Kwon, SW 2002, 'Social capital: Prospects for a new concept', *Academy of Management Review*, 27(1), 17–40.

Canals, J 2014, 'Global leadership development, strategic alignment and CEOs commitment', *Journal of Management Development*, 33(5), 487–502.

Carroll, B & Simpson, B 2012, 'Capturing sociality in the movement between frames: An illustration from leadership development', *Human Relations*, 65(10), 1283–1309.

Cavallaro, L 2007, 'Action learning accelerates innovation: Cisco's action learning forum', *Organization Development Journal*, 25(4),107.

Contractor, NS, DeChurch, LA, Carson, J, Carter, DR & Keegan, B 2012, 'The topology of collective leadership', *The Leadership Quarterly*, 23(6), 994–1011.

Cullen, KL, Palus, CJ, Chrobot-Mason, D & Appaneal, C 2102, 'Getting to "We": Collective leadership development', *Industrial & Organizational Psychology*, 5(4), 428–32.

DeRue, DS, Nahrgang, JD, Hollenbeck, JR & Workman, K 2012, 'A quasi-experimental study of after-event reviews and leadership development', *Journal of Applied Psychology*, 97(5), 997–1015.

Edmondson, AC & Lei, Z 2014, 'Psychological safety: The history, renaissance, and future of an interpersonal construct', *Annual Review of Organizational Psychology and Organizational Behavior*, 1(1), 23–43.

Ellis, S, Carette, B, Anseel, F & Lievens, F 2014, 'Systematic reflection: Implications for learning from failures and successes', *Current Directions in Psychological Science*, 23(1), 67–72.

Grant, AM 2012, 'ROI is a poor measure of coaching success: Towards a more holistic approach using a well-being and engagement framework', *Coaching: An International Journal of Theory, Research and Practice*, 5(2), 74–85.

Hazy, JK & Uhl-Bien, M 2014, 'Changing the rules: The implications of complexity science for leadership research and practice', in DV Day (ed.), *The Oxford handbook of leadership and organizations*, 709–32, Oxford University Press, New York.

Hezlett, SA 2016, 'Enhancing experience-driven leadership development', *Advances in Developing Human Resources*, 18(3), 369–89.

Ibarra, H & Hunter, M 2007, 'How leaders create and use networks', *Harvard Business Review*, 85(1): 40–7.

Jick, TD 1979, 'Mixing qualitative and quantitative methods: Triangulation in action', *Administrative Science Quarterly*, 24(4), 602–11.

Kotter, JP 1990, *A force for change: How leadership differs from management*, Free Press, New York.

Leech, NL & Onwuegbuzie, AJ 2009, 'A typology of mixed methods research designs', *Quality & Quantity*, 43(2), 265–75.

McCall, MW, Jr 2010, 'Recasting leadership development', *Industrial and Organizational Psychology: Perspectives on Science and Practice*, 3, 3–19.

McCall, MW, Jr & McHenry, JJ 2014, 'Catalytic converters: How exceptional bosses develop leaders', in CD McCauley & MW McCall, Jr, (eds), *Using experience to develop talent: How organizations leverage on-the-job development*, 396–421, Jossey-Bass, San Francisco.

McCauley, CD & McCall, MW, Jr 2014, *Using experience to develop talent: How organizations leverage on-the-job experience*, Jossey-Bass, San Francisco.

McCauley, CD, DeRue, DS, Yost, PR & Taylor, S 2014, *Experience-driven leader development*, John Wiley & Sons, San Francisco.

Preston-Dayne, LA 2014, 'PARR: A learning model for managers', in CD McCauley, DS DeRue, PR Yost, & S Taylor (eds), *Experience-driven leader development: Models, tools, best practices, and advice for on-the-job development*, 151–5, John Wiley & Sons, San Francisco.

Raelin, JA 2010, *The leaderful fieldbook: Strategies and activities for developing leadership in everyone*, Davies-Black, Boston.

—— 2013, 'The manager as facilitator of dialogue', *Organization*, 20(6), 818–39.

—— 2016, 'It's not about the leaders: It's about the practice of leadership', *Organizational Dynamics*, 45, 124–31.

Van Katwyk, P, Hazucha, J & Goff, M 2014, 'A leadership experience framework', in CD Mccauley, DS DeRue, PR Yost, & S Taylor (eds), *Experience-driven leader development: Models, tools, best practices, and advice for on-the-job development*, 15–20, John Wiley & Sons, San Francisco.

Yammarino, FJ, Salas, E, Serban, A, Shirreffs, K & Shuffler, ML 2012, 'Collectivistic leadership approaches: Putting the "we" in leadership science and practice', *Industrial and Organizational Psychology*, 5(4), 382–402.

Chapter 12

References

1. Raelin, JA 2016, 'It's not about the leaders: It's about the practice of leadership', *Organizational Dynamics*, 45(2), 124–31.

2. Schwarz, R 2002, *The skilled facilitator: A comprehensive resource for consultants, facilitators, managers, trainers, and coaches*, Jossey-Bass, San Francisco.

3. Heron, J 1999, *The complete facilitator's handbook*, Kogan Page, London.

4. World Institute for Action Learning 2017, 'What is Action Learning?', http://wial.org/action-learning.

5. McGill, I, & Beaty, L 2001, *Action Learning: A guide for professional, management and educational development*, Kogan Page, London.

6. Keys, L 1994, 'Action Learning: Executive development of choice for the 1990s', *Journal of Management Development*, 13(8), 50–6.

7. Pedler, M 2011, *Action learning in practice*, Gower Publishing.

8. Revans, R 2011, *ABC of action learning*, Gower Publishing.

9. McGonagill, G & Doerffer, T 2010, *Leadership development in the U.S.: Principles and patterns of best practice*, Bertelsmann

Stiftung, http://mcgonagillconsulting.com/download/
Leadership_Development_Best_Practices.pdf.

10. Marquardt, MJ 2013, *Michael Marquardt Action Learning
    lecture*, video, www.youtube.com/watch?v=ZtVG8kF8qf4.

11. Giber, D, Lam, SM, Goldsmith, M & Bourke, J (eds) 2009,
    *Linkage Inc's best practices in leadership development handbook:
    Case studies, instruments, training*, 2nd edn, Pfeiffer, San
    Francisco.

12. Foxon, MJ 1998, 'Closing the global leadership competency
    gap: The Motorola GOLD process', *Organization Development
    Journal*, 16(4), 5–12.

13. Marquardt, MJ 2003, 'Developing global leaders via action
    learning programs: A case study at Boeing', *Thai Journal of
    Public Administration*, 3(3), 133–57.

14. —— 2000, 'Action learning and leadership', *The Learning
    Organization*, 7(5), 233–41.

15. Dotlich, DL & Noel, JL 1998, *Action learning: How the world's
    top companies are re-creating their leaders and themselves*, Jossey-
    Bass, San Francisco.

16. Boshyk, Y 2012, 'History, evolution and some varieties of.
    action learning: A roadmap', conference presentation (expanded
    version), *New Dimensions in Action Learning: Reinventing
    Leadership Development*, MIT Action Learning, 2 August,
    http://mitsloan.mit.edu/actionlearning/media/documents/
    conference2012/YuryBoshyk.pdf.

17. Heifetz, RA, Grashow, A & Linsky, M 2009, *The practice of
    adaptive leadership: Tools and tactics for changing your organization
    and the world*, Harvard Business Press, Boston.

18. Heifetz, RA & Linsky, M 2002, *Leadership on the line: Staying
    alive through the dangers of leading*, Harvard Business Review
    Press, Boston.

19. Johnstone, M & Fern, M 2010, 'Case-in-point: An experiential methodology for leadership education', *The Journal Kansas Leadership Center,* 2(2), 98–117.

20. Shapiro, E & Carr, A 2012, 'An introduction to Tavistock-style group relations conference learning', *Organisational and Social Dynamics,* 12(1), 70–80.

21. Owen, H 2008, *Open space technology: A user's guide,* Berrett-Koehler, Oakland, CA.

22. Lindfield, M 1995, 'Open Space Technology', Open Space World, www.openspaceworld.org/files/tmnfiles/lindfield.htm.

23. Herman, M 2006, *Open space technology: Inviting leadership practice,* www.michaelherman.com/publications/inviting_leadership.pdf.

24. Jones, D 2001, 'Sociometry in team and organisation development', *British Journal of Psychodrama and Sociodrama,* 16(1).

25. Lippitt, R 1943, 'The psychodrama in leadership training', *Sociometry,* 6(3), 286–92.

26. Freeman, L 2004, *The development of social network analysis: A study in the sociology of science,* BookSurge, North Charleston, SC.

27. Center for Creative Leadership 2015, *Leadership development state of practice,* Center for Creative Leadership, Greensboro, NC.

28. Macnamara, D 2014, '5 Dynamics of networking leadership', *Leadership Acumen,* 19, Banff Executive Leadership Inc.

29. Grayson, C & Baldwin, D 2011, *Leadership networking: Connect, collaborate, create,* Center for Creative Leadership, Greensboro, NC.

30. Cullen-Lester, KL, Maupin, CK & Carter, DR 2017, 'Incorporating social networks into leadership development: A conceptual model and evaluation of research and practice', *The Leadership Quarterly,* 28(1), 130–52.

31. Cullen, K, Willburn, P, Chrobot-Mason, D & Palus, C 2014, *Networks: How collective leadership really works*, Center for Creative Leadership, Greensboro, NC.

32. Ibarra, H & Hunter, M 2007, 'How leaders create and use networks', *Harvard Business Review,* 85(1): 40–7.

33. Puccio, GJ, Mance, M & Murdock, MC 2010, *Creative leadership: Skills that drive change*, Sage Publications, Thousand Oaks, CA.

34. Puccio, G & Grivas, C 2009, 'Examining the relationship between personality traits and creativity styles', *Creativity and Innovation Management,* 18(4), 247–55.

35. Gliddon, DG 2006, 'Forecasting a competency model for innovation leaders using a modified delphi technique', PhD thesis, Penn State University.

36. Horth, D & Buchner, D 2014, *Innovation leadership: How to use innovation to lead effectively, work collaboratively and drive results*, Center for Creative Leadership, Greensborough, NC.

37. Ekvall, G 1996, 'Organizational climate for creativity and innovation', *European Journal of Work and Organizational Psychology,* 5(1), 105–23.

38. Hackman, JR & Wageman, R 2005, 'A theory of team coaching', *Academy of Management Review,* 30(2), 269–87.

39. Hawkins, P 2014, *Leadership team coaching: Developing collective transformational leadership*, Kogan Page, London.

40. Edmondson, AC 2012, *Teaming: How organizations learn, innovate, and compete in the knowledge economy*, Jossey-Bass, San Francisco.

41. —— 2012, 'Teamwork on the fly', *Harvard Business Review,* 90(4), 72–80.

Suggested reading

Andrews, HB 1995, *Group design and leadership: Strategies for creating successful common-theme groups*, Allyn & Bacon, Boston.

Argyris, C, & Schön, D 1978, *Organizational learning: A theory of action perspective*, Addison Wesley, Reading, MA.

Balkundi, P, & Kilduff, M 2006, 'The ties that lead: A social network approach to leadership', *The Leadership Quarterly*, 17(4), 419–39.

Barnes, LB, & Kriger, MP 1986, 'The hidden side of organizational leadership', *Sloan Management Review*, 28(1), 15.

Bens, I 2012, *Advanced facilitation strategies: Tools and techniques to master difficult situations*, John Wiley & Sons, San Francisco.

———— 2012, *Facilitating with ease! Core skills for facilitators, team leaders and members, managers, consultants, and trainers*, John Wiley & Sons, San Francisco.

Bidart-Novaes, M, Brunstein, J, Gil, AC, & Drummond, J 2014, 'Sociodrama as a creative learning strategy in business administration', *Creative Education*, 5(14), 1322–33 .

Borgatti, SP, & Cross, R 2003, 'A relational view of information seeking and learning in social networks', *Management Science*, 49(4), 432–45.

Boshyk, Y (ed.) 2002, 'Action learning worldwide: Experiences of leadership and organizational development', Springer.

Burke, CS, DiazGranados, D, & Salas, E 2011, 'Team leadership: A review and look ahead', in A Bryman, D Collinson, K Grint, B Jackson & M Uhl-Bien (eds), *The Sage handbook of leadership*, 338–51, Sage Publications, London.

Cacioppe, R, & Edwards, M 2005, 'Seeking the Holy Grail of organisational development: A synthesis of integral theory, spiral dynamics, corporate transformation and action inquiry', *Leadership & Organization Development Journal*, 26(2), 86–105.

Carr, W 1996, 'Learning for leadership', *Leadership & Organization Development Journal*, 17(6), 46–52.

Carroll, B, Levy, L, & Richmond, D 2008, 'Leadership as practice: Challenging the competency paradigm', *Leadership*, 4(4), 363–79.

Cilliers, F, & Koortzen, P 2000, 'The psychodynamic view on organisational behaviour', *The Industrial-Organizational Psychologist*, 38(2), 59–67.

Cross, R, Borgatti, SP, & Parker, A 2002, 'Making invisible work visible: Using social network analysis to support strategic collaboration', *California Management Review*, 44(2), 25–46.

Daloz Parks, S 2005, *Leadership can be taught*, Harvard Business School Publishing, Boston.

de Novaes, MBC, Brunstein, J, & Gil, AC, *Sociodrama as a learning process in organizations: A support tool for creativity and change in action research*, http://www.academia.edu/3774179/sociodrama_as_a_learning_process_in_organizations_a_support_tool_for_creativity_and_change_in_action_research.

Dick, B 1991, *Helping groups to be effective: Skills, processes and concepts for group facilitation*, Interchange, Chapel Hill, QLD.

Dixon, NM 1998, 'Action learning: More than just a task force', *Performance Improvement Quarterly*, 11(1), 44–58.

Galaskiewicz, J, & Shatin, D 1981, 'Leadership and networking among neighborhood human service organizations', *Administrative Science Quarterly*, 26(3), 434–48.

Goldstein, IL 1993, *Training in organizations: Needs assessment, development, and evaluation*, Thomson Brooks/Cole Publishing Co.

Gould, LJ, Stapley, LF, & Stein, M (eds) 2006, *The systems psychodynamics of organizations: Integrating the group relations approach, psychoanalytic, and open systems perspectives*, Karnak Books, London.

Grayson, C, & Baldwin, D 2007, *Leadership networking: Connect, collaborate, create*, vol. 125, Center for Creative Leadership Greensboro, NC.

Heron, J, & Reason, P 1997, 'A participatory inquiry paradigm', *Qualitative Inquiry*, 3(3), 274–94.

Hirschhorn, L 1990, *The workplace within: Psychodynamics of organizational life*, vol. 8, MIT Press, Cambridge, MA.

Hirschhorn, L 1998, *Reworking authority: Leading and following in the post-modern organization*, vol. 12, MIT Press, Cambridge, MA.

Hogan, C 2005, *Practical facilitation: A toolkit of techniques*, Kogan Page, London.

Hoppe, B, & Reinelt, C 2010, 'Social network analysis and the evaluation of leadership networks', *The Leadership Quarterly*, 21(4), 600–19.

Isaksen, SG, & Treffinger, DJ 2004, 'Celebrating 50 years of reflective practice: Versions of creative problem solving', *Journal of Creative Behavior*, 38, 75–101.

Latham, GP, & Dello Russo, S 2008, 'The influence of organizational politics on performance appraisal', in C Cooper & S Cartwright (eds), *The Oxford handbook of personnel psychology*, 388–410, Oxford University Press, New York.

Lucius, RH, Kuhnert, KW 1997, 'Using sociometry to predict team performance in the workplace', *Journal of Psychology*, 131(1), 21–34.

Marsick, VJ, & O'Neil, J 1999, 'The many faces of action learning', *Management Learning*, 30(2), 159–76.

Mehra, A, Smith, BR, Dixon, AL, & Robertson, B 2006, 'Distributed leadership in teams: The network of leadership perceptions and team performance', *The Leadership Quarterly*, 17(3), 232–45.

Mescon, MH 1959, 'Sociodrama and sociometry: tools for a modern approach to leadership', *Academy of Management Journal*, 2(1), 21–8.

Moreno, JL 1951, *Sociometry, experimental method and the science of society: An approach to a new political orientation*, Beacon House, Oxford.

—— 1953, *Who shall survive? Foundations of sociometry, group psychotherapy and socio-drama*, Beacon House, Oxford.

Neri, C 1998, *Group*, Jessica Kingsley Publishers, London.

Osborn, A 1953, *Applied imagination-principles and procedures of creative writing*, Charles Scribner's Sons, New York.

Parks, SD 2005, *Leadership can be taught: A bold approach for a complex world*, Harvard Business Review Press, Boston.

Pedler, M, Burgoyne, J, & Brook, C 2005, 'What has action learning learned to become?', *Action Learning: Research and Practice*, 2(1), 49–68.

Puccio, G 1999, 'Creative problem solving preferences: Their identification and implications', *Creativity and Innovation management*, 8(3), 171–8.

Puccio, GJ, & Cabra, JF 2010, 'Organizational creativity', in JC Kaufman, & RJ Sternberg (eds), *The Cambridge handbook of creativity*, 145–73, Cambridge University Press, Cambridge, NY.

Raelin, J 2011, 'From leadership-as-practice to leaderful practice', *Leadership*, 7(2), 195–211.

Revans, RW 1982, 'What is action learning?', *Journal of Management Development*, 1(3), 64–75.

Saam, NJ 2004, 'Towards a rational foundation of Open Space Technology', *Organization Development Journal*, 22(1),76–92.

Schuman, S (ed.) 2012, *The IAF handbook of group facilitation: Best practices from the leading organization in facilitation*, vol. 1, John Wiley & Sons, San Francisco.

Shapiro, ER 2016, 'Learning from the director's role: leadership and vulnerability', *Organisational and Social Dynamics*, 16(2), 255–70.

Slaughter, AJ, Yu, J, & Koehly, LM 2009, 'Social network analysis: understanding the role of context in small groups and organizations', in E Salas, GF Goodwim & S Burke (eds), *Team effectiveness in complex organizations: Cross-disciplinary perspectives and approaches*, 433–59, Taylor and Francis, New York.

Smith, PA 2001, 'Action learning and reflective practice in project environments that are related to leadership development', *Management Learning*, 32(1), 31–48.

Sutanto, J, Tan, CH, Battistini, B, & Phang, CW 2011, 'Emergent leadership in virtual collaboration settings: A social network analysis approach', *Long Range Planning*, 44(5), 421–39.

Thakadipuram, T, & Stevenson, L 2013, 'Turnaround: from breakdown to breakthrough with Open Space Technology', *Human Resource Development International*, 16(1), 116–27.

Thornton, C 2010, *Group and team coaching: The essential guide*, Routledge, London.

Tichy, N, Tushman, M & Fombrum, C 1979, 'Social Network Analysis for Organizations', *Academy of Management Review* 4(4), 507–20.

Wexley, KN, & Latham, GP 1991, *Developing and training human resources in organizations*, HarperCollins.

Wiener, R 2009, *Creative training: Sociodrama and team-building*, Athenaeum Press, Cambridge, MA.

Zohar, D, & Tenne-Gazit, O 2008, 'Transformational leadership and group interaction as climate antecedents: A social network analysis', *Journal of Applied Psychology*, 93(4), 744.

Chapter 13

References

1. Yule, P & Woolner, D 2008, *The Collins Class submarine story: Steel, spies and spin*, Cambridge University Press, Cambridge, MA.

2. Cameron, K & Lavine, M 2006, *Making the impossible possible: Leading extraordinary performance: The Rocky Flats story*, Berrett-Koehler Publishing, San Francisco.

3. Shepherd, J 2012, *The gift of acceptance*, Allan & Unwin, Sydney.

4. Erez, M & Zidon, I 1984, 'Effect of goal acceptance on the relationship of goal difficulty to performance', *Journal of Applied Psychology*, 69(1): 69–78.

5. Zaffron, S & Logan, D 2009, *The three laws of performance: Rewriting the future of your organization and your life*, Jossey-Bass, San Francisco.

6. Leibner, J, Mader, G & Weiss, A 2009, *The power of strategic commitment: Achieving extraordinary results through total alignment and engagement*, AMA, New York.

7. Bass, BM 1985, *Leadership and performance beyond expectations*, Free Press, New York.

Suggested reading

Bass, BM, Dong, IJ, Avolio, BJ & Berson, Y 2003, 'Predicting unit performance by assessing transformational and transactional leadership', *Journal of Applied Psychology,* 88(2), 207–18.

Cullen, JB, Johnson, JL & Sakanoc, T 2000, 'Success through commitment and trust: The soft side of strategic alliance management', *Journal of World Business,* 35(3), 223–40.

Dvir, T, Eden, D, Avolio, BJ & Shamir, B 2002, 'Impact of transformational leadership on follower development and performance: Á field experiment', *Academy of Management Journal,* 45(4), 735–44.

Forward, J & Zander, A 1971, 'Choice of unattainable group goals and effects on performance', *Organizational Behavior and Human Performance,* 6, 184–99.

Thompson, KR, Hochwarter, WA & Mathys, NJ 1997, 'Stretch targets: What makes them effective?', *The Academy of Management Executive,* 11(3), 48–60.

Ward, K; Bowman, C & Kakabadse, A 2007, *Extraordinary performance from ordinary people: Value creating corporate leadership,* Butterworth Heinemann, Oxford, UK.

Zenger, J & Folkman, J 2010, *Leadership Development 6.0: Connecting leadership development with drivers of business results,* www.zengerfolkman.com.

INDEX

action
— bold 283–291
— call to 283–290
— language of 37–38, 40
— learning 235, 236–238
— moving others to 35
— preparing for 283–291
— readiness for 37
adaptive challenges 19–21
— examples 19–21
— leadership and 20–21
Alcoa 237
Alcoholics Anonymous (AA)
200–202, 288
All Blacks rugby team example
198–199
Ameritech 209, 215, 237
Australian Football League story
203–204, 206, 227–228, 288
aviation industry 194, 195

Bannister, Roger 264, 269, 270
BAU (business as usual) mindset
272, 273–274
behavioural dimension 78, 79
being (attitudinal) dimension
106, 287

blame, handling 34
blind spots 43–47, 132, 179,
239, 240, 286; *see also* models
of leadership, naive
bliss, follow your 115
Boeing 209, 215, 237
bonding capital 215–216
boy psychology 105–106
BP 209, 222
brainstorming 18
Branson, Richard 140, 169
bullying 105, 187–188, 288
bystander effect 191–193

change agents 235
character 106
— building 142–145
— strengths 156, 157
Chase Manhattan Bank 212
chicken story, two boys and
290–291
Churchill, Winston 39, 40, 51,
143, 169
Cisco organisation example
197–198, 209, 213, 215, 237,
288
Citibank 209, 215, 237

fight/flight 242
flow, experiencing 141–142
followers, role of 61
Ford Motor Credit (FMC) 140
four-minute mile story 264, 269, 270
frogs story 163–164, 287–288

Garden of Eden story 109–110
General Electric (GE) 209, 211, 215, 237
global village 16–17, 23–24
GLOBE (Global Leadership and Organizational Behaviour Effectiveness) 62–63
— evaluation 65–68
goals
— attainment 171
— setting 169–176, 196, 270–272
gratitude 153, 154–156
— barriers to 155–156
— benefits of 14–155
gurus, village that believed in 13–15, 285–286

Harvard Business School 237
helping others 131–132
HERO (hope, efficacy, resilience, optimism) 147
hero's journey 115
Hewlett-Packard (HP) 209, 211
hope 124, 147
human capital 52–53, 70, 76, 77, 132, 174, 208, 251–252
human error 194–195
humility 107–108, 113–114

IBM 209, 212, 222
IDEO company 199–200, 288
impostor syndrome 126–127, 129
influence 21, 55–56
initiation
— defined 104
— humility and servitude 113–114
— leadership 104–122, 287
— liminal space 111–112
— men, 103–104, 110
— myths 105, 108–110, 113–114
— phony 116
— rites 104, 105, 108–110, 287
— self-transformation 114–115
— story 103–104, 287
— 21st century leadership 118–120
innovation 9–10, 63, 97, 99, 196, 254–256
— leadership 256–258
innovative workplace behaviour (IWB) 63
integrity 88–89, 144, 145–146
— model of leadership 73–100
iPhone 73–74

Jasmine's story 187–188, 288
Jean-Pierre's story 151–152, 287
Jobs, Steve 32, 39, 50–51, 73–74, 140
Johnson & Johnson 209, 211, 215, 237

leadership ... (*cont'd*)
— assumptions about 46–47, 49, 57, 64, 70
— attributes effective 63
— best practice 203–229
— capacity 251–252
— capabilities 16, 24, 33, 82–86
— collaborative 43–44, 197, 198
— competencies 57–59, 63, 70, 119, 143–144, 254
— control vs 105
— credibility 92–94
— ethical 145–146, 159–161
— gurus 13–15
— honour 117–120
— impact 77–80, 94–98
— influence 55–56
— innovation 256–258
— mental illness 51
— network 252–253
— pluralistic 189, 205
— positive integrity 88–89
— recent forms of 205–206
— relational (RL) 59, 60–61, 64, 73–100, 144, 189–190, 208, 285
— relationships 59, 60–61, 82–86, 118, 144
— research on 80–82
— role of 208
— shared 197
— skills 207
— social context 56
— stereotypes 44–47, 84
— styles 48
— traditional 21, 55, 84, 119

leadership capability development tools 73–100; *see also* leadership
— employee engagement model 73
— leader development model 73
— leadership development model 73, 75–77
— leadership model 73
leadership development 54–55, 77, 203–229, 287;
see also leadership
— approaches to 231–260
— best practice 203–229
— defined 207–209
— evaluation 64–70
— failure of 49
— leader development vs 207, 208–209
— management vs 207–208
— methods 231–260
— programs (LDPs) 214
— ROI 64–65
leadership development best practice 209–226
see also leadership
— assessment 212
— benefit of evaluations 226
— CEO commitment 210
— clear goals 211
— coaching 213–214
— evaluation 217–228
— experiential approach 214–215
— feedback 226
— integration of principles 225–226

targets, performance (*cont'd*)
— stretch 274, 275, 276–280
— pie in the sky 274, 276
— poor/mediocre 274, 275
teams, high-performing
195, 232
teamwork 3–7
thinking
— patterns 127–128
— styles 128–129
3M 212
transformation 120
— process 112
— self 114–115
Trump, Donald 32
trust 16, 8–9, 93–94, 98. 195
tsunami, village chief and
283–285

University of Michigan 237

values 106, 114, 119
— overrated? 158–159
victimisiation story 187–188,
288
Virgin Airlines 140
virtues 156–157, 159–161
vision 120, 168–169
visioning 16
Vodafone 209, 214
VUCA world 15, 29

wake-up calls 106–107
Walt Disney Company 31–32
Wandoo Offshore Oil Platform 5
Weihenmayer, Erik 268
Winkler, Don 140

CONNECT AND SHARE

Thank you for reading *Leadership Results*. I trust that you have enjoyed it and gained some new insights that you can now put into practice.

I would love to hear about your breakthroughs.

As you would know from your own experience, implementation can be challenging. I, and any of my colleagues around the world, would be happy to assist you to explore any ideas or implement any of the strategies presented in this book to take your self-leadership, or that of your team or organisation, to the next level.

Best regards,

Sebastian

Ways to connect:

- LinkedIn: Sebastian Salicru
- Twitter: @Seb_PTS
- Google Scholar: Sebastian Salicru
- ResearchGate: Sebastian Salicru
- website: www.leadershipresults.com.au
- email: ss@leadershipresults.com.au
- website2: www.pts.net.au
- email2: sss@pts.net.au

Initiate ▶ Activate ▶ Deploy ▶ Impact